THE BRITISH
ICE HOCKEY
HALL OF FAME

THE BRITISH ICE HOCKEY
HALL OF FAME

MARTIN C. HARRIS

Dedicated to members of Ice Hockey Journalists UK (previously the British Ice Hockey Writers Association), who down the years have striven to obtain exposure for ice hockey in the British media.

Also, to three giants of the written word who left records of the sport that serve as shining beacons to future generations: Vic Batchelder (1940-2001), Phil Drackett (1925-2005), Bob Giddens (1906-1963).

First published 2007

STADIA is an imprint of
Tempus Publishing
Cirencester Road, Chalford,
Stroud, Gloucestershire, GL6 8PE
www.tempus-publishing.com

British Library Cataloguing in Publication Data.
A catalogue record for this book is available from the British Library.

ISBN 978 0 7524 4447 5

Typesetting and origination by NPI Media Group
Printed in Great Britain

CONTENTS

PHOTO CREDITS

Author's collection (HIHA):	Anning; Beach; Borland; Brenchley; Campbell; Coward; Dailley; Dryburgh; Elvin; Erhardt; Giddens; Glennie; Halpin; Hodgins; Kewley; Kilpatrick; Lauder; Marsh; Murray; Petries; Poirer; Rost, 'Sonny'; Sexton; Snider; Strongman; Thomas; Weeks; Wyman; Zamick
Bartram, Lorne:	Nicklin
Bayley, C.R.:	Knott
Bayliss, Walter:	Batchelder; Curry; Dempster; Stevenson; Swinburne
Bone, Alan:	Urquhart
cardtraders.co.uk/Mike Smith	
Clarion:	Lee, Bobby
Collins, Andrew:	Goldstone
Dpa – Fotoesport:	Ahearne
Gordon, David/Brennan Archive/Syme collection:	Brennen B.; Syme, Tuck
GRA:	Foster; Key
Hill, R&J Ltd:	Archer
Ice Hockey Annual:	Booth; Brennan, A.; Carlyle; Imrie; Kerr; Lee, Benny; Meredith
Ice Hockey Annual/Bayliss, Walter:	Johnson
Ice Hockey Annual/Benbrook, Trevor:	Clark; Wight
Ice Hockey Annual/Hutton, John:	Toemen
Ice Hockey Annual/McEwan, Lynne:	Kelland
Ice Hockey Annual/Smith, Mike:	Adey; Brebant; Conway; Dampier; Hope; Neil.
IHNR:	Cooper, I; de Mesquita; Miller; Stefan
IHNR/Hutton, John:	Blaisdell; Latto; Matthews
IHNR/Smith, Mike:	Lawless
IHNR/Wilson, Alec:	Reilly
IHW:	Carlson; Davey; Hutchinson; Kellough; Kewley; Leacock; Lovell; McNeil; Shepherd; Smith; Syme, 'Tiny'; Zamick
LEE:	Monson, Peer
Rigny, Jason:	Conway
Skating Times:	Patton
Smith, Mike:	S. Cooper; Lynch
S.N.A.:	Chappell
Taylor, Mike:	Dampier
The Hockey Fan:	Spence
Wallace, C.F.:	Bates; Child; Stapleford
Wills, W.D. and H.O.:	Beaton

ACKNOWLEDGEMENTS

First and foremost I must thank Stewart Roberts, who as chairman of Ice Hockey Journalist UK and former secretary of its immediate predecessor. the British Ice Hockey Writers Association, offered support and encouragement when I first mentioned my proposal for a book publishing the exploits of Hall of Fame members.

Annually I composed the majority of the citations of the inductees of yesteryear. Others with greater awareness of the exploits of more recent members added to the press releases issued each spring by British Ice Hockey Writers Association/Ice Hockey Journalists UK.

I must acknowledge the debt owed to these enthusiasts, who over, the years, have compiled some of the profiles which formed a basis for further extensive research. Most are, like the author, first and foremost fans and devotees of the sport who placed their writing skills at the disposal of the British Ice Hockey Writers Association and its successor.

Particular thanks are therefore due to Tony Allen (Vic Batchelder, Norman de Mesquita); Anthony Beer (Stephen Cooper, Shannon Hope, Ian Wight); Tony Boynton (Terry Matthews and Icy Smith); the late Phil Drackett (Gib Hutchinson and Archie Stinchcombe); David Gordon (Billy Brennan, Marsh Key, Keith Kewley, Tom 'Tuck' Syme); David Hall (Ken Swinburne); Ivor Hobson (Mike Urquhart); Richard Stirling (Willie Kerr); John Vinicombe (Bobby Lee).

Also to Dennis Fill for kindly acceding to my request to utilise his interviews in *Champions On Ice*. A special thank you must go to fellow writer David Gordon for freely making available the results of his many hours of research at Glasgow's Family History Centre and New Registry House, Edinburgh.

I am grateful for additional information provided by Alan Batchelder, Joanne Collins, Mick Drackett, Norman de Mesquita, Bill Fitsell, David Hall, Corey Hartling, Ronnie Herd, Richard Hodgins, Rob JonanPat Marsh, Ronnie Nichol, Annette Petrie, Pauline Rost, Kevin Shea, Pat Smith, Gary Stefan, Richard Stirling, the GMC, Ian Wight and Andy Weltch.

Yearly elections to the British Ice Hockey Hall of Fame have been recorded by Stewart Roberts in his *Ice Hockey Annual*. This is a labour of love that is an essential work of reference. As is the now defunct *Ice Hockey News Review* produced by the late Vic Batchelder. Grateful acknowledgement is made to both publications.

The use of Gordon Wade's player statistics for the 'modern era' is appreciated as is those of the late Peter Green, particularly for his research on the 1958-1960 seasons.

Each profile between the covers of this book is supported by a photograph, and where known the photographer has been credited.

David Huxley, whose company Midlands Publishing Holdings Ltd, as owner of the title to *Ice Hockey News Review*, kindly granted permission for the reproduction of photographs from that magazine. As did the late Phil Drackett, for use of pictures taken for the weekly and monthly *Ice Hockey World*.

I am most grateful to Walter Bayliss who, although suffering from ill health, has been kind enough to take the time to supply several excellent portraits from his archives.

My gratitude, as always, to Barbara for enduring with fortitude my hours at the PC.

Any errors of fact are entirely mine.

INTRODUCTION

The intention of the author in compiling this book is for it to act as a complementary volume *Homes of British Ice Hockey*, which Tempus Publishing published in November 2005. *Homes* primarily featured all ice rinks within the United Kingdom where any form of ice hockey had taken place. Facts and figures concerned steel, concrete and the bricks and mortar that sheltered the teams which predominated within.

This work concentrates on and honours those personages, who down the years, since the close of the nineteenth century, gave outstanding service to British ice hockey. Therefore, it is only natural that the players, whose on-ice skills have thrilled the fans, should fill the majority of these pages. However, their coaches and those who have 'built' the sport such as club owners and administrators are not excluded, along with outstanding members of the media and the officiating panel.

Having built up a large archive of material over thirty-five years of covering the sport in Britain, I am in the fortunate position of being well placed to compose the profiles of the majority of the inductees to the Hall of Fame. I have also, down the years, been privileged to enjoy at least a passing acquaintance with nearly half of those featured here. All previously published profiles have been revisited and most redrafted and expanded with additional information and statistics.

Details of the exploits and personal history of some of the early pioneers have sometimes proved elusive. Consequently their stories are not as fully explored as the later members.

Regrettably, player statistics are incomplete or sometimes missing from earlier eras. Pre-1935 they were almost never compiled or published. Even after the introduction of the semi-professional English and Scottish National Leagues, the number of games played and penalty minutes accrued were not noted until after the Second World War. There are also gaps in the records of amateur hockey, at the Durham-based Northern Tournament for instance, and also during the life span of the 1966-82 Northern League. Coaching statistics are given for the non-playing role only.

The profiles that follow are intended to demonstrate the outstanding service provided to their sport by those so honoured with election to the 'Hall'. They are not intended to be full biographies, rather to provide a background and highlight the qualities, on and off the ice, as appropriate, that gave rise to their consideration and then elevation to the British Ice Hockey Hall of Fame.

Martin C. Harris

Ealing, London W5

July 2007

BRIEF HISTORY OF HALLS OF FAME

Contrary to popular belief, the first 'Halls of Fame' were built not in the USA but in Germany, and in the nineteenth, not the twentieth, century although they were not quite the 'Halls' we have come to know today, which usually as a physical entity are more often than not a shrine to outstanding personalities combined with a museum.

The first building to be graced with the title Hall of Fame opened in Bavaria in 1853. Conceived by King Ludwig I of Bavaria and located above Theresienwiese in Munich, it took ten years to construct. The building consists of three open colonnade wings, in Greco-Roman style, housing marble busts on pedestals of outstanding Bavarians. Since 1966 the tradition has recommenced with the addition of new figures.

The Berlin Hall of Fame, in the oldest surviving building on the Unter den Linden, ran from 1877 to 1924. It was housed in the Berlin Arsenal, which opened in 1730 and was converted into a Hall of Fame to honour the Prussian Army. It was more of a military museum as we know them today. There is no record of individual inductees.

The first to open outside Europe was the Hall of Fame for Great Americans at University Avenue and West 181 Street in New York City. Located on the campus of what is now Bronx Community College, it was the vision of NY University Chancellor Henry Mitchell MacCraken. It was financed by a gift of $100,000 from Mrs Finley J. Shepard and designed by Stanford White as a 500ft open air semi-circular granite colonnade. When opened on 30 May 1901 there were twenty-nine inductees including George Washington, the only unanimously elected member. There are now 102, with ninety-eight honoured by a bronze sculptured bust or plaque.

Probably the first sports Hall of Fame is that in the pastoral village of Cooperstown, NY State in the USA, dedicated to baseball, which opened on 2 June 1939. First proposed in 1935, five inaugural members were elected the next year. They now number 278, as at January 2007.

Canadians borrowed baseball's example for their national winter sport of (ice) hockey. The first reference to a 'mythical hockey hall of fame' was published in a December edition of the *Montreal Gazette*. The concept was further discussed during 1941. Two years later the National Hockey League (NHL) and the Canadian Amateur Hockey Association (CAHA) granted a charter to Kingston, Ontario, to organise an International Hockey Hall of Fame. The first twelve members were elected in 1945, although funding failed to materialise in Kingston.

Following a temporary exhibition during August 1957 at the Canadian National Exhibition grounds in Toronto, a permanent NHL Hall of Fame, combined with Canada's Sports Hall of Fame, was opened in August 1961 in a building costing $500,000. The number of members inducted had risen to thirty-three. By 1986 the NHL determined that the facility at Exhibition Place had outgrown the site.

Two years later Toronto City Council approved the inclusion of the redundant late nineteenth-century ornate Bank of Montreal premises, on the corner of Yonge and Front Streets, into the new BCE Place office complex.

This historic landmark now houses some 61,000 square feet devoted to a unique and outstanding display of rare artefacts, creating a veritable museum of hockey. Plaques honouring the 348 (as at June 2007) Hall of Fame members and trophies, including the original Stanley Cup, are on display below a stained-glass domed roof in the timber-panelled former banking hall.

Support for the Kingston project was withdrawn by the NHL in 1958. Money was therefore raised locally and a building opened on the Kingston Memorial grounds in 1965. Billed as the 'Original Hockey Hall of Fame' and the oldest sports hall in Canada, it contains 10,000 square feet of exhibition space.

Windsor, Nova Scotia and Bowmanville, Ontario, boast museums devoted to hockey. Most of Canada's provinces now possess a sports museum come hall of fame, with generous space devoted to hockey.

Sports halls of fame and museums have proliferated in recent years, mainly in the USA where they range from basketball, bicycling, bowling and boxing through to pro football, tennis, skiing and wrestling.

Even in Britain one can visit and view historical sports objects in venues devoted to archery, badminton, cricket, cycling, golf, football, horse and motor racing, surfing, rugby, rowing and tennis but not, as yet, ice hockey.

BRITISH ICE HOCKEY HALL OF FAME

It was Bob Giddens – owner, editor and publisher of the world's first regular journal devoted to ice hockey, who – in the autumn of 1948, founded the British Ice Hockey Hall of Fame.

Without prior announcement or editorial the London based weekly *Ice Hockey World* of 2 December 1948 blazed, at the head of page four in large type, 'No.1 Name For Hall Of Fame'. That name being the veteran Canadian-born player Keith William 'Duke' Campbell.

In a box alongside details of Campbell's career on ice, Paul King wrote:

> This is the first in a series of articles on men whom the 'World' regards as worthy of a niche in the 'Ice Hockey World' Hall of Fame. This distinction will not be lightly awarded. And will go to puck chasers who by their sportsmanship, value to their team and service to hockey generally, have set an example for all aspiring youngsters.

From the perspective of nearly sixty years it is illuminating to observe that it was only men who were to be considered. Women's hockey then, and for many decades to follow, was considered, if mentioned at all, more of a gimmick than an aspect of the sport to be taken seriously. The phrase, 'who by their sportsmanship' strikes a welcome, if somewhat old fashioned note in this more cynical era.

Three more profiles followed that spring and the next season. With no mention of the method of selection, or by whom, we must assume that Bob Giddens, maybe in consultation with some of his experienced reporters, determined those to be so honoured.

The next two batches of inductees, seven per year, were first highlighted in the *World's Annuals* of 1950/51 and 1951/52. Pioneers such as 'Peter' Patton, 'Doc' Kellough and Blaine Sexton, all born in the nineteenth century, were added, bringing the total to eighteen.

Additions every twelve months were by no means automatic. In fact the *Ice Hockey World Annual* published three years on made a point of saying:

> For the second successive year the *Ice Hockey World* elected no new members... The reasons were similar to those which promoted the previous year's decision... there were a number of outstanding candidates... it was felt that these men had not made it apparent by their actions that they had the interests of the game at heart.

Interestingly this article refers to a 'Committee', probably more a figure of speech than a formal body.

Spring 1955 saw three more names added; the last for thirty-one years. With the closure to hockey of two of London's three large capacity arenas – Empress Hall in 1953 and Harringay Arena five years later – the *Ice Hockey World* also ceased publication. No other body took up the task of honouring the heroes of the sport.

Not, that is, until the spring of 1985. Tony Allen, the secretary of the recently formed British Ice Hockey Writers Association (BIHWA), proposed to his fellow committee members that the Hall should be reactivated.

A perfect vehicle for carrying the good news now existed in the form of the fortnightly *Ice Hockey News Review,* founded in 1981 by then BIHWA member Vic Batchelder who seconded Tony's suggestion.

J.F. 'Bunny' Ahearne, Bob Giddens, Roy Halpin, 'Red' Stapleford and Sam Stevenson were the first new members. An administrator, journalist, two players and a coach provided an inspired first mix to pass through the reopened doors of the 'Hall' in April 1986.

The agreed rules for eligibility being:

Any Player, Referee, Official or Administrator who is, or has been distinguished in British ice hockey:

1. Candidates for election as Players shall be chosen for their ability, integrity, character and their contribution to their team and the game of ice hockey in general.
2. Candidates for election in other categories shall be chosen for their service, achievement and contribution towards the development and growth of the game in Britain.
3. Candidates shall be elected by a Selection Committee comprising current members of BIHWA, this Committee to be appointed by the full BIHWA Committee.

A further refinement soon followed, in that a player must be retired for a minimum of twelve months before being eligible for consideration. Also, one member of the selection committee retires in rotation each year.

This selection or sub-committee of five or six in number sift the journalists' nominations, a maximum of five per member each winter. More recently these are required in writing with reason(s) for the choice of candidate. The final decision as to whom is worthy of entry is now made by means of a telephone conference.

Press releases are then prepared giving details of the new Hall of Fame members. These are issued in time to make the maximum media impact in the days leading up to the end of season play-offs. In the days of the Heineken-sponsored Wembley Arena finals the newly enshrined inductees were guests at the writers' annual dinner and presented with their framed citation certificate.

Unfortunately with the British finals moving away from the capital, first to Manchester then to Nottingham, an annual formal dinner is no longer viable in the absence of the majority of the London-centric media.

Citation presentations are now usually made at the recipient's home rink, or posted to the new Hall of Famer or his nearest traceable relative in the case of posthumous awards.

Since 1984 yearly elections to the British Ice Hockey Hall of Fame have been recorded by Stewart Roberts in his *Ice Hockey Annual.* The now sadly defunct *Ice Hockey News Review,* until its sudden closure under new ownership in 2002, also devoted generous space each spring to those newly elected to the Hall.

Bob Giddens, the British Hall's founder, may well have been influenced and inspired by the success and consequent publicity attached to the first elections in Canada, during 1945, to an International Hall of Fame, then yet to be constructed.

The concept of a physical stand-alone building to house the memories of those so honoured in Britain was not, and still is not, a viable prospect. The 1950 feature article highlighting the second group of inductees headed 'Wall of Fame' (sic) noted '…we have not aspired to erecting a special building, so for the present a "Wall" it is.' Even this only existed within the pages of the *Ice Hockey World* and its *Annual.*

During the construction of the Nottingham Ice Centre in the late 1990s the British Ice Hockey Association (BIHA) announced that they would relocate there, with office accommodation in the new complex. It was hoped that space would also be found to bring together the scattered surviving archives and memorabilia of the sport to form a permanent home. Approaches were therefore made to the trustees and management of the NIC, and by the Writers Association for wall-mounted, framed outline biographies, complete with a photo of each Hall of Fame member, to be located within the NIC.

Regrettably the BIHA failed to conclude an agreement with the NIC and soon folded. Neither did the writers receive a positive response to their suggestions. So prior to the publication of this volume the only location for the complete British Hall of Fame outline profiles was in cyber-space at www.ihjuk.co.uk.

A physical presence is still awaited, hopefully within the construction of a future arena, with the capacity, will and desire to honour the heroes and heritage of British ice hockey.

MEMBERS OF THE BRITISH ICE HOCKEY HALL OF FAME 1948-2007
with Year of Induction

PAUL ADEY (2006)
JOHN F. 'BUNNY' AHEARNE (1986)
LES 'RIMOUSKI ROCKET' ANNING (1999)
Alex 'Sandy' ARCHER (1993)★

Vic BATCHELDER (2000)
Lou BATES (1950)
George 'Regina Peach' BEACH (1989)
Joe BEATON (1950)
Mike BLAISDELL (2004)
'Bill' BOOTH (1989)
Jimmy BORLAND (1993)★
Rick BREBANT (2004)
Edgar 'Chirp' BRENCHLEY (1993)★
Alastair 'Ally' BRENNAN (1990)
Billy BRENNAN (2004)

Keith 'Duke' CAMPBELL (1948)
Earl CARLSON (1998)
Johnny CARLYLE (1998)
Jimmy CHAPPELL (1993)★
Art CHILD (1993)★
Willie CLARK (1993)
Kevin CONWAY (2005)
Ian COOPER (2002)
Stephen COOPER (2003)
Johnny 'Red' COWARD (1993)★
Michael 'Micky' CURRY (1994)

Gordon DAILLEY (1993)★
Alex DAMPIER (1995)
Gerry DAVEY (1949)
Norman de MESQUITA (2002)
Frank DEMPSTER (1992)
Phil DRACKETT (2007)
Jack 'Jackie' DRYBURGH (1991)

Sir Arthur ELVIN MBE (1990)
Carl ERHARDT (1950)

Jimmy FOSTER (1950)

R.G. 'Bobby' GIDDENS (1986)
Bill GLENNIE (1951)
Alec GOLDSTONE (1992)

Roy HALPIN (1986)
Art HODGINS (1989)
Shannon HOPE (1999)
Gib HUTCHINSON (1951)

Thomas 'Red' IMRIE (1987)
Peter 'Jonker' JOHNSON (1989)
Chris KELLAND (2002)
T.M. 'Doc' KELLOUGH (1950)
Willie KERR Snr (1990)
Keith KEWLEY (2005)
Marsh KEY (2007)
Jack KILPATRICK (1993)★
Charles J. KNOTT Jnr (2004)

Gordon LATTO (1990)
Tommy LAUDER (1951)
John LAWLESS (1997)
Ernie LEACOCK (1987)
Benny LEE (1995)
Bobby LEE (1949)
Lawrie LOVELL (1992)
Jim LYNCH (2001)

Pat MARSH (1988)
Terry MATTHEWS (1987)
George McNEIL (1951)

Frederick MEREDITH (2003)
Alfie MILLER (1989)
Wally 'Pop' MONSON (1955)
Johnny MURRAY (1996)

Scott NEIL (2007)
Percy NICKLIN (1988)

B.M.' Peter' PATTON (1950)
Bert PEER (1955)
Alan & Annette PETRIE (2005)
Gordie POIRIER (1948)

Derek 'Pecker' REILLY (1987)
Clarence 'Sonny' ROST (1955)
John ROST (1991)

Blaine SEXTON (1950)
Roy SHEPHERD (1999)

J. J. Icy SMITH (1988)
Floyd SNIDER (1951)
Jimmy SPENCE (2006)
Harvey 'Red' STAPLEFORD (1986)
Gary STEFAN (2000)
Sam STEVENSON (1986)
Archie STINCHCOMBE (1951)
Les STRONGMAN (1987)
Ken SWINBURNE (2006)
James 'Tiny' SYME (2006)
Tom 'Tuck' SYME (2005)
Glynne THOMAS (1991)
Nico TOEMEN (1993)

Mike URQUART (2007)

Alan WEEKS (1988)
Jack WHARRY (1994)
Ian WRIGHT (1993)
Bob WYMAN (1993)⋆

Victor 'Chick' ZAMICK (1951)

⋆ Elected en bloc as members of Great Britain's 1936 Olympic Champions (Davey, Erhardt, Foster, Nicklin and Stinchcombe previously inducted individually)

FREQUENTLY USED ABBREVIATIONS

Governing Bodies, etc.

BIHA — British Ice Hockey Association
BIHHofF — British Ice Hockey Hall of Fame
BIHWA — British Ice Hockey Writers Association
CAHA — Canadian Amateur Hockey Association
EIHA — English Ice Hockey Association
GRA — Greyhound Racing Association
ICHL — Inter-City Hockey League
IHJUK — Ice Hockey Journalists United Kingdom
IHUK — Ice Hockey United Kingdom
IIHF — International Ice Hockey Federation
LIHG — Ligue Internationale de Hockey sur Glace
NIHA — Northern Ice Hockey Association
SIHA — Scottish Ice Hockey Association

League and Cup Competitions

AC — Autumn Cup
AHL — American Hockey League
B&H AC — Benson and Hedges (Autumn) Cup
BNL — British National League (various eras)
CC — Challenge Cup
EL — English League (various eras)
ENL — English National League (various eras)
EPL — English Premier League
HBL P — Heineken British League – Premier Division
HBL D1 — Heineken British League – Division One
ICL — Inter-City Senior League
IHL — International Hockey League (North America)
NHL — National Hockey League (North America)
NL — Northern League
NU AC — Norwich Union (Autumn) Cup
SNL — Scottish National League (various eras)

Publications

IHNR — *Ice Hockey News Review*   *IHW* — *Ice Hockey World*

Statistics

GP	Games Played	SO	Shut-out
G	Goals Scored	W	Games Won
A	Assists	L	Games Lost
Pts	Points (total of goals plus assists)	D	Games Drawn
PIM	Penalties in Minutes	W%	Percentage of Games Won from
---	Not available		Games Played (ignoring draws)

Paul ADEY

Inducted 2006

Paul Adey spent eleven consecutive years as centre-ice/right-wing for Nottingham Panthers, setting club records that still stand. He held the Autumn Cup aloft four times and led his team to their only triumph in the British finals at Wembley Arena.

Canadian-born Adey joined Nottingham as the lone import forward, from the three imports permitted in the Heineken-sponsored British League. He relates that 'my agent called on the Monday and asked if I'd come to Nottingham. I had never been to England so I thought I'd give it shot.' Panthers' coach Alex Dampier said 'he scored consistently for three years in the IHL and I'm sure he is going to do a good job for us.' Prophetic words indeed.

On his debut during 8 October 1988 Adey notched three assists. Next evening he scored his first goal. By the following spring his total stood at 88 goals plus 83 assists, the top Panthers points scorer. In front of 8,996 spectators in his first British play-off final at Wembley, Adey pulled his team level at 1-1 in the first period. Panthers concluded the sixty minutes on 22 April 1989 with a triumphant 6-3 defeat of Ayr. The losers' star Danny Shea said of Paul: 'He really is a tough cookie.'

Paul Adey waits for his turn on the ice from the Nottingham Panthers' bench.

The next winter he continued as the Panthers' sole import forward and leading scorer in all three competitions. Brian McKee of Murrayfield, who overcame Nottingham by the odd goal in nine in a pulsating semi-final, said, 'Paul is a non-stop battler whose work rate is quite superb.'

For the third consecutive season Adey set the pace in scoring for Nottingham with 151 points from fifty NU AC, league and play-off matches. In 1991/92 Adey, with 33 points, took the Panthers to an Autumn Cup final victory. He notched two goals and three assists in the loss to Durham in the Wembley final. A rival coach commented '… his value to the side is quite outstanding.'

In early 1994 a knee injury shortened his season and nearly put an end to his on-ice career. He slipped to second in the Panthers' points-scoring chart and maintained that placing the following winter. Adey enjoyed a second Autumn Cup victory in the Sheffield Arena as Cardiff were crushed 7-2. The granting of a testimonial night at Nottingham Ice Stadium came in late autumn 1995, in front of nearly 2,000 fans. He now held the club record for the most games played, goals and assists.

The formation of the fully professional Ice Hockey Superleague Ltd for 1996/97 virtually ended all limits on imported players. Adey raised his game, taking over again as the Panthers top marksman. The B&H Autumn Cup was regained. His 1,000th league point came in front of Sky TV cameras, to be followed by a first All-Star team selection in the spring.

Probably his greatest on-ice exploits came during his final full season in a Panthers uniform. A fourth B&H Autumn Cup was secured with a 2-1 victory over Ayr. He went on to clinch his first league scoring title with 21+35, by one point, from his wingman Greg Hadden, to earn a place on the All-Star 'A' team.

By summer 1999 it became apparent that he would not be returning to Nottingham, at least for the time being. Adey wanted a two-year contract which Neil Black, the club owner, was not prepared to grant. In the meantime he moved to Italy where in twenty-five games with Milan Vipers he contributed 14 goals and 12 assists. The following autumn saw a shock move to Panthers' closest and deadliest rivals Sheffield.

Former Nottingham coach Mike Blaisdell offered Adey a job. Despite lack of match fitness he netted twice in his debut for Steelers. 'I was really impressed,' said Blaisdell. 'All I wanted him to do was take a regular shift.' Adey commented, 'The game, though strengthened, is simpler now because they play with "a system".' Sheffield won all the silverware on offer. He contributed 12+13. 'The great thing about Sheffield was I got to win the league championship which was something I'd never done,' Adey said. 'For us to win all four trophies was a miracle as far as I'm concerned.'

Looking to the future he returned to his old club in May 2001 as coaching assistant to Director of Hockey Alex Dampier. 'This is a challenge for me but I'm ready to take it on,' noted Adey. He served his apprenticeship and replaced Dampier behind the Nottingham bench within two years. In the second leg of the Elite League's CC final, on 17 March 2004, with Adey in control, Panthers defeated Steelers 3-2 in overtime, on Sheffield ice.

Now eligible for a British passport the 5ft 10in-tall forward was a valuable addition to the national team. In his first tournament, the 1995/96 Olympic qualifier, he topped Great Britain scoring as he did in Pool B the same season and the 2000 Olympic qualifier. He competed in a further six competitions, ending in 2001, aged thirty-seven.

By June 2005, Adey's association with Nottingham ended. His No.22 shirt was retired by the club before he left and it hangs high above the ice at the NIC. He now coaches in Italy.

He was born on 28 August 1963 in Montreal where from the age of sixteen he progressed through the Quebec youth leagues with Richelieu, Hull and Shawinigan. Stints with Toledo, Fort Wayne and Peoria of the IHL followed, totalling 94 goals and 89 assists.

We will leave the final words with Paul. Reflecting on his years in a Panthers jersey he told the press: 'we were always competitive, in the eleven years I played for the club: we won five trophies and played in another six finals.' On his time as Nottingham's coach he added:

In the [first] year I was head coach I feel we accomplished plenty. Being the first team to beat Sheffield in a final was something special and playing in another three finals in only three seasons was an accomplishment... success come from hard work and believing in one's self.

Competition Statistics	GP	G	A	Pts	PIM
Nottingham Panthers	595	787	746	1,533	707
Sheffield Steelers	36	12	13	25	12
Great Britain	55	27	26	53	79

Coaching	GP	W	L	D	W%
Nottingham Panthers	134	75	43	16	54

John Francis 'Bunny' AHEARNE
Inducted 1986

J.F. 'Bunny' Ahearne was a charismatic, shrewd and controversial Irishman, who dominated the organisation of ice hockey in Britain from the early 1930s to the mid-1960s. He was equally forceful in the committee rooms of the world governing body the IIHF in the three decades immediately after the Second World War.

For many years in Britain (mainly in England) he managed to balance the conflicting financial interests of the owners of small rinks and the large capacity arenas promoting ice hockey. He also insured the continuance of the flow of imported Canadian players, with the necessary skills, to maintain the interest of the paying public. Immediately before and then after the Second World War his endeavours to persuade the rinks to invest ice time in developing local players met with some limited success. On the world stage his merits are hotly debated, principally by Canadians. They claim he favoured the interest of the European nations, especially regarding Olympic player eligibility. It is acknowledged in Europe that he pioneered the use of board advertising and TV coverage at World Championships, negotiating favourable revenues greatly to the benefit of the IIHF.

Bunny Ahearne, seen here aged seventy-seven in 1977.

John Francis Ahearne was born on 19 November 1900 in the hamlet of Kinnagh, Co. Wexford in Ireland, then still part of the United Kingdom. Educated at the Good Counsel College in New Ross and Rockwell College, Co. Tipperary, he joined the British Army under age, at sixteen and a half. With its lower age limit, seven years at sea with the Merchant Navy followed, where he rose to the rank of senior radio operator. Ahearne then continued his education, qualifying as a member of the National Association of Secretaries and lectured for two years on accountancy. He settled in London, working in a travel bureau, then in 1928 he set up his own agency, British-American Tours Ltd, which later became Blue Riband Travel Ltd. He was also director of a fashion house.

He first saw ice hockey in 1931 at the Golders Green rink in north London, where he also met George Brown of Boston, and quickly grasped the potential benefits of the sport to his travel company. Soon he was handling transportation arrangements for the North American teams that visited Europe each winter. At a meeting in a New York hotel in 1934 he became an honorary member of the Eastern Arenas Union, which included Brown, an organisation that ran ice hockey as a business. A year later, with a change at the top of the CAHA, he was appointed their European representative.

Ahearne became assistant secretary of the BIHA from autumn 1933, and secretary twelve months later, serving in that role until 1971 when he became president. He took the lead in stamping his authority on the sport, debarring Streatham from the English National League in spring 1938 over their use of suspended players. He constantly clashed with the Scots, before and after the Second World War, whose rink/club owners formed their own association. He insisted that, as the British governing body affiliated to the LIHG, later IIHF, all player registration, including imported Canadians, had to be via the BIHA, to whom a levy per player was due.

The first dispute with the Canadian authorities occurred in summer 1935. Promoters in London signed sixteen players direct, bypassing the CAHA. Ahearne smoothed ruffled feathers by travelling to Toronto to negotiate an amicable agreement. The sixteen included British netminder Jimmy Foster and Alec Archer both British born and earmarked by Ahearne, as manager of the Great Britain team, for that winter's Olympics. Jim Coleman, author of *Hockey is Our Game,* alleged that Ahearne 'had a mole working in the registry office of the CAHA and by 1934 had obtained a complete list of all Canadian-registered players born in the British Isles'.

There was an almighty row on the eve of the Olympics in Germany. The disputed pair were suspended by the LIHG, although the Canadian delegation agreed to the lifting of the ban for the duration of the games. Noone had foreseen that Britain would defeat Canada and go on to win gold. This brought on the next confrontation. The Canadians claimed that rather than carry the result forward to the final round, the two countries should meet again. Ahearne defended his team and the ensuing vote by the LIGH delegates went his way. Some Canadians to this day claim they were beaten in the committee room rather than on the ice. Next year he was listed as the BIHA representative to the LIHG and in receipt of their 'Diploma of Honour'.

Further spats between Ahearne and the Canadians occurred over the awarding of the World Championships to Canada for 1969 and the agreement they could use nine reinstated minor pros, subsequently vetoed by the IOC. He was also accused of denying Canada bronze medals at the 1976 Olympics.

In 1946 the LIHG became the IIHF, as an agreement was reached at a meeting in New York between the former and a rival world governing body, the International Ice Hockey Association, which included Scotland. Ahearne was of course in attendance. Five years later he was appointed vice-president of the IIHF and was president by 1957; alternating continuously in these posts for a further eighteen years. The three serving presidents during Ahearne's years as vice-president were, to accord with the IIHF statutes, from North America, but were generally of a weaker character. This enabled Ahearne to virtually control world hockey for almost a quarter of a century.

The sport in Britain struggled in post-war austerity, losing out financially to other choices for the leisure pound. Youth development with structured leagues was absent, prompting the question that Ahearne may have diverted his energy to his IIHF activities. However, judging by the state of ice hockey in Britain in the first decade of the twenty-first century, it seems unlikely he could have stopped the slide provided by commercial pressures. Maybe the firm smack of a near autocrat was, and still is, necessary.

Karl Scherer in his book *70 Years of LIHG/IIHF* quotes Dr Fritz Kaatz's description of Ahearne, his successor as vice-president: 'An Irishman, fiery-haired, arrogant, quick on the uptake, a fine businessman, obstinate, capable of marvellous warm feelings and then acting unscrupulously in pursuit of his own advantage'. A biased view maybe, as he was awarded the Cross of Finland, the Order of Yugoslavia and the Gold Cross of Austria. Also the Canadian dominated NHL elected him to their Hall of Fame in 1977, only the third European hockey personality to be so honoured.

J.F. Ahearne stood down at the IIHF Congress in 1975 and from the BIHA seven years later, to be made a life member of both bodies. He retired to Toddington in Gloucestershire where he died on 11 April 1988.

Les 'Rimouski Rocket' ANNING

Inducted 1999

Les Anning was one of the fastest skaters and most consistent scorers in the pre-1960 era of British ice hockey. He was one of the top ten scorers in six of his twelve years here.

He first came to England as a nineteen year old in the autumn of 1946, joining Wembley Monarchs for the inaugural post-war season of the semi-pro ENL. Anning, at 5ft 8in and 154lb, finished the season as Monarchs' leading scorer with 86 points as right-wing on the 'Kid Line' with Mauno Kauppi and George Steele. The line was briefly reunited in autumn 1949.

Next year, back in Canada, Les played for Montreal Royals and Shawingan Cataracts of the Quebec Senior League. Having married a London girl during 1947 they returned to the capital where he re-signed for Monarchs. He spent the next twenty years in Britain and the Continent, where he also coached. Monarchs won their first silverware since being formed in 1936, clinching the league formatted Autumn Cup and International Tournament during 1948/49. Les contributed 21 goals and 17 assists.

Eight games into the following season, Monarchs' last, he was transferred to Wembley Lions. From 1950 to 1953 Anning wore the orange and black of Earls Court Rangers. He made up the BAR line with Kenny Booth and Cliff Ryan. In his first winter on Lillie Road he ended fifth overall in the ENL scoring chart with 56 points, to be named in the All-Star 'A' team. He bettered this by one place the following year to earn a second 'A' rating.

In an extensive interview with Dennis Fill in the late 1990s, Anning considers his most memorable time was playing for his adopted country: 'We beat both Canada and the USA to win the Churchill Cup.' He played in all four matches of the two Churchill series. 'England' was entirely composed of Canadians, apart from Art Green, and beat the USA twice and Canada, the Olympic and World Champions, 6-4 at Wembley in March 1952. Anning drew England level at 2-2 in the twenty-sixth minute. He had scored the third goal in the Canadian 4-3 defeat of England the previous winter.

His first spell on the Continent saw him at Basel in the Swiss B League, and the best part of 1954/55 in Scotland with Ayr Raiders in the newly formed BNL. He moved back to Wembley for the next three winters assisting the Lions to gain the league crown in spring 1957 and win the Autumn Cup later that year. Anning again got his hands on the Autumn Cup as he moved south to Brighton for 1958/59, before returning to the Lions for the last year of the BNL.

Les Anning, of Wembley Lions during the 1949/50 season.

With the collapse of semi-pro league hockey in Britain he moved to Switzerland to play and coach for a further six years.

Although born in Montreal on 17 March 1927, he grew up in Ottawa and spent his summers in Rimouski where his father worked. Hence the later 'Rocket' tag provided by writer Phil Drackett. He explained his speed, 'It was partly due to my skates being ground pretty well flat, little or no rocker, plus playing with a lie 3 stick, which kept me low to the ice.'

In an interview with Phil, Les noted that he was first recruited to Wembley by their pre-war star Lou Bates. 'That call from Lou Bates completely altered my life. Hockey gave me a good living, a life in Europe for twenty-five years and a fistful of great moments and memories.'

He retired from paid hockey in 1971, working first as a golf pro then owning a fast-food outlet. Today he resides in Barrie, Ontario.

Competition Statistics	GP	G	A	Pts	PIM
Wembley Monarchs	112	97	75	172	79
Wembley Lions	249	212	167	379	98
Earls Court Rangers	180	157	112	279	74
Ayr Raiders	21	22	13	35	6
Brighton Tigers	50	56	32	88	12

Alex 'Sandy' ARCHER

Inducted in 1993 as a member of the Great Britain 1936 Olympic and World Champions

Alex Archer was a member of the Great Britain team that defeated Canada to win the gold medal at the 1936 Winter Olympic Games in Germany. He was one of sixteen players

who joined English clubs without a release from the Canadian authorities, leading to a row prior to the Olympics. The dispute did not seem to affect his performance as he iced in all seven matches, scoring goals against Japan and Hungary.

Returning to the land of his birth in the autumn of 1935, he signed for Wembley Lions in the ENL. He remained at Wembley until the war, winning silver medals at two World Championships for his country, and returned to coach when hostilities ended.

Born on 1 May 1910 in West Ham, London, of Scottish parents, they moved to Winnipeg in Canada when Archer was three years old. There he learnt to play ice hockey, graduating via Elmwood Maple Leafs, including a game in the Memorial Cup, to commence 'Senior' hockey in 1929 with Winnipeg Native Sons. A season split between Tacoma Tigers and Quebec Castors followed, then three winters with Selkirk Fishermen. Two years running he was among the Manitoba League's top scorers. The winter prior to joining Wembley was spent with Saint John Beavers where he notched up 22 points in the play-offs.

Alex Archer – resplendent in his Wembley Lions top on a 1939 cigarette card.

In his six seasons at the Empire Pool he was a major force at right-wing, contributing to the half dozen trophies captured by the Lions. Two consecutive league championships, between 1935-37 with the London Cup which was decided on a league basis, were won the next season and again in 1939/40. The similarly organised National Tournament silverware entered Wembley's trophy cabinet in 1937/38, to remain there the next winter. Ranking among the top ten scorers in the majority of these competitions earned Archer three consecutive All-Star 'A' team ratings.

War saw him back in Canada, turning out three times for Yorkton Terriers during 1940/41. After nearly four years as a corporal attached to Canadian Army Records, he skated out for the Lions first post-war match in December 1945. Next March in an English League side against the Swedish club Hammarby at Wembley, his playing career came to an end as he suffered a skull fracture.

His first coaching assignment at Nottingham for 1946/47, in their opening campaign, which earned him an All-Star 'B' rating. Back at Wembley for the next winter he repeated as an All-Star 'B' coaching the Monarchs. The following season he guided them to Autumn Cup and National Tournament victory. Archer managed and coached Edinburgh Royals for 1952/53 in their first year in the SNL. After a second season behind the bench he became rink manager.

A quiet thoughtful person, he died in the early 1980s.

Compe/tition Statistics	GP	G	A	Pts	PIM
Wembley Lions	---	108	97	205	---
Nottingham Panthers	1	0	0	0	0
Great Britain	24	14	10	24	---

Vic BATCHELDER

Inducted 2000

Victor Batchelder was the founder, editor and publisher of *The Ice Hockey News Review*, a fortnightly journal of record unsurpassed in Britain.

He came late into journalism, spending his earlier working life in the transport police. Ice hockey was not Vic's first sporting passion. He played football in a local league at Kidderminster until the age of twenty-nine and then decided to take up officiating, working up the refereeing ladder, to reach the status of linesman in the Football Combination. He called it a day after twenty-five years in soccer, when he realised that by the time he reached the heights of the Football League, he would be nearing the compulsory retirement age for officials at that level.

Born on 27 August 1940 at Ruislip, Middlesex, he had seen a few games of ice hockey as a youngster. In the late 1950s, from his home in Worcester he spent weekends in London and watched the Lions at Wembley. When living in Chaddesden, not far from Derby, he became aware of the re-launch of the sport at nearby Nottingham in 1980.

A year later he approached the officials of the regional ICL who were effectively running ice hockey in England, other than in the North East and North West. He proposed enhancing news of the league's activities by means of an insert to be placed in every club's match night programme. He was invited to a meeting in London where the committee promptly approved his ideas and created the post of assistant-secretary to provide him with the necessary backing.

Issue No.1 of his four-page A5 insert appeared in the last week of September 1981 under the title of *Ice Hockey News Review* and every fortnight thereafter during the season. Vic was his own man and the insert soon diverged from the ICL, to be sold as a stand-alone publication.

His editorial always took a tough and independent line, often highly critical of those running the sport and on rare occasions the match officials. In only his second issue he was unhappy with their pre-season stance but also suggested that critics volunteer to see if they 'could do any better'. From then on these editorials always concluded with the homily of 'Happy Hockey Days Folks'. In No.3 he urged the regional associations to settle their differences and work towards parity in playing standards.

The following year Batchelder took on the additional task, as well as continuing in his day job of credit manager with a financial company, of secretary to Nottingham Panthers. He fulfilled this role for about sixteen months, as by now he had plans to expand the magazine. Years later, Vic admitted he was fortunate to be in the right place at the right time, 'it started as a hobby and grew with the sport.' A spate of ice rink building saw more teams and spectators, leading to sponsorship by Heineken, Norwich Union and later Benson & Hedges, plus for a while, a game a month was broadcast on television by the BBC.

At the end of the second year he added two summer issues. Issue No.40, geared to the Wembley finals of May 1984 was a milestone – twenty pages of tabloid newsprint.

Five months later Volume 2 Issue No.1 appeared on twenty-four pages with photos. A month on and the page size was full A4, moving to a glossy, with colour banding on the cover by mid-December. This momentous season for *IHNR* closed with the introduction of full-colour photos and four summer newsletters.

The additional pages permitted coverage of youth hockey, feature articles, NHL and international news, a nostalgic look back at past glories and expanded game reports plus statistics.

Naturally with growth came difficulties. After the first two issues the printers went bankrupt, this in hindsight was a lucky break. Being forced to find another printer enabled production of a more professional publication. The sweat, toil and late nights lead to Batchelder, with the full support and backing of his wife Yvonne (who passed away in February 2006), to go full-time with the magazine, initially running the business from home.

Vic Batchelder stands proudly on the ice at Manchester Arena with
his newly presented Hall of Fame certificate.

The move to office premises at nearby Stapleford was soon necessary as reporting on all aspects of the sport continued to expand. Page numbers increased to thirty-two by 1985 to thirty-six the next year, stabilising at forty from 1987. His son Alan also joined the enterprise on a full-time basis. Occasionally end of season 'Specials' were added to the range, along with a foray into a history of Nottingham Panthers. Page numbers dropped back to thirty-two from late summer 1997.

The idea for an annual award for the most promising British lad under twenty-one was Batchelder's. From 1985 to 1994 he persuaded the Government of Alberta, Air Canada and the Calgary Flames to sponsor a trip to an NHL training camp. Ian Cooper, Tony Hand and David Longstaff were among the prize winners.

He also added to his workload, from the late 1980s, the role of ice hockey correspondent of the *Guardian* newspaper. His nose for a story produced an almost daily column, probably the best coverage of any national daily newspaper.

Sadly the constant deadlines took their toll on Batchelder's health and by 1999 he sold his successful venture to Pinegen Ltd. Based in Surrey they had been responsible for pagination and printing for some years. He continued to contribute articles on a regular basis, as he did to the *Guardian* until a week before his passing. Their sports pages contained two obituaries, a rarity for a freelance.

He was presented with his certificate of membership to the Hall of Fame on the ice at Manchester Arena during the play-off weekend. In a subsequent interview to his erstwhile magazine he said: 'It's an honour when you look at the names of people who are on the list… it is still an elite club… it's always nice to be accorded something by your peers.'

Vic was always generous in acknowledging a debt to his contributors and photographers. They held him in high regard as Tony Allen, his one time international editor, said at his induction, 'He built *Ice Hockey News Review* from nothing into the small-leading magazine of the time… he has helped serve the sport'.

He died on 11 October 2001 after a brave battle with stomach cancer.

Lou BATES

Inducted 1950

Lou Bates, as the most popular player in pre-Second-World-War England, featured on a Wills cigarette card and a pull out strip of sports stars issued with a boys comic.

in summer 1934 he was one of the first signings for the inaugural Wembley Lions, and was immediately named captain. A natural leader with skills above average he wore the 'C' for six years. As a 196lb defenceman with a right-hand shot, Bates captured the imagination of the thousands who flocked to witness ice hockey in the first arena built for that purpose in Britain. Tall with good looks, he had charisma on as well as off the ice, with a near English accent, plus an impeccable dress sense. From right defence he would rush up ice, with his sleek black hair flopping all over the place, to distribute accurate passes to his wingmen. Massed shouts of 'Lou-oo-oo-oo' echoed around the newly opened Empire Pool in west London. Good natured, he was never too busy to sign an autograph or talk to a fan.

He led the Lions to silverware in four of those six years. The ENL title

Lou Bates on the ice at the Empire Pool, Wembley, during 1937.

was captured in 1935/36 along with the Inter-Paris Tournament. Recognition came with election to the league's All-Star 'B' sextet. The following winter the ENL crown was retained.

In 1937/38 the London Cup joined the National Tournament trophy which remained in the display cabinet the following season. He took over as coach to the Lions from ex-NHL netminder Clint Benedict in the new year of 1938. He continued in that role until the events of May 1940, earning an 'A' rating that fateful spring.

When league hockey returned for autumn 1946 Bates was back, this time increasingly guiding the Lions from the bench. By January he was also named manager. The following winter he only coached, standing down as 1947 closed. He returned in 1950 to guide Great Britain to a fourth-place finish at the World Championships in London. He briefly came back to the sport in January 1952 as coach to Streatham, leaving by the October to devote more time to his business ventures.

John Louis Algenon McVicar Bates, born in Ottawa in 1912, was a distant relative of Prime Minister Herbert Asquith. Both his parents were English, dividing their time between Britain and Canada. Lou (he hated being called Louis), arrived in the world two months after they returned to Canada. In 1936 he was quoted as saying: 'There is nothing I should have liked better than to have been able to play for Great Britain at ice hockey'. Country of birth was the deciding factor by the mid-1930s.

Lou received a good education at Asbury College. He first played ice hockey at the age of eight and in organised hockey at seventeen with Ottawa New Edinburghs. In twenty games he scored seven goals and an equal number of assists. He spent time first with Rideaus, then Shamrocks, both from the capital in 1930 to 1933, with an appearance in the Allan Cup. In his second trip to Europe with Shamrocks, including games in Britain, he scored 19 goals to finish 1933/34 in Paris with Francais Volants before moving to England.

Lou continued to live in Wembley and died in London on 30 July 1987.

Competition Statistics	GP	G	A	Pts	PIM
Wembley Lions	---	55	54	109	---

George 'Regina Peach' BEACH
Inducted 1989

George Beach, a Canadian, joined Wembley Lions of the ENL in October 1947 shortly after his twenty-first birthday and was an instant success. He tallied two goals and four assists in his first match, an Autumn Cup contest against Harringay Greyhounds. As a centre-ice with a right-hand shot he went on to top the club scoring for the league and National Tournament.

For the next two seasons he was with Lions' rink mates, the Monarchs, helping them to win the Autumn Cup and National Tournament during 1948/49. In the spring of the following season, after leading his club in points, he was named to the All-Star 'A' team. Wembley's management ceased to operate Monarchs from the autumn of 1950 so he rejoined the Lions, staying for the next four years. In the first campaign the Lions won the ENL championship and Beach a spot on the All-Star 'B' squad as he gained most goals and assists for his club. By April 1951 he was given the Curtis Bennett Bowl to keep. Presented by Wembley for sportsmanship, he had won it three years in a row.

With increasing prosperity on mainland Europe, Beach, like many other Canadians at that time, commenced to play and coach on the Continent. With their generally shorter season he either began or finished in England, or both. Initially with Milan, he soon moved to Martigny, staying with the Swiss club for three winters. From 1954 to 1957 he appeared consecutively in the colours of Brighton Tigers, Harringay Racers and Nottingham Panthers. Following two full seasons in Switzerland he rejoined the Lions for the final year of the BNL, piling up 106 points. This brought another All-Star 'B' accolade.

George Beach of Wembley Monarchs during the 1949/50 season.

With the collapse of semi-pro hockey, Beach joined Southampton Vikings in late 1960. Games were now staged as 'home' tournaments, taking the place of league hockey, due to the disparity in clubs' ice availability. The following winter he became the player-coach. The generally lower standard in the amateur ranks can be seen by Beach's increase in goals and assists. Rank's bought the Southampton rink in summer 1963 and promptly barred any form of hockey. The majority of the players, including Beach, who signed for a resurrected Lions, who played mainly challenge games at the Empire Pool until 1968.

Beach was born on 4 October 1926 in Regina, Saskatchewan – hence the nickname. He told an issue of *IHW* in November 1947: 'Guess I've always been around on skates right from the time my Ma bought my first set when I was three years old.' After leaving school he sold hardware in a co-op store and was regularly picked for the Regina All-Star softball team. His hockey was played with Regina Commandos. Whilst a teenager, a scout for Chicago Black Hawks of the NHL invited him to their autumn training camp. From there he turned pro with Kansas City Pla-Mors in the US Hockey League. In thirteen games during 1945/46 he turned in a respectable 2+4.

Asked in 1962 for the greatest influences on his hockey he cited Russian-born Johnny Gottselig – a former Black Hawks veteran, Lou Bates and 'Sonny' Rost, both from Wembley.

Although Wembley folded the Lions in 1969, George kept in touch with the sport. After returning to the ice for a few games with the homeless Wembley Vets he became chairman of the supporters club of the Detroit-backed London Lions. They called Wembley home during 1973/74. Two years on he was appointed to coach Great Britain in the 1976 Pool 'C' World Championships in Poland.

Beach, a hustling and bustling playmaker, who stands fifth in the points rankings among pre-1960 members of English 'senior' hockey, now lives in retirement in the west of England.

Competition Statistics	GP	G	A	Pts	PIM
Wembley Monarchs	171	163	168	331	116
Wembley Lions*	319	284	332	616	94
Brighton Tigers	17	15	28	43	2
Harringay Racers	23	18	19	37	4
Nottingham Panthers	19	10	13	23	2
Southampton Vikings	56	93	141	234	8
Wembley Vets	4	7	10	17	0

* Excludes 1963-68 challenge games.

Joe BEATON

Inducted 1950

Joe Beaton is another star of pre-war English ice hockey to be featured on a cigarette card. He was 'A stick handler with unlimited skills' and, at the time of his retirement, the leading all-time scorer in ENL competitions with 330 points.

Joe Beaton, immortalised upon the ice at Richmond in 1937.

He crossed the Atlantic from his native Nova Scotia in October 1934 to join the newly formed Richmond Hawks, who then finished fourth in the English League. Hawks ended top in Pool 'B' of the International Tournament above Paris, Prague and Berlin.

The following season he captained Richmond to the runners-up spot, with 'National' added to the league title, losing out to Wembley Lions on goal difference. Joe, a diminutive centre-ice, clinched the scoring crown by a margin of six points, with 29 goals and 15 assists. Richmond only won one game in the London Cup, but Beaton, third in points, was the only Hawk in the top ten. Consolation came in an All-Star 'B' team accolade. Although for 1936/37 the ENL expanded to eleven teams, Richmond could not sustain the pace, in spite of Beaton's skills, and ended in the cellar.

By the time the next season commenced, the Richmond Hawks were no more and Beaton had moved north-east across London to Harringay Greyhounds. His team finished fourth but he gained an All-Star 'A' award. For the next two winters the Greyhounds swept to two consecutive ENL and London Cup titles. Joe put in solid performances with 81 points by April 1940 to gain a further 'A' rating. He moved to Wembley for the first post-war season which was to be his last.

Lions' veteran defenceman 'Sonny' Rost said in an interview with Phil Drackett: 'One of the best I ever played against was Beaton, Joe was a centreman… always had his head up and was a real smart playmaker and scorer.'

Beaton was born on 18 June 1910 at Stellarton, Nova Scotia, one of seven brothers. By the time he was ten years old he was quite proficient on the ice. He played hockey for his high school and moved onto the intermediates. His breakthrough into senior hockey came with Old Stellarton Oaklands. Now a journeyman he played for St Xavier X-Men in 1928, moving to New Glasgow Tigers the following year where he was league MVP and leading scorer. During 1930-32 he helped Fredericton Capitals twice win the Brunswick league title. Before coming to England he attended Boston Bruins training camp.

He married the daughter of Jack Olding, a major importer and modifier of tractors with a factory in Hertfordshire. The family were frequent spectators at Harringay Arena and Joe entered the family business. He died at the comparatively early age of fifty-five at Stanmore, Middlesex, on 26 October 1965. He is honoured by membership of the Nova Scotia Sports Hall of Fame.

Competition Statistics	GP	G	A	Pts	PIM
Richmond Hawks (1935-37 only)	---	54	30	84	---
Harringay Greyhounds	---	95	71	106	---
Wembley Lions	47	44	36	80	2

Mike BLAISDELL

Inducted 2004

Mike Blaisdell guided his teams to twelve trophies at the top level, more than any other coach in recent times in Britain.

He initially crossed the Atlantic as a player, joining Durham in January 1991 at the age of thirty-one. His impressive debut at right-wing, in a defeat of Murrayfield Racers, all but sealed the HBL P title for the Wasps. His coach, Paul Smith, son of Durham's owner Tom said: 'His vision of the game is excellent, he settled straight into the first line, knew where he should have been.' He should have, as the previous season he played fifty games for the Canadian national team, including a tour of Europe. Before that he had appeared in 349 games in the NHL.

Wasps cleared up with Blaisdell, at 6ft 1in tall and weighing 196lb in the roster. He immediately clicked with Rick Brebant, as Durham won the Norwich Union Autumn Cup. 'I struck it lucky, Durham could have signed another import,' he told *IHNR*. In his second final, the Heineken-sponsored British Championships at Wembley, Durham defeated Nottingham 7-6 with Blaisdell contributing a goal and an assist in front of 9,000 spectators. By the following Christmas he was gone: the Wasps had slumped and he was axed.

He turned to coaching, joining Nottingham for the start of the 1993/94 season. The injured and cash-strapped Panthers made it to the Wembley finals; this speaks volumes for the rookie coach's influence. Winning the B&H Autumn Cup at Sheffield Arena in December was his first success behind the bench. He also gained his first 'Coach of the Year' title, although injuries forced him to lace up the skates on fourteen occasions. They stayed on his feet the next winter as he took the third import position, due to financial constraints, scoring 35 goals. He won admiration for recruiting a competitive side that reached two major finals.

Mike Blaisdell, who spent his ice hockey apprenticeship with NHL farm teams, came to prominence in Great Britain as a record-breaking goalscorer for the Durham Wasps. He also enjoyed influential spells in Nottingham and Sheffield before turning to coaching with both the rival clubs. He was particularly successful with the Steelers, leading them to a league record finish before retiring from ice hockey in 2006.

At the end of the first year of the all-pro Superleague Blaisdell said,:'I can't be disappointed with the year we've had, after all there were only three teams that won a trophy this year, and we were one of them.' The trophy was his second B&H Cup. It was retained twelve months on in a 5-3 defeat of Ayr at the Ice Stadium. He was again forced to get back onto the ice during 1998/99 but not for the B&H Autumn Cup final, a 2-1 victory over Ayr, his fourth triumph. He claimed the win was down to his system: 'It's easy, we get at teams and try and create havoc. Get the puck in and go and hit someone, that's easy to play.'

Triumph turned to drama as twelve games into the following season Blaisdell walked away from the Panthers, claiming breach of contract and lack of financial backing from the club. He did not have far to 'walk', moving thirty-five miles north to Sheffield, the Panthers' arch rivals. He soon delivered the first silverware for the Steelers and their new owner Darren Brown as, irony of ironies, Nottingham were beaten 2-1 in the CC final, held at the London Arena in March 2000.

The run-and-gun style of hockey favoured by 'Blazer' continued as the Superleague's Grand Slam was delivered to Steelers voluble fans next year.

His recruiting skills produced a team of characters that stuck together when the going got tough, on and off the ice. Losing only 17 out of 70 contests, the B&H Autumn Cup was the first to enter the trophy cabinet via a 4-0 blanking of Newcastle Jesters. A 19-point margin separated the Steelers from the league runners-up. Amidst the end-of-season tussle for club ownership a determined London Knights were overcome 2-1 at Nottingham's new Ice Centre. Three weeks earlier Blaisdell and his boys had to travel to Belfast to gain the third of their four pieces of silverware as they defeated Ayr 4-2 for the CC. Their coach remarked: 'I guarantee that every one of these players will go home with good memories'. He earned the 'Coach of the Year' title.

Delays in the transfer of Sheffield to new owner Norton Lea inhibited recruitment, and this, combined with a reduced budget, meant that a place in the final four was a coaching achievement of high order, culminating in a pulsating Steelers penalty shoot-out defeat of Manchester. Two more trophies were gained the following season. Blaisdell's ability to continue to coax gritty performances from a team with limited finesse and finances resulted in a Superleague title and a CC win. A third 'Coach of the Year' award followed.

A change of title, to Elite, did not deflect the Steelers' coach and his charges from holding onto the league crown. His superior recruiting and man-management skills also led to a play-off weekend 2-0 blanking of Cardiff and a sweet 2-1 defeat of Nottingham in the final at the NIC in April 2004. 'We strapped four guys across the blue line and it worked,' Blaisdell told the press as he retained the 'Coach of the Year' title, his fourth.

That summer he returned to Canada and took a job as assistant coach to his old team the Regina Pats, now a major junior team in the West Hockey League. A year later he was back where he cut his coaching teeth – Nottingham. This time there was no silverware. Key players were injured, so third in the league was a proud achievement. At the end of April 2006 he decided not to renew his contract and went back to Canada. Despite the final fallow season, Mike Blaisdell's place in the Hall of Fame was already assured.

Born in Moose Jaw, Saskatchewan, on 18 January 1960, Michael Walter Blaisdell progressed through the junior ranks of hockey to spend 1977/78 with Regina Pats and a trip to the Memorial Cup. After a short spell at Wisconsin University he rejoined the Pats. As a first draft pick by Detroit in 1980, he turned pro with their farm team Adirondack that autumn and was almost immediately called up to the NHL Redwings. During the next nine years he accumulated 71 goals and 86 assists with Detroit, New York Rangers, Pittsburgh and Toronto.

Competition Statistics	GP	G	A	Pts	PIM
Durham Wasps	75	137	113	250	230
Nottingham Panthers	87	268	120	204	204
Sheffield Steelers	4	0	1	1	0

Coaching	GP	W	L	D	W%
Nottingham Panthers	477	272	158	47	57
Sheffield Steelers	606	366	182	58	60

Bill Booth, who, despite a post-hockey career as the North East Correspondent for *Ice Hockey World*, is best remembered as an influential long-term coach to the mainly British-bred players of the Durham Wasps.

William Walton 'Bill' BOOTH

Inducted 1989

Bill Booth, at 5ft 8in in height and weighing 173lb, spent three years immediately following the Second World War on the blue line with Brighton. But his real place in the Hall of Fame was gained as an influential coach and father figure to the mainly English-bred boys of Durham Wasps.

In the summer of 1946 he was invited to join Brighton Tigers. From September he became resident in Britain. His 16 goals and 26 assists in 55 matches aided the Tigers in their clean sweep of the ENL, by a ten-point margin, and the National Tournament. The inaugural Autumn Cup was swept up with a seven-point gap between the Tigers and Wembley Monarchs. Spring saw him named in the All-Star 'B' team. Brighton retained the ENL crown next winter.

Booth moved north in the summer of 1949 after Icy Smith, owner of Durham Wasps, visited Brighton to interview him for the post of player-coach. Financial arrangements were resolved which included a fully furnished house, rent and rate free.

His first game was in front of 4,500 spectators at the Wearside rink on 1 October. He played a full sixty minutes as the Wasps beat Falkirk Cubs 2-1. Booth shaped and coached Durham into one of the top three senior amateur outfits in Britain. Durham Wasps headed the Northern Tournament standings seven times and won the finals on three occasions during eleven seasons from 1949 to 1961. Many of his players progressed to represent England and Great Britain including Dave Lammin, Bobby Green, Derek Elliott, Hep Tindale, Ian Dobson, Derek Adamson, Ronnie Stark, Derek Metcalfe and many others. Between 1961 and 1963 the team fell out with the rink and lost home ice. Booth kept the club going, as the Wasps appeared in rinks all over Britain.

Born in Montreal on 20 August 1919 he learnt to skate at the age of eight, although he did not start to play hockey, with Crane in the Mount Royal Junior League until he was fourteen. Lachute provided a taste of senior hockey before moving to Valleyfield Braves. Joining the army in 1942 he was posted to Kingston where he was on the ice with NHL stars Red Hamill and Gus Giesbrecht. A month after D-Day he was in France as a driver in the Royal Canadian Ordnance Corps. As hostilities drew to a close Booth again donned the skates to play service hockey in Belgium, Holland and Germany. Back in England he saw action on the ice at Brighton, Wembley and in Czechoslovakia with a Military HQ team.

He married Isobel, a local Durham girl, and after retiring from the ice made a new career in insurance, whilst keeping in touch with hockey. In the early part of the 1960s he contributed articles to the monthly *Hockey Fan* and in the 1980s became North East correspondent for *IHW*, which had been revived as a glossy monthly journal. He died on 25 September 1986.

Competition Statistics	GP	G	A	Pts	PIM
Brighton Tigers	156	26	41	67	250
Durham Wasps (1950-53 & 1954-55 only)	112	77	115	192	64

Jimmy BORLAND

Inducted in 1993 as a member of the Great Britain 1936 Olympic and World Champions

Not much is known about the short life of Jimmy Borland, who gained gold medals playing for Great Britain in the 1936 Olympic, World and European Championships.

James Andrew Borland was born at Stalybridge, eight miles east of Manchester on 25 March 1911 and grew up in Lakeshore, Ontario, and Montreal where he learnt his skills in ice hockey.

He returned to the land of his birth in 1933 to sign for Grosvenor House Canadians, partnering Gordon Dailley on defence. Grosvenor House's rink was at basement level, in the upmarket hotel of the same name located on Park Lane in London's West End. Canadians, along with the nearby Queens club in Bayswater, pioneered the importation of paid players. Grosvenor won all of their home games in the English League along with the league title in Borland's first season in the capital.

Almost as soon as he arrived in England, Borland was chosen for the national side. The first occasion was on 20 November when England lost 2-1 to France at the Hammersmith rink. He was on the ice again the following month opposing Ottawa Shamrocks and on 3 January in England's 3-3 tie with the USA at Queens. These appearances, plus the foreign opposition faced with his club, clinched a place with Great Britain for the World Championships held in Milan during early February. Eliminated on goal difference, Jimmy scored in Great Britain's 3-0 win over Belgium and again in the 4-1 victory against Italy in the consolation group.

He had a year away from the rinks before signing for Brighton in the autumn of 1935. The Tigers did not enjoy a particularly successful first season as Borland centred the second forward trio. Selected for Britain's 1936 Olympic bid at Garmisch in Germany, the winter games were his finest hour. He was on defence in Great Britain's 1-0 shut-out of Sweden on 7 February. Next day, as a forward, he scored in the 3-0 victory over Japan. His final appearance came on 13 February in the second round 5-1 defeat of Hungary.

The next winter was a tough one. He started as captain of the Tigers, but a troublesome knee was further injured during early November in a collision with a visiting Toronto Dukes player. The cartilage had to be removed. Borland returned to the ice spasmodically from late February, but in total he only iced 13 times for Brighton.

The Great Britain Olympic and World Champions of 1936. Jimmy Boland is kneeling on the far left of the front row.

At 5ft 9in in height and weighing 168lbs, Jimmy Borland was very versatile. He could play on defence or up front, preferring right-wing although sometimes used at centre-ice. He was even tempered, cheerful, a good mixer and not easily upset. An electrician by trade he also enjoyed golf, fishing and baseball.

He is reported to have died in 1937, at the age of twenty-six.

Competition Statistics	GP	G	A	Pts	PIM
Brighton Tigers	---	2	3	5	---
Great Britain	8	3	---	3	---

Rick BREBANT

Inducted 2004

Rick Brebant, a centre-ice, played with eight different clubs during his long career in Britain, his fierce competitiveness being a major factor in their success. His teams won seven play-off championships, seven league titles and six cup competitions.

He arrived in England midway through 1987/88 to join Durham Wasps of the HBL P. He said many years later: 'I was only supposed to be here for the short term when a friend of mine got injured and I came over here instead.' He soon found his way into the affections of the Durham fans with his no nonsense all-action game. That first spring he contributed 4 assists as Wasps defeated Fife 9-5 for the British championship in front of a capacity 7,900 crowd at Wembley on 24 April.

The following season he led the league in goals and total points as Durham carried off the league title and play-offs plus the NU AC. His first of five All-Star awards followed. The second arrived in the spring of 1991 along with the 'Player of the Year' title from the journalists. Mike Blaisdell had joined Durham in the January and the duo achieved instant chemistry. The NU

AC was mopped up as Brebant hit 1+7 in the final. The league title was next, with Rick as leading scorer, followed by the play-off championship at Wembley. His three assists contributed to the 7-4 victory over Peterborough. Recognition of his influence continued with a successive selection to the All-Star team as Durham held onto the league and play-off titles.

He had been the leading Premier Division scorer in three separate seasons and was now third in the all-time scorers' list. These figures attracted Cardiff with whom he signed a two-year contract in September 1993. He commented that it was 'a tough decision to leave Durham,' adding 'it's [Cardiff] the most professional set-up in British hockey.' Cardiff Devils manager John Lawless told *Powerplay* magazine: 'Rick is already well known to the Cardiff fans and is sure to make an immediate contribution to the team.' This he did as the Devils swept to the Premier Division title of the British League and the championships at Wembley. Sheffield were brushed aside 12-1 in the final.

With Blaisdell coaching at Nottingham the club negotiated Rick's release from Cardiff for an undisclosed sum. Here he added another Autumn Cup medal to his collection, contributing 2+2 as the Panthers defeated his previous club 7-2 in front of 8,200 spectators at Sheffield. Maybe seeing his ex-winger's success at coaching inspired Brebant to emulate him.

He signed as player-coach to Durham Wasps, now owned by Sir John Hall's short-lived Newcastle Sporting Club. Home was the small capacity Sunderland rink, located above retail units.

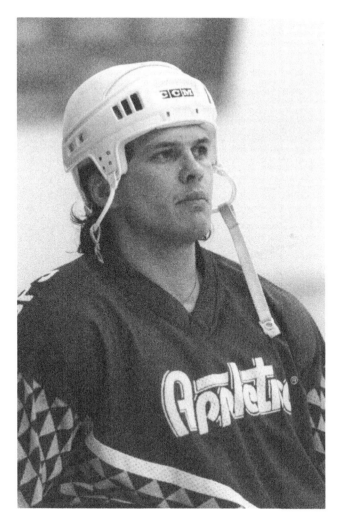

Rick Brebant during his spell as a Durham Wasp.

Autumn 1996 saw the club, renamed as the Cobras, move into Newcastle Arena for the first campaign of the Superleague. Disappointed at poor results, he branded his team 'a bunch of prima donnas.' The following autumn was no better and following seven consecutive defeats he resigned in early November, to move to Manchester. A few years later he commented on this episode saying: 'I coached and managed at Newcastle... it was a job I should never have taken on. I was thirty and in my prime as a player but I took on too much, that's why I left. But I don't regret it... I learned a lot.' Greater support from the club's upper management would have helped.

The move assisted Storm to lift the Superleague title. That Brebant was able to maintain his place at the top at the age of thirty-five was demonstrated at the B&H Autumn Cup final in December 1999. Deadlocked at 3-3 with Chris McSorley's London Knights, he was the only one of nine shooters to beat the netminders. He moved to London the month after in a player swap between the two sides. He had asked for his release from Storm, commenting it would be 'better for the team and myself if I moved on.' Back at Manchester he netted the game-tying goal for London at 15.55 as his new club powered on to a 7-3 finals triumph.

Brebant made another move in summer 2000 for a third spell with coach Blaisdell, this time at Sheffield, where he helped the Steelers achieve the Grand Slam. Tenacious and tireless at both ends of the ice, Brebant added four further medals to his growing collection. The next winter Sheffield held onto the play-off crown and he ended as club top scorer. In a third and final year with the Steelers he was hampered with a shoulder injury whilst collecting league and CC medals. His last season in England was as coach to a resurrected Manchester club. With a tight budget he was forced, within weeks, to don the blades again, as he worked tirelessly with Phoenix owner Neil Morris to achieve the play-offs. In February, on his fortieth birthday, he announced that he would be retiring in the summer, to return to Canada to work with young players.

In 1994 he acquired a British passport in time to join the national team for their first Pool 'A' venture in the World Championships for thirty-two years. His only goal came, fittingly, against Canada, as Great Britain lost 8-2. 'The experience was awe inspiring' he said later. Six more tournaments with Great Britain followed. He contributed eight points at Pool 'B' in 1998 and again two years later.

Before leaving England he stated his philosophy: 'You play the game to win championships and titles. You must believe in yourself. What made me stay was the fact that I was enjoying my hockey, I did it as a living but to me it is [also] a hobby... lots of fun, very enjoyable and a lot of great memories.'

Richard 'Rick' Joseph Brebant was born at Elliot Lake, Ontario, on 21 February 1964, the middle of two taller but less-competitive brothers. He left home at the age of seventeen to join Pembroke Lumber Kings, racking up high numbers in the Canadian Junior League. He spent three years at Ohio State University with the Buckeyes then played fourteen games with Carolina in the All-American League prior to the move to Durham.

Competition Statistics	GP	G	A	Pts	PIM
Durham Wasps	326	705	849	1,554	706
Cardiff Devils	63	119	154	273	130
Nottingham Panthers	59	85	156	241	106
Newcastle Cobras	45	24	39	63	119
Manchester Storm	143	44	93	137	172
London Knights	28	13	22	35	42
Sheffield Steelers	166	42	102	144	343
Manchester	36	2	26	28	64
Great Britain	32	10	13	23	78

Chirp Brenchley in his Hershey uniform in 1935. This photograph was taken before he joined the British league and became a member of Great Britain's Olympic and World Championship winning team the following year.

Edgar 'Chirp' BRENCHLEY

Inducted as a member of the Great Britain 1936 Olympic and World Champions

'Chirp' Brenchley wrote himself into the record book by scoring the game-winning goal against Canada ninety seconds from time at the 1936 Olympics.

British-born and taken to Canada at a young age, he returned in the autumn of 1935 to join Richmond Hawks of the ENL. The Hawks were coached by Percy Nicklin, who was also coach to Great Britain. Richmond came second, tying on points with Wembley Lions. Brenchley, at 5ft 8in and weighing 155lbs, skated on the right-wing to contribute a goal and four assists, His season had started slowly but he then improved with every game.

With a five-match series between Great Britain and the Resident Canadians of the ENL, and an Olympic trial meet with Wembley Lions, Brenchley had a chance to impress the selectors. This he did, scoring against the Lions and again in the final 'Test Match' at Brighton on Boxing Day. He iced in all of Great Britain's seven Olympic games. In the opener with Sweden, a few minutes from the start, he fired a long shot at the netminder to score the game's only goal. Next day, at the ten-minute mark, he collected the loose puck to draw the Japanese netminder out, giving Britain their first goal in the 3-0 shut-out. His third against Canada on 11 February was decisive in the gold medal quest. Deadlocked at 1-1 Brenchley, against the run of play, calmly flicked the puck past the goaltender. His fourth Olympic goal came in the 5-1 win over Hungary.

That autumn he moved with Nicklin to the newly opened Harringay Arena, and the Greyhounds. London hosted the 1937 World Championships where Canada regained the world crown. In the final group, Brenchley's fast backhand drove the puck into the corner of the Swiss net, breaking the 0-0 tie five minutes into the second overtime period. He also netted twice against Germany in the last game which gave Britain the European championship. The *IHW* reported: 'Brenchley showed the spirit of a Lions throughout the series [and] worked hard all the way…'

Born on 10 February 1912 at Sittingborne in Kent he was brought up in Canada, attending Niagara Falls Technical School. He spent two seasons in junior hockey with the home town Rockets, moving onto the Hershey Bars in the Eastern Amateur League. His moniker of 'Chirp' referred to his liking of practical jokes.

Brenchley returned to Niagara Falls in the summer of 1937 to a long and successful career in hockey: playing, coaching and ending as a scout. He appeared on the ice for Hamilton, Toronto Army Shamrocks (1942/43) and in America with Washington, New York Rovers (1947/48 US Senior champions), Atlantic City and Johnston. Appointed head coach of Johnston Jets in 1953 he moved on to guide Philadelphia, New Haven, Toledo, Sudbury, and St Catherine. Between 1966 and 1973 he was the eastern scout for Pittsburgh Penguins of the NHL. He died in 1975.

Competition Statistics	GP	G	A	Pts	PIM
Richmond Hawks	---	5	5	10	24
Harringay Greyhounds	---	6	8	14	22
Great Britain	16	12	---	12	11

Alastair 'Ally' BRENNAN

Inducted 1990

Alastair Brennan first played senior amateur hockey in the early 1960s for the Paisley Mohawks, who were player-coached by his elder brother Billy. He enjoyed a long mid-career on defence before reverting to skating on the wing during his final season.

The first skates he wore were figure skates given to him by his brother's wife for use on a local pond one winter. Roller skates came next before hockey skates, brought back from a trip to Sweden by Billy. He soon started attending Sunday practices for youngsters during 1956/57 at the nearby original Paisley rink on East Lane. Several players with the semi-pro Pirates of the BNL sometimes helped out. Progress to the senior amateur Mohawks scrimmage sessions followed.

At sixteen 'Ally' started playing for the Mohawks all over Britain at opposing teams' 'home' tournaments. The NL commenced in 1966 comprising a mix of Scottish teams including the Mohawks plus Durham and Whitley Bay from north-east England. Paisley headed the league for the first three years, with Ally one of the top-ten scorers in the inaugural campaign gaining election to the All-Star 'B' team. By the end of the next season he was voted onto the 'A' squad.

When Paisley folded in 1970 due to closure of their rink, he moved to Ayr Bruins, until he suffered a broken neck in a car accident two years later. Although told by doctors that he must never play again, he fought back to full fitness. Then the Ayr rink closed in 1972. Back on the ice practising in Glasgow he was invited to join Fife Flyers that autumn. He spent seven years playing the best hockey of his life for the Kirkcaldy team. He helped them win the Autumn Cup in his first campaign and again in 1975-77, together with the play-offs for the Spring Cup. The NL title was captured in 1977-79 along with the Icy Smith Cup, then emblematic of the British Championships. Brennan's performances were marked with a 'Player of the Year' award for his first winter with the Flyers. Moving back to defence gained him four successive 'A' team All-Star selections in 1976-79.

Ally Brennan, a Scottish stalwart.

With an impending marriage and a new home in Ayrshire, the travelling to Kirkcaldy became a burden. He returned to Bruins reluctantly as player-coach. His preference was for a player role only. Here he gained his fifth All-Star 'A' rating in spring 1980. Ayr were not very strong on the ice and by Christmas 1982, following a dispute with a committee member, he left. Ally accepted an invite to join Dundee Rockets whose owner Stewart pioneered the 1980s import of paid Canadians. He won a championship medal with Dundee in 1983 at the first Heineken-sponsored British championships, held over one April weekend at Streatham in south London.

With a change of management at the Ayr club, plus the attraction of joining three good quality imports, he returned to Bruins that autumn. Ally's last goal for Bruins, at 45.21, gave his team a 4-2 lead in the semi-final at the inaugural Wembley finals weekend in April 1984. The last of his 102 international appearances came eight days later at Dundee in Scotland's 7-4 victory over England.

He then retired from playing although briefly ran the bench at Ayr the following winter and helped start youth coaching at the newly opened Lagoon Centre rink at Paisley in 1992.

Ally made the first of his forty-seven World Championship appearances for Great Britain in 1965 in Finland, going on to play in a further seven tournaments against twenty-two nations. The best figures were achieved in Holland in 1971 in Pool C where he contributed 3+3 from Great Britain's seven matches. Ten years on, in his last World Championship, in Beijing, China, the team was as far from Britain as it had ever been.

Alistair Brennan was born on 17 February 1945 at Paisley, where he received his education. He was the youngest of four children. Following an apprenticeship at the firm where he worked for the next twenty years, he moved to the Caledonian paper mill near Irvine as a maintenance engineer. Taking early retirement in 2003 he now enjoys the occasional round of golf.

Competition Statistics	GP	G	A	Pts	PIM
Paisley Mohawks*	134	144	81	225	251
Ayr Bruins	143	91	114	205	263
Fife Flyers**	45	43	70	113	78
Dundee Rockets	9	0	1	1	12
Great Britain	47	7	3	10	29

★ 1963-65 & 1966-70 only

★★ 1975-78 only and 1976/77 Icy Smith Cup only

Billy BRENNAN

Inducted 2004

Billy Brennan was a precocious talent on the ice, making his debut in the Canadian-dominated semi-pro SNL at the age of seventeen. He also enjoyed a prolonged international career and helped keep hockey alive in Scotland in the 1960s.

He vaguely recalls watching his first ice hockey match as a five year old at Ayr. In March 1939 his father's cousin Mickey and his Trail Smoke Eaters teammates opened the new rink, in a challenge encounter with the Scottish Select. It was another five or six years before Billy learnt to skate at his home rink in Paisley. At fourteen he joined the pee-wee team, soon moving on to the junior Wildcats. Not long after, youth hockey folded at Paisley, as it did in the other Scottish rinks around 1950. Young Brennan then travelled the short distance to the Crossmyloof rink in Glasgow, initially joining the weaker Mustangs coached by old-timer Jim Kenny. He soon moved up to the Mohawks.

During 1951 he was invited to Ayr by their Canadian coach Keith Kewley to fill in for the injury-hit Raiders. At the end of that season he got a chance to join Paisley Pirates of the SNL, now coached by Kewley. Within ten weeks he had surprised his coach by gaining a regular place on the team. Kewley converted him into a checking right-wing. Pirates won the league that winter, plus the Scottish Autumn and Canada Cups, with Brennan contributing 35 points. The following year, the first of the combined English and Scottish BNL, Paisley finished third in the Autumn Cup and BNL. They also won the Scottish Cup.

By 1958 the Pirates had a new coach but he and Brennan fell out, and so the next year Billy took over as player-coach to the senior amateur Mohawks, now based at Paisley. They competed with some success at 'home' tournaments in England, mainly at Altrincham, Brighton and Southampton, and later at Wembley, as well as in the Scottish League which ran for three seasons from 1962. The Southampton-based Southern Cup was won in 1960. Mohawks were also Northern Tournament finalists that spring, as they were at Altrincham two years later and at the Brighton Tournament in 1965. The BBC Television *Grandstand* Trophy was captured twelve months later. During this period Brennan's abilities was rewarded with two All-Star 'B' ratings, and in 1965 one for defence and one as coach – both in the 'A' category.

With the formation of the NL in 1966 the Brennan-coached Paisley topped the new league for three years. His team also won the play-offs, Autumn Cup and Icy Smith Cups for 1967/68. These achievements were recognised with successive All-Star 'A's for defence and a 'B' as coach in 1968 and 1969. An innovative coach and one of the very few, other than Anatoli Tarasov, the father of Russian ice hockey, to utilise the ideas in Lloyd Percival's 1951 *Hockey Handbook*. 'I used that book for years as a grounding. Percival was way ahead of his time,' he told author David Gordon.

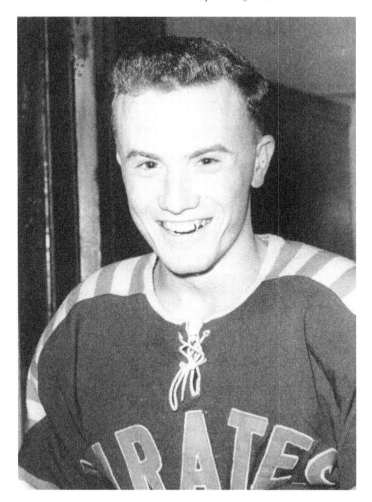

Billy Brennan, seen here in 1953/54 during his time with Paisley Pirates, was a precious talent who did much to keep Scottish ice hockey alive.

Billy's domestic career ended in Glasgow after eighteen months in retirement. He joined the Dynamos halfway through the 1970/71 season, helping them to a NL runners-up place. His performances were such that he gained an All-Star 'A' for his work from the blue line and a recall to the national team.

Great Britain returned to the World Championships after an interval of five years. He played on the wing in the seven games in Pool C held in Holland, then retired from the ice for good.

His international career had begun as a winger in 1953 when, aged nineteen, Britain competed in Pool 'B' of the World Championships held in Switzerland. Seven years elapsed before Great Britain was again seen on the world stage. Brennan was part of that silver medal winning Pool 'B' side at Geneva and Laussane in 1961. The following year he captained Great Britain at the 'A' tournament in the USA and served as player-coach in the 1965 and 1966 Group 'B' events.

William Brennan was born on 13 January in Paisley where he commenced his education, before moving to St Mungo's Academy in Glasgow. He left school at seventeen to take an apprenticeship as an engineering draughtsman. His job took him to Birmingham by the early 1970s then to Aberdeen in 1975 to join a Norwegian-based firm. He retired as their UK managing director in 1999.

When a rink opened in the Granite City in 1992 Billy helped out coaching the youngsters for a while. He and his wife now live at nearby Bridge of Don, where he enjoys an occasional game of golf.

Competition Statistics	GP	G	A	Pts	PIM
Ayr Raiders	10	0	1	1	2
Paisley Pirates	218	35	66	101	202
Paisley Mohawks*	84	32	57	89	143
Glasgow Dynamos	13	6	10	16	30
Great Britain	36	8	6	14	62

* 1963-65 & 1967-69 only

Keith 'Duke' CAMPBELL

Inducted 1948

'Duke' Campbell was the first member to be inducted into the British Ice Hockey Hall of Fame. At that time he held the record of 389 consecutive league and cup appearances in English National League competitions.

The nickname 'Duke' stuck during his school days in Winnipeg. His burgeoning hockey skills were likened to 'Duke' Keats an NHL star of the 1920s and at that time one of the best passers of the puck.

Campbell arrived in London for the autumn of 1935 to join the Percy Nicklin-coached Richmond Hawks. Hawks tied with Wembley Lions for the league title, losing out on goal difference. The following autumn, as with several other teammates he moved with his coach to the newly opened 8,200-seat Harringay Arena. He spent the following four seasons with the Greyhounds. Moved from left- to right-wing by Nicklin he initially formed a line with Wib Hiller and Earl Nicholson, taking the team to a third-place finish in the league. Two years later, combining with Joe Beaton and Fan Heximer he helped Greyhounds win the ENL and London Cup. Winter 1940, with Dunc Cheyne replacing Heximer, made no difference as the league title was retained along with the capture of the National Tournament. Seventh overall in league scoring gained an All-Star 'A' for Keith.

With the war over he played briefly for Brighton in the first Autumn Cup, before switching to Harringay Racers. He continued where he left off seven years earlier. At season's end with a total of 21 goals and 51 assists, he was again voted onto the All-Star 'A' sextet, with Racers second in the league and London Cup. Now captain and assistant coach his team won the 1947 Autumn Cup and the following campaign the league crown. Racers picked up the Autumn Cup again in 1949 followed by an All-Star 'B' rating for Campbell.

With an opportunity to move up to be a full player-coach and with the blessing of his previous club, he crossed London to sign for Earls Court Rangers. Skating on defence since the war, he was still able to outwit younger players with rink craft and cunning. By April 1952 he had guided Rangers to second in the ENL, their highest post-war finish. The previous three years they had finished in the cellar. This time, the first that he had personally selected the team, the end of season vote of the experts named him as coach on the 'B' squad. He only suited up for seven matches. The next winter he saw action in thirty-one outings, retiring in the spring.

At the time he left the sport, as a forty-four-year-old veteran, this 5ft 8in tall former forward, weighing in at 178lbs, had earned a reputation as an outstanding skater with stick handling skills to match. He was a team player, coupled with a will to win.

Keith William 'Duke' Campbell was born on 21 September 1909 at Stratton, Ontario, moving to Winnipeg at the age of two. Educated there, he graduated from the University of Manitoba in engineering. Commencing in organised hockey at the age of thirteen in the

Duke Campbell – British ice hockey's first Hall of Fame inductee –
photographed during the 1949/50 season he spent with Harringay Racers.

midgets with the local St Pats he progressed to the junior St Vital Saints. By twenty, as a centre-ice, he was in senior hockey with Elmwood Millionaires and then the Selkirk Fishermen. On the way he had visits to the Memorial and Allan Cup play-offs. During 1934/35 he iced for Moncton Hawks, coached by Nicklin, and Pittsburgh Yellowjackets.

Working in an aircraft factory during the Second World War, he continued to play hockey at Brighton in their Sunday League. He also turned out for the Canadian Forces in Europe team at Wembley in early 1946.

Whilst with the Harringay Racers he was employed by the GRA at their greyhound track adjacent to the arena. Married to an English girl, they lived at Hounslow, west London, in the early 1950s.

He died in the early 1980s in Winnipeg, Canada.

Competition Statistics	GP	G	A	Pts	PIM
Richmond Hawks	---	10	11	21	24
Harringay Greyhounds	---	64	64	128	---
Brighton Tigers	12	6	11	17	10
Harringay Racers	199	63	139	202	113
Earls Court Rangers	98	16	30	46	20

Earl CARLSON

Inducted 1998

Earl Carlson became a key member and captain of Durham Wasps from their formation in 1947 and the core of the team in the Northern Tournament throughout the 1950s.

He was born at Kenora, Ontario, and came to Britain, aged seventeen, with the Royal Canadian Air Force during the Second World War. Based at Middleton St George, then at Croft

airfield in north-east England he was instrumental in forming the Croft airmen's team that played at Durham in the Canadian Bomber Group League.

The original rink at Durham was an open air facility, later protected from the vagaries of the weather by a tarpaulin roof supported by substantial timber posts, some of which were located down the centre of the ice. What the hundreds of Canadian servicemen including Carlson, thought of it remains a mystery. A press report of February 1945 said of him: 'The little white haired centre-ice man for Croft was the outstanding player of the match.' Several of the flyers married locally and settled in the area post-war. With a permanent structure now in place to enclose the ice they became mentors to the native lads and together formed Durham Wasps.

Carlson at 5ft 9in and weighing 165lbs was an outstanding stick handler, scoring hat-tricks in his first two appearances with Wasps. Three goals once entered the net within twenty-six seconds. His dazzling speed, solo rushes and weaving skating style down the ice brought the packed 4,000-strong Durham attendances to their feet week after week.

Earl Carlson was Durham Wasps' first captain and at the core of their team in the 1950s.

From the inception of the Northern Tournament at Durham in the autumn of 1948, Wasps headed the table for most of the twelve years of the competition. Playing on average thirty or so games against amateur teams each winter, Durham won the play-offs five times. Unfortunately individual player records are sparse but Carlson headed his teammates in every one of the five seasons that have been published. Named Player of the Week in the 18 January 1958 edition of *IHW*, a rare distinction for a non-professional National League player, he became the second player in Britain to score more than 500 goals.

He retired in spring 1963 from the briefly renamed Durham Bees. With the advent of the NL for 1966/67 he made a short-lived comeback for Durham, now again labelled the Wasps, scoring five times and adding two assists in his seven appearances.

Earl married Catherine, a local girl, and after a brief spell in Canada, soon after the war ended, they returned to England to settle in Darlington. A modest and reserved man, very popular with his fellow Wasps and fans alike, he firmly believed in team spirit and fairness. He died suddenly in hospital at his adopted town of Darlington on 15 April 1970, aged forty-four.

Competition Statistics	GP	G	A	Pts	PIM
Durham Wasps*	134	262	179	441	71
Durham Bees**	5	6	1	7	2

* 1948/49, 1950-53 & 1954/55 only,

** 1962/63 only

Johnny CARLYLE

Inducted 1988

Johnny Carlyle is another of Scotland's outstanding players to emerge in the early post-war years. He played professionally in the Scottish National League and later the BNL until 1960, and then became a well respected coach in senior amateur hockey.

He learnt to skate at the local rink in Falkirk around the age of fourteen during the Second World War and was soon involved in ice hockey. As a big lad it was not long before he graduated to the junior Cubs. He credits his first coach Nelson McCuaig with showing him how to hold a stick and shoot correctly. He made his debut for the Canadian-dominated Falkirk Lions at the age of seventeen. He substituted for an injured player in November 1946 against Paisley Pirates.

National Service in the Argyll and Sutherland Highlanders took him away from the rinks for two years. On his return Lions' coach George McNeil moved him from centre to a defensive left-winger, then back to defence. He gained a regular place with the Lions as his team won the SNL play-offs for the Anderson Trophy three times. On the second occasion – season 1951/52 – Falkirk also collected Scottish and Canada Cups. The latter remained in the trophy cabinet the next year,

Senior hockey folded in Falkirk in 1955, to be replaced by the Scottish Amateur League which lasted one year, won by a

A Scot in exile – Johnny Carlyle of Harringay Racers in 1956.

Carlyle-inspired Lions. With the sport ceasing in his home town he moved to London, joining Harringay Racers. Here he credits his coach Bill Glennie with completing his hockey education. The Racers came second in the Autumn Cup and league. Johnny gained All-Star 'B' recognition, a rare occurrence for a British player in an era dominated by Canadians. The following winter he became the first home-bred player to captain Racers. With Harringay closing he moved first to the reformed Edinburgh Racers who folded at Christmas 1958, then to Nottingham and Brighton next winter. On the south coast he again grasped silverware as the Tigers triumphed in the first, and last, play-offs of the pro BNL. Taking a 3-2 first leg lead to Nottingham on 6 May 1960, Carlyle drove the deciding game into overtime with the fifth goal of the evening at 33.10. Brighton tied the match in the sixty-sixth minute for 6-5 victory on aggregate.

He commenced his coaching career that autumn as Edinburgh resumed hockey, Royals defeated Durham in the last of the classic Northern Tournament finals and swept up the Southampton and Brighton 'home' tournaments. Murrayfield dropped hockey so Carlyle came south once more, signing for Brighton. He stayed two years as player-coach, gaining All-Star honours at 'A' and 'B' for coach and defence slots.

Back to Murrayfield in autumn 1963, to stay for ten years, he soon hung up the sweater to concentrate on coaching. He moulded the Racers into a powerful outfit. Runners-up in the inaugural NL campaign of 1966/67 led to a similar finish in the following year's Autumn Cup.

With this performance came the first of four consecutive All-Star 'A' accolades as coach. In 1968/69 Racers won the play-offs and picked up the Autumn and Icy Smith Cups. Both were retained the following two winters as was the NL title, for the third consecutive time.

The BIHA previously acknowledged his talent in selecting and motivating a winning combination by naming him player-coach in 1961 for Great Britain's return to the World Championships.

Eleven years earlier he made his debut for Britain as London hosted the world event, to finish fourth. He scored three goals in the opening match, a 9-0 blanking of France. The following year in Paris, in an almost all-Scottish roster, he netted Great Britain's only goal in a 5-1 defeat by Sweden and another in the 6-6 tie with America.

In his first stint as coach in Pool 'B' in Switzerland he played in all six games. The team missed out on promotion, tying with Norway, with an inferior goal difference. He was recalled ten years on to mastermind Britain from the bench in two Pool 'C' tournaments. In Holland in 1971 and 1973 he coaxed a total of three wins and two ties from a mix of veterans and rookies, hampered by lack of funding, and consequently a lack of preparation.

A rugged defenceman, Carlyle was very much a hockey players' player. As a coach he knew exactly what he wanted from his charges, they needed to work hard, which had a great deal to do with his success in improving their game.

John Cumming Carlyle was born on 31 July 1929 at Falkirk. His paternal grandparents were American from Pennsylvania. He went to school in Falkirk and served a long apprenticeship as a painter and decorator, following his father's trade.

After hockey finished at Brighton he settled in Falkirk to work as a sales rep in electrical goods before setting up a decorating business, moving on to own a couple of shops and a café. He and his wife live in retirement in the town where he first saw the light of day.

Competition Statistics	GP	G	A	Pts	PIM
Falkirk Lions	329	81	120	201	345
Harringay Racers	102	6	36	42	87
Edinburgh Royals	20	3	10	13	34
Nottingham Panthers	27	1	6	7	14
Brighton Tigers	121	46	55	101	95
Murrayfield Racers*	12	4	9	13	28
Great Britain	16	9	3	12	8

* 1964/65 only

Jimmy CHAPPELL

Inducted as a member of the Great Britain 1936 Olympic and World Champions

Jimmy W. Chappell scored twice in the seven matches that gave Great Britain the 1936 triple crown of Olympic, World and European Champions. He also contributed 7 goals and 9 assists as Britain retained the European title for the following two years.

Born in Huddersfield, Yorkshire on 25 March 1915 his parents moved to Perth, Ontario, when Jimmy was ten years old before settling in Oshawa. He first appears in organised hockey in 1932 with Oshawa Blue Imps and next winter in the Majors of the Ontario Junior Hockey Association. He had one year at intermediate level in Whitby and skipped a university course to join the increasing number of British-born hockey players returning to the land of their birth.

Signing for Earls Court Rangers in west London he centred the second attack trio. Quickly snapped up by Great Britain, he secured his Olympic place by scoring in four of the five Test matches against Resident Canadians. In Bavaria he netted in the 5-1 win over Hungary in the group semi-finals and again next day in the 5-0 final round shut-out of Czechoslovakia.

Jimmy Chappell on the ice for Brighton Tigers in 1947/48.

Rangers won the London Cup in his first season at Empress Hall and secured the knock-out National Tournament the next season in a two-leg final with Manchester Rapids. In February London staged the World Championships with Chappell alternating at centre and right-wing. His playmaking was vital in the struggle for European supremacy with Switzerland. On 20 February 10,000 spectators at Wembley saw his hard work assist Dailley in netting the opening marker. Chappell took a perfect pass to score the third goal at the fifty-minute mark in the 3-0 shut-out of the Swiss. Five days later, at the same venue in the four-team final pool, the first goal did not arrive until ten minutes into the second overtime. Five minutes later a short pass from Chappell gave Great Britain a 2-0 victory; a second triumph over the Swiss. His third European gold medal was secured in Prague where he played in all eight of Britain's matches.

After a third year with a near bottom-of-the-table Rangers he moved to Scotland's emerging semi-pro National League. He joined Fife Flyers in their inaugural season, operating out of Kirkcaldy in his first year there. By mid-March 1939 Flyers ended third and he was fifth overall in points in the league tournament for the Canada Cup. The following autumn he was with the rookie Dunfermline Vikings which won the knock-out Scottish Cup.

For the next three years he played for teams in Toronto and Oshawa and the Ordinance Corps in Ottawa after joining the Army. He rose to the rank of captain, seeing action in Germany. He turned out for the Canadian HQ team at Wembley prior to the resumption of league hockey in autumn 1946 when he signed for Brighton. His three years on the south coast saw the Tigers roar to two successive league titles, plus the inaugural Autumn Cup and the National Tournament.

In the twilight of his career he again suited up for Great Britain when they endeavoured to retain the Olympic title at St Moritz in 1948. In the eight games he scored three times including one in the opening 5-4 win over Austria on 31 January.

The following winter injuries restricted him to 20 matches as he moved into refereeing for a couple of seasons, including the 1950 World Championships.

Pre-war Chappell ran a skate shop and milk bar at Earls Court and by 1947 worked as a London-based sales manager for a South African export company. The experience served him well when he finally settled in Toronto with his family, developing a successful business. A modest man, who still spoke with traces of a Yorkshire accent, he was a keen cricketer who represented Canada and once faced Don Bradman.

He died whilst on holiday in Florida during April 1973.

Competition Statistics	GP	G	A	Pts	PIM
Earls Court Rangers	---	26	15	41	46
Fife Flyers	---	11	18	29	---
Dunfermline Vikings	---	23	17	40	---
Brighton Tigers	130	72	64	136	79
Great Britain	30	12	9	21	---

Art CHILD

Inducted in 1993 as member of the Great Britain Olympic and World Champions

Art Child was Great Britain's back-up netminder to the gold medal winning team at the 1936 Winter Olympic Games in Germany. Although an integral member of the Great Britain squad, appearing in all the group and informal photos taken at Garmisch, he was not tested. The brilliant performances of first choice, Jimmy Foster, kept him on the sidelines.

Arthur 'Art' John Child was born on 15 September 1916 in West Ham, London. His family emigrated to Canada when he was about three years old. He started in hockey as a forward and switched to goal when the regular netminder was injured. Between 1932 and 1934 he was with West Toronto Nationals in the Junior Ontario Hockey Association. He graduated from the Ontario School of Baking with a diploma for scientific bakery. As a very determined and adventurous nineteen year old he spent the summer travelling across Canada to the Pacific by jumping freight trains and walking.

Child came to England on the assumption that someone would give him a chance, it duly came in January 1936 when he took over guarding the Wembley Lions' net. The next winter he acted as back-up at Earls Court to the Rangers and Royals. He turned out a couple of times for Southampton Vikings in mid-December as their regular netminder returned to Canada due to a family bereavement. Perivale Rovers, the equivalent to one of today's recreational teams, and backed by the Philco Radio manufacturer, also called upon Art on occasions.

He regained a starting position with Wembley Monarchs for 1937/38, replacing Jackie Nash. This was Art's most successful season here and the only one for which his statistics are available. He back-stopped the Monarchs to a runners-up place in the league with four shut-outs. In the National Tournament, with a 2.42 goals-against average per match, he helped Monarchs win a preliminary pool although they lost 6-5 on aggregate to Wembley Lions in the semi-finals.

Art Child, a successful
netminder for the Wembley
Monarchs between 1937 and
1939.

He maintained his place the next winter, but not the glory of the previous year as 1939/40 saw him moving aside to a back-up slot with Monarchs in the first and only wartime league campaign.

During 1941 in Canada, as a member of the British Technical Commission, he set up a munitions department at the American Can Co. Later he became their director of Marketing and Government Affairs. Hockey still played an important part in his life. He back-stopped Hamilton Majors/Tigers from 1942 to 1951 in senior hockey, including the Allan Cup finals in 1946.

Moving into politics, Art Child served as a member of the Canadian Parliament from June 1955 to May 1959. As a seventy year old he was still active in business but in 1996 he collapsed and died whilst playing golf.

Competition Statistics	GP	GA	GAA	SO
Wembley Monarchs*	29	64	2.20	4

★ 1937/38 only

Willie CLARK

Inducted 1993

Willie Clark was an outstanding goalminder for Murrayfield Racers in the heyday of the NL in the early 1970s, and went on to become involved in the management of Scottish ice hockey.

Virtually a one-club man, his involvement in ice hockey dates back to around 1954, a couple of years after the Murrayfield rink opened for business. His first wore skates whilst acting as a steward on hockey nights. Edinburgh Royals dropped out of the pro BNL in the spring of 1955 and the ice stewards formed their own team. Clark started playing on defence, until one evening the regular goaltender failed to appear. He liked the position and stayed to make it his own.

Very soon he was acting as back-up goalkeeper to the unbeaten senior amateur Royals in the North British League, which flourished during 1957/58. The following season he moved to Glasgow Flyers and by mid-season became their No.1 keeper.

With the Royals back in hockey for 1959/60 he naturally moved to his original club. He back-stopped Edinburgh to triumph in the 1961 Northern Tournament held at Durham and Whitley Bay, the BIHA Cup at Southampton and the Brighton Tournament. It was this season that saw his first visit to the World Championships. He played in three of Great Britain's games in Switzerland, with a goal-against average of 2.33.

Willie Clark with his Hall of Fame certificate at the 1993 Writers' Dinner at Wembley. He was a stalwart for Scottish ice hockey on and off the ice, particularly for the Murrayfield Racers.

As facilities for the sport were withdrawn by the Murrayfield rink, the Royals faded away for a couple of years. Racers slowly evolved as a reserve team from new younger players, benefiting from the coaching of Johnny Carlyle. Clark spent some of 1965/66 with Fife. However, with the introduction of the NL in 1966 he returned to Murrayfield for some of his finest years between the pipes. Racers won the Icy Smith Cup five times between 1968 and 1975, the NL title and play-offs four times and the Autumn Cup three times. Willie was named to the All-Star 'A' team from 1969 for four consecutive seasons and again three years later, as well as two 'B's.

He hung up the pads for good in summer 1976 to serve as the Racers team manager for the next ten years and chairman for the following two. Also, until 1994 he was team manager for Scotland for eighteen seasons having played in several of the annual clashes with England. By the mid-1980s Clark was a member of the SIHA in charge of senior development and soon representing the SIHA on a regular basis at BIHA Council meetings in London until he resigned in 1996. Clark also served two terms as manager of the Great Britain Under-20 side in Holland and Yugoslavia.

He was selected for Great Britain in four further World Championships. In Pool 'B' in 1963 and 1965 he was not called upon to face a puck. In his last trip with Great Britain, to Holland in 1971, he was between the pipes for all seven matches in Pool 'C' with three wins and a tie.

William McLean 'Willie' Clark was born in Edinburgh on 24 May 1931. As a young adult glazing was his trade. This stood him in good stead when many years later he took on the role of Projects Manager at the Murrayfield rink where he remained until retirement at the age of sixty-five.

He now runs a cattery from the house he built at Newbridge on the outskirts of Edinburgh.

Competition Statistics	GP	GA	GAA	SoG	SO
Edinburgh Royals	---	---	---	---	---
Glasgow Flyers	---	---	---	---	---
Murrayfield Racers*	141	497	3.52	3,502**	7
Fife Flyers	---	---	---	---	---
Great Britain	34	---	---	---	0

* 1967-73 only
** excludes 1967/68

Kevin CONWAY

Inducted 2005

Kevin Conway is one of the most talented players from Canada to play in Britain in the modern era. In twenty seasons, ending in spring 2004, he piled up a total of 2,574 points from 805 games in competitions at four different levels.

He arrived in Britain in 1985 to sign for Ayr Bruins in the Premier Division of the HBL. Conway immediately topped the Division with 129 goals to gain his first of five All-Star ratings. After spending the early part of the next winter with Indianapolis Checkers he returned to join Durham. He helped the Wasps win the British play-offs at Wembley by assisting on the first two goals in the final, a 9-5 defeat of Murrayfield.

Conway was released the next October to be snapped up by Division One Telford, where he was reunited with Tim Salmon. They had previously been together at Ayr in the push for promotion. In their first weekend together they accumulated 56 points in two matches. The Tigers duly won the division with Conway topping the points table. He was named 'Player of the Year' and collected an All-Star place. Despite leading Telford in scoring for the next campaign, Tigers and Conway slipped to fourth respectively in the league and points chart he needed to find another team at the season's end.

Kevin Conway, who appeared 363 times for Basingstoke as a Beaver or Bison, awaits some ice time from the bench.

Cleveland moved quickly to sign him in summer 1989 as Conway joined his fourth club in five years. He stayed for two winters. In the first he was second overall in league scoring only to go one better in the promotion play-offs, won by Bombers. The pundits named him to the All-Stars for a third time. Conway ended on 57+55 by spring 1991 although his club slid to ninth and relegation. His next move saw him settle for seven years in Hampshire.

Linking up with previous scoring partner Salmon during his first winter, then Mario Belanger the following year, he gained two consecutive All-Star accolades. Beavers topped Division One and their four-team group of the promotion play-offs in spring 1993. Several coaching changes during the first year in the Premier Division for a ninth-place finish still saw Conway with 111 points. He totalled his fourth century in goals since arriving in Britain. He upped his league points total by twelve the next season to hold Beavers' records for most goals and points. With a change of ownership and name, to Bison, for his fifth season at Basingstoke, he remained top scorer, adding most assists to his club records.

He gained his British passport in 1992 and was immediately called up for Great Britain. In his first venture at the World Championships, staged at Hull, his 13 goals and 10 assists helped Great Britain to gain promotion from Pool 'C' to the 'B' group.

Born on 13 July 1963 at Sault Ste Marie, Ontario, the 5ft 10in winger, weighing in at 179lbs, played in a further six World Championships for Great Britain, including Pool 'A' in Italy in 1994. He also skated in two Olympic qualifying tournaments. His total points haul of 66 places him second-highest since Britain re-entered the world scene in 1989.

With the coming of the out and out high professional Superleague he maintained his position on Bison's roster.

Conway's final year in Hampshire coincided with the Bison's second and last campaign in the expensive Superleague. In one of their four home victories, Kevin scored the overtime winner against Mancester Storm, the eventual runners–up. In summing up the season coach Peter Woods said: 'It was always just one line that produced all our offence.' Of course, that line included Conway.

He left Basingstoke as their all-time leading scorer with 946 points, including 478 goals, to sign for Newcastle, now re-labelled as Riverkings. Aged thirty-five and in his last season at the highest level of competition he still had the skills and commitment that yielded 51 points as the team's leading scorer. This zest for the sport was recognised with a recall to the Great Britain squad.

The following winter proved difficult. He commenced at the second level of British hockey with Hull Thunder in the BNL. A change of ownership and lack of funds lead to his release at the close of 1999. In January he put pen to paper for Chelmsford Chieftains in the Premier Division of the English League. Director John Blundell said: 'We are naturally delighted to have landed a player of Kevin's class and quality.' He made an immediate impact in his first game in Essex with a wrap-around goal eighty-six seconds from the opening face-off. Chieftains proceeded to win the league and play-offs.

The next move was to the Solihull Barons, revived after a four-year absence. His 41 goals tied as the Premier Division's best. In his second winter in the Midlands, a better-balanced Barons outscored the opposition to lose out on the Premier title by a single point. Kevin was fifth in league scoring with 27+34 and fourth in the English Cup. He sat out the 2002/03 season, returning to the ice at Solihull the following autumn with the renamed Kings. Initially the team's only non-British-trained member, his experience proved invaluable to the younger players in raising morale at the cash-starved club. His 32 points total was ten higher than the next player.

Until he resumed his playing career at Dumfries from the spring of 2004, his only involvement in hockey was coaching the Under-10s at Hull. The following year he was honoured at Basingstoke in a ceremony where his No.10 shirt was raised to the rink rafters.

Aged forty-three, and two years after entering the Hall of Fame, he came out of retirement. As the sole permitted import for Solway Sharks of the Scottish National League his silky smooth skating and scoring skills inspire a new generation.

Competition Statistics	GP	G	A	Pts	PIM
Ayr Bruins	47	163	123	286	88
Durham Wasps	34	80	95	175	38
Telford Tigers	61	252	220	472	206
Cleveland Bombers	88	206	173	379	158
Basingstoke Beavers/Bison	363	478	468	946	333
Newcastle Riverkings	56	23	28	51	14
Hull Thunder	20	12	16	28	6
Chelmsford Chieftains	12	9	9	18	6
Solihull Barons/Kings	124	111	108	219	96
Solway Sharks	47	47	59	106	42
Great Britain	58	33	33	66	54

Ian COOPER

Inducted 2002

During Ian Cooper's long and distinguished career in British ice hockey he made significant contributions to the sport, both on and off the ice. On the ice he contributed at left- or right-wing by assisting Durham Wasps and Cardiff Devils to five consecutive league and play-off championship doubles, including two grand slams, and eighty World Championship appearances for Great Britain. Off the ice he contributed with many unpaid hours devoted

Ian Cooper proudly shows off his
Ahearne Medal.

to the duty of chairman of the Players Association. He represented them on the now
defunct BIHA Council and for a time on the competitors section of the British Olympic
Committee.

Ian Cooper was born on 29 November 1968 at Peterlee, Co Durham, the younger brother
of Stephen. At the first ice hockey match he was taken to as a seven year old, at the newly
opened Crowtree rink in Sunderland, he decided 'to have a go with an old hockey stick
and a pair of skates'. Living half way between Sunderland and Durham he was soon skating
six days a week, and playing across two or three age groups. By the time he was fifteen he
topped the scoring in the Northern Section of the English Junior League with 31 goals and
12 assists from 12 matches. He netted twice for Durham Mosquitoes as they won the all-
England play-offs.

At the same time he was gaining experience with the older Hornets in the second division
of the British League, heading the points scoring chart for 1984/85 with a total of 70. He
first suited up that same winter with the senior Durham Wasps, seeing limited ice time in
thirty games to score three times. In an interview in 2000 he commented that 'Stephen [his
older brother] and I spurred each other on.' Ian's parents were praised for their support in his
development. 'It became a big part of their social life when we were growing up through the
sport. They have spent a few bob'.

His senior career took off the following season with 38 goals and 36 assists as Durham
retained the HBL P title. Wasps proceeded to win the British Championship finals at London's
Wembley Arena for the next two campaigns. The team added the Autumn Cup in the second
of those years, as Ian's points total rose to 139, earning him an All-Star rating. The same spring
he was awarded the accolade of Young British 'Player of the Year' with a sponsored trip to the
Calgary Flames training camp in Canada.

Then the ambitious Cardiff Devils, newly promoted to Division One of the HBL, offered enough money for Ian to quit his day job. He said later 'It was a huge gamble for us to go to Cardiff. We both quit our jobs… it was a big risk at the time.' He risked dropping a level in playing standard to become a full-time professional. The gamble paid off as the Devils won the Autumn Trophy, lifted the divisional title and the promotion play-offs to the HBL P. He gained his second consecutive All-Star British selection at left-wing.

Back in the top flight of the sport in Britain, Ian's points total for the season increased to 163 as Cardiff clinched the 1990 Premier title and the British Championship. The double overtime twenty-four-penalty shoot-out victory over Murrayfield Racers in front of a packed Wembley is one of his most enduring memories.

That summer Durham offered full professional wages. With the call of home proving strong, Ian's return coincided with Durham's grand slam of HBL, Heineken British Championship and Norwich Union Autumn Cup titles. Ian's points total topped out at 178. After helping the Wasps retain the league and Championship crowns he returned to Cardiff in 1992. During the next six years three league titles, two championships and an Autumn Cup medal were added to his own trophy cabinet.

Two years into his six years as chairman of the Players Association he was awarded the Ahearne Medal for his services to the sport. This was presented by the then president of the BIHA, Frederick Meredith at an on-ice ceremony during the Wembley finals weekend.

His fiftieth senior cap for Britain came at an Olympic qualifying tournament in Holland the following December. Of his Pool 'B' gold medal in 1993 he said, 'that was something special.' Alex Dampier, his coach at the time, added: 'He displays pride when he plays. He gives his all.' Ian first represented his country at Under-19 level in 1984, collecting a gold medal in Spain (Pool 'C') two years on. This partly paralleled a four-year stint with Great Britain Under-21s

After the Cardiff management failed to renew his contract in 1998 Cooper nearly joined Phoenix of the USA West Coast League before moving to London. Here he captained the Knights in their inaugural campaign, a rare privilege in an all-import roster. Eighteen months later his Superleague career ended, as Knights coach Chris McSorley arranged a move to Guilford in the BNL. This Millennium year also saw the last of his fourteen consecutive tournaments for Great Britain since the national side re-entered the World Championships in 1989.

The following winter a couple of games at Basingstoke and a few weeks at Chelmsford closed out Ian's illustrious playing career for club and country. He left the ice, aged thirty-two, to move from working part-time for a sponsor's agent into media management. For the past few years he can be found in southern Spain, selling property.

Ian Cooper was as much a playmaker, or more so, than a pure goalscorer, with a tough-but-fair approach to his game. By sustaining a professional career for many years, with playing standards increasing as the number of imports rose, he serves as an outstanding example to aspiring young Brits. His Great Britain coach of the mid-1990s, Peter Woods, said of him, 'Game in, game out he has always been consistent and I think the sport has benefited from the approach and attitude that Ian has brought.'

Competition Statistics	GP	G	A	Pts	PIM
Durham Wasps	272	306	316	622	600
Cardiff Devils	412	449	506	955	997
London Knights	59	10	20	30	95
Guilford Flames	13	2	12	14	20
Basingstoke Bison	2	1	0	1	0
Chelmsford Chieftains	10	5	18	23	16
Great Britain Under-19	14	8	6	14	6
Great Britain Under-21	22	10	13	23	18
Great Britain Senior	80	30	31	61	128

Stephen COOPER

Inducted 2003

During Stephen Cooper's long and distinguished career he has been the outstanding British-born-and-trained defenceman. At left defence he assisted Durham and Cardiff to five consecutive league and championship play-off doubles, including two Grand Slams. He also made 61 appearances in the World Championships for Britain in their rapid climb from Pool 'D' to the top Pool.

Along with his younger brother Ian, Stephen epitomised professionalism and the impact the two brothers made, along with the future Hall of Famer Tony Hand, helped fuel the boom in the sport in the late 1980s. Their example encouraged the belief that Brits could earn a living playing hockey.

Stephen Cooper was born on 11 November 1966 at Peterlee, Co. Durham. Whilst skating with his brother he saw a poster for a testimonial match for Kenny Matthews, a veteran player from the north-east of England. A few weeks after watching that game he went to his first training session armed with an old stick. Most of his early coaching between the ages of nine and fourteen was at Sunderland's Crowtree rink, mainly as a forward.

By the time he was thirteen he was also playing at Durham with the Mosquitoes in the junior league and for the older Hornets, usually donning his skates around six times a week. It was in this period that he moved back to the blue line, being encouraged by Mick Curry before he turned to refereeing.

He made his debut with the senior Durham Wasps during 1980/81. The following year he was awarded the Montfort Trophy as 'Rookie of the Year' in the final season of the NL. Two years later he won silverware as the Wasps topped Section B in the first winter of the revived British League. In the following seven seasons Cooper's reputation as a defender grew rapidly, so much so that his skills were eventually on a par with an import. By the time Cardiff came knocking in the summer of 1988 he had added two Premier Division and British Championship play-off medals to his collection. All-Star recognition first came in 1985, then two years later and again the following spring.

As with his brother Ian, the money offered by Cardiff meant gambling on giving up the day job to go full-time as a hockey player. The opportunity to practice every day provided additional strength and endurance. He regularly spent forty-five to fifty minutes on the ice during a match as the Devils won the Division One title and two-leg promotion play-off and the Autumn Cup Selection to the All-Star team was a mere formality.

Back in the top division Cooper's performance was a factor in Cardiff overturning the bookies odds of 500-1 to clinch the Premiership crown. In the championship final he shook off the attentions of Murrayfield's defenders to connect with a pass from his brother Ian, which tied the game 6-6 with ninety-five seconds remaining. The subsequent twenty-four-penalty shoot-out at Wembley, won by the Devils, will long be remembered.

That summer Durham offered professional wages so Stephen and his brother returned home. Durham Wasps duly raced to a Grand Slam of NU AC, league and the championship play-off titles.

Cooper racked up 118 points, often clocking up fifty minutes on the ice. After helping the Wasps retain the league and championship he returned to Cardiff in 1992. During the next four years with the Devils an Autumn Cup, two league and two championship medals were added to his collection, plus two further All-Star citations. He also featured in Cardiff's European venture in the autumn of 1994. The Devils defeated two former Soviet Elite teams, becoming the first British team to reach the Europa Cup semi-finals, which Ian missed due to injury.

In the summer of 1996 he signed for Manchester Storm for the inaugural Superleague season. In the second winter his points production increased to 25 as Storm ended league

Stephen Cooper – as featured
on a 2004 hockey card
produced by Cardtraders.

runners-up. Now at the veteran stage he spent a winter at Newcastle with the league-operated Riverkings. He moved again, this time to Nottingham. For his third team in as many years Stephen chose Hull, one of six signings from the Superleague and was pure class on the blue line in the BNL and a linchpin with his rasping shot. When Thunder's funding ran out he was forced to move south to the first year Coventry Blaze. Here he completed his career on a high note, as by the close of the 2001/02 campaign Blaze were BNL runners-up and finalists in the play-offs and Challenge Cup. His knack of scoring crucial goals almost single-handedly put Coventry into the play-off final. For his steady play and rock-like anchoring of the defensive corps he was honoured with the retirement and raising to the ceiling of his No.55 shirt.

His career for Great Britain commenced in 1982 at the Under-19 European Championships, being named as the tournament's Best Defenceman, at the age of sixteen. Two years on, he was made captain and named Best British Player, and his team took home the silver medal. That same winter he made the Under-21 side and again in 1986. He moved to the senior squad in 1989 for eleven tournaments at World and Olympic qualifying level, including the 1994 Pool 'A' against the might of Canada and Russia. Named 'Outstanding Defenceman' twice, at Pool 'D' and three years later in the Pool 'B' is a rare distinction for a Brit.

Over the twenty-two years at the upper levels of the sport Stephen Cooper proved to be a hard-hitting, hard-working physical defenceman and nine-times winner of the Alan Weeks Trophy. As an example of how to play this difficult position, his is a hard act to follow.

Upon leaving the sport in 2002 he and his wife set up home in Manchester where he is employed selling high-quality motor cars.

Competition Statistics	GP	G	A	Pts	PIM
Durham Wasps	379	202	359	561	627
Cardiff Devils	292	154	362	516	498
Manchester Storm	110	10	28	38	70

Newcastle Riverkings	54	6	8	14	14
Nottingham Panthers	59	2	12	14	40
Hull Thunder	38	11	29	40	58
Coventry Blaze	78	22	57	79	187
Great Britain Under-19	13	7	4	11	22
Great Britain Under-21	9	2	4	6	14
Great Britain – Senior	61	11	27	38	54

Johnny 'Red' COWARD

Inducted in 1993 as a member of the Great Britain 1936 Olympic and World Champions

Johnny 'Red' Coward played left-wing for Great Britain in the 1936 Olympic Winter Games triumph at Bavaria, Germany. Coward participated in six games, sitting out the opener against Sweden. Used mainly as a backchecker, he scored a goal in the final four-nation pool 5-0 shutout of Czechoslovakia on St Valentine's Day.

Red Coward, a 1936 Olympic and World Champion

He was born on 8 February at Ambleside, Westmoreland, in the midst of the English Lake District. His family probably emigrated to Canada when Johnny was quite a young child. He grew up at Fort Frances in north-western Ontario.

It was Percy Nicklin, coach of the British national team, who identified Coward as a suitable player for Richmond Hawks, also coached by Nicklin. Returning to England in the autumn of 1935 he wore sweater No.9 and skated on the second forward line with fellow Olympian 'Chirp' Brenchley at right-wing. Nicklin used the pair, centred by Ivor Nicholson, as a checking line, limiting Coward to a single assist. Hawks contested for the ENL title all season long with Wembley Lions, tying on points but losing the crown due to an inferior goal difference. Richmond finished fifth in the nine game London Cup. Johnny netted a pair and contributed an assist.

Scoring twice in Great Britain's 7-4 test-match series over the Resident Canadians at Wembley in December 1936, plus a goal in the 8-7 loss at Brighton the next month assured his retention in the national side. The World and European Championships were held in London in February, at Wembley and Harringay, where Great Britain finished second to Canada. He iced in five of Britain's nine games, being used by Nicklin as the seventh forward.

Weakened by the defections to the new Harringay teams, Richmond performed poorly in Coward's second season, despite his increased points tally. The club folded at the end of the schedule. Johnny returned to Canada with his haul of gold medals, two European, one Olympic and one World Championship medal to go alongside the 1937 silver medal. His 1936 Great Britain jersey was donated to the Toronto Hall of Fame in 2001 by a friend of the family to whom it had been given.

Growing up in Fort Frances, Johnny first appears in the hockey records in 1924 with the local junior Cadets. Moving on to senior hockey he spent three winters with Fort Frances Tigers in the Thunder Bay League. This was followed by spells with the local Orfuns (sic) and Royals and Duluth Hornets during 1933/34 in the USA Amateur Hockey Association.

From 1937 he spent four years with Fort Frances Maple Leafs in the International American League, including a trip to the Allan Cup play-offs in 1940. Four years overseas followed as an instructor in the Military Police. After the war he worked in a paper mill until 1969, then ran a pro golf shop and coached minor hockey. He died at Fort Frances, where he spent most of his life, on 8 February 1989.

Competition Statistics	GP	G	A	Pts	PIM
Richmond Hawks	---	7	6	13	22
Great Britain	11	1	0	1	---

Michael 'Micky' CURRY

Inducted 1994

'Micky' Curry was a top-level referee and a rising star in the international ranks of officiating when his life was cruelly cut short at the age of thirty-seven.

He began his association with ice hockey as a player in the Durham youth system. Curry broke into senior hockey with the Wasps at the age of twenty in the days of the NL and its associated competitions. Some statistics are missing but those that are available show him with a total of 13 goals and 18 assists from 69 matches with the same number of penalty minutes. He retired five games into the 1982/83 season, after an on-ice eye injury had forced him to sit out most of the previous two seasons.

Unable to keep away from the sport, he turned to officiating. He was soon handling contests in the newly formed Heineken-sponsored British League, first as a lineman then with the red arm bands as a referee. In total he appeared in 234 Premier Division matches, 166 as a referee plus sixty-eight as a linesman. These included seven Wembley Championships commencing in 1985 on the lines. He refereed a semi-final in 1990, 1991 and 1992 and was tipped to work the 1993 final.

Micky Curry, a leading official, who tragically died in a road traffic accident after a match in Peterborough on 7 March 1993.

His international career began in March 1988 as a linesman in the European Pool 'B' Junior Championships at Briancon, France. The next year he lined the World Junior Championships Pool 'C' held in the west of England and Wales and 1990 at Eindhoven in Holland. Six months later he was assigned to a European Cup quarter-final group at Rouen, France. By early 1992 he was moved up to referee Pool 'B' of the senior World Championships in Austria. In November he was in Milan for the European Cup semi-finals. This was followed by a New Year trip to Sweden to handle the best youngsters from Canada and Russia in the World Junior Championships 'A' Pool.

On the evening of 7 March 1993 he was driving north to his home at Hetton-Le-Hole with a linesman, after officiating at Peterborough. He was killed as his car was struck head-on by a van travelling in the opposite direction on the wrong side of the A1 dual carriageway. A nineteen-year-old student, who had been driving the other vehicle involved, was convicted of driving whilst drunk and jailed for eighteen months.

Had he lived there is no doubt that he would have progressed to the senior A Pool and possibly fulfilled his ambition to call games at the Olympics. Many tributes were paid at the memorial game held at his home rink on 17 March between Durham Wasps Select and the British All-Stars. Among them was erstwhile teammate and coach Peter Johnson, who paid this tribute: 'As a referee, Micky had a totally professional attitude and always kept himself in fit condition. His calming influence, either talking to you or telling you to keep your mouth shut, is something I will always remember about him.'

Michael Curry's ability to communicate his commitment to officiating influenced and provided encouragement to beginners at the numerous seminars and training camps he attended up and down the country. The BIHA instituted an annual award in his name to be presented to the most improved young official.

Gordon DAILLEY

Inducted in 1993 as a member of the Great Britain 1936 Olympic and World Champions

Gordon Dailley served on defence in all seven matches in Great Britain's triple-crown triumph at the 1936 Winter Olympics in Bavaria, Germany.

At the core of the multi-medal-winning national team of 1935–39 he was also one of the

few players to be featured on a British cigarette card. He first came here in 1933 as a twenty-two year old from his native Canada, having worked his passage across the Atlantic on a cattle boat. He found a spot with Grosvenor House Canadians, who lost just one game on their way to the English League title. Having only arrived a few weeks earlier he was soon appearing in the English team opposing France, Canada and the USA at various London rinks. He provided a goal and an

George Dailley was an ever-present member of Great Britain's triple-crown success at Winter Olympics in Bavaria, Germany, during February 1936. He played his club hockey in London, mainly at Wembley with the Lions and then the Monarchs.

assist in the 4-5 loss to the Americans at Streatham and the goal in the 1-0 victory over France at Purley.

That summer Dailley moved a few miles west to join Wembley Lions at the newly opened Empire Pool. Here he skated at left-wing on the first forward line. Next year he dropped back to the blue line, switching to Wembley Monarchs two years later. Whilst with the Lions he assisted them to two successive league titles, plus the London-Paris Tournament in 1935/36. He had less luck with the Monarchs who he captained. The best they achieved in his two seasons was a league runners-up position.

He first represented Great Britain at the 1935 World Championships in Davos, scoring four goals to win bronze. He took over as captain of Britain from the injured Carl Erhardt at the 1937 London world event, scoring the first goal in the opening 6-0 blanking of Germany. He continued to amass goals, ending on nine, as Great Britain won European gold. Twelve months on, the European crown was retained in Prague as Dailley contributed 2+2. At his final World Championship he captained and bolstered a younger and less-experienced squad in Switzerland.

Gordon Debenham Dailley was born on 24 July 1911 in Winnipeg. Educated at St John's College he graduated from the University of Manitoba. Spending the Second World War in England, he attended the Canadian Staff College in 1943, attaining the rank of major. After the war he held posts in Ottawa and was with the United Nations Armistice Commission in Korea. Promoted to colonel in 1955 he was assigned to Belgrade as Military Attaché and by 1960 was base commander at Gagetown in New Brunswick.

Retiring from the military in 1964 he founded the African Safari Park at Rockton five years later, the first such park in Canada. An instigator of the Canadian Association of Zoological Parks, he also assisted in the formation of the Atlantic and New Brunswick Junior Symphony orchestras. Gordon Dailley died on 3 May 1989, aged seventy-seven at Cambridge, Ontario, Canada.

Competition Statistics	GP	G	A	Pts	PIM
Grosvenor House Canadians	---	---	---	---	---
Wembley Lions*	---	14	11	25	62
Wembley Monarchs	---	18	10	28	34**
Great Britain	36	15	5	20	---

* Excludes 1934/35
** Excludes 1938/39

Alex DAMPIER
Inducted 1995

Appointed in 1990 as head coach of the Great Britain national team, Alex Dampier took them from Pool 'D' to face the might of Canada and Russia in the top ranked Pool 'A' in five years – a huge achievement.

Like most Canadians he grew up playing ice hockey, developing from a left-winger into a defenceman. Whilst on holiday in Scotland as a twenty-three year old, visiting his girlfriend Sally (who was later to become his wife), he discovered British ice hockey. He stayed, turning out for Murrayfield Racers from autumn 1978 Racers, then a member of the NL. A year after joining Murrayfield Alex became player-coach, to be named an All-Star 'A' three winters in succession for his achievements. Racers won the league and the Icy Smith Cup three times and the Autumn Cup twice, plus the 1978/79 play-offs. He was also honoured with an 'A' and three successive All-Star 'B's as a defenceman.

A revived British League commenced from autumn 1982 and from the next season Dampier made only occasional appearances on the ice as he moved behind the bench. Two further

Alex Dampier played a massive part in re-establishing Great Britain as a competitive international team. In five years the team had gone from World Championship Pool 'D' to Pool 'A'. This achievement can not be underestimated.

All-Star 'B' coaching awards followed. He guided the Racers to a finals appearance in the first two years at Wembley Arena. At the third attempt, in late April 1986, his team triumphed in the 4-2 defeat of Dundee in front of a 7,657 crowd.

Moving south to fulfil the same function for Nottingham from autumn 1986, he spent seven years in the Lace City. Named runner-up as 'Coach of the Year' the following spring, he proceeded to gain the accolade two years running. On 15 November 1986 he steered the Panthers to a 5-4 victory over Fife Flyers at the NEC. Fifteen months later, at Wembley in front of 8,996 spectators, the Nottingham team held aloft the British Championship trophy. Defeating Humberside 7-5 at Sheffield on 23 November 1991 provided a second Autumn Cup and a record attendance for the competition final of 6,061. With Nottingham ninth in the ten-team Premier Division of the HBL, Dampier quit in mid-December 1992 to immediately move north to Sheffield. The parting was described as 'by mutual consent'. Alex commented: 'Seven years is a long time, it was getting to the stage where the players really needed someone fresh… Sheffield presents me with the opportunity to consolidate the position of an established team'.

He steered his new club to twenty victories from twenty-five remaining games, losing only once in their promotion group. Next winter, the Steelers, who were first in the HBL Premier Division, finished as runners-up, and later dropped to third for breaching the wage-cap. Undeterred, in the first encounter of this now-classic rivalry, Sheffield blanked Dampier's previous club 8-0 in the British Championship semi-final at Wembley. Spring 1985 saw Alex lead Steelers to the British League and Championships titles. Next year they repeated the triumph and added the B&H Autumn Cup. The coach commented: 'It's marvellous for the club and its fans to win three competitions when the standards in the sport have risen so high.' From autumn 1996 and the introduction of the Superleague he became general manager with Clyde Tuyl taking the coaching role. Two campaigns later, with Sheffield in ownership turmoil he resigned, moving further north to coach the Superleague-operated Newcastle Riverkings with a below-average budget.

A takeover of the club by a new Finnish owner saw Dampier back at Nottingham as director of hockey, ten games into their league campaign. He left in 2002 to accept a fresh challenge back at Newcastle, helping to put together a new team in the BNL. Two years later he made the decision to leave British hockey.

He was appointed to coach Great Britain in 1981 in the World Champioships Pool 'C' held in China, when the sport here was virtually amateur. He commented on his return: 'The opposition was so much better than us in every way. They were almost professional; some of the players had competed in the NHL.' Three years later when Britain entered the World Junior (Under-21) Championships for the first time he was put in charge, winning bronze twice at Pool 'C' over the next six tournaments.

His reputation as a thinking man's coach with a modest self-deprecating manner saw Dampier promoted back to the senior Great Britain side for 1990. Held at Cardiff, his reign started in The World Championships Pool 'D', with four wins from four starts. The second successive Pool 'C' was again a clean sweep, this time on home ice at Hull. The following winter the BIHA found sufficient resources for eight warm-up games between November and early March, enabling Dampier to select and weld a potentially winning team. The unknowns of Pool 'B', after a twenty-seven-year gap, were swiftly resolved. On the first morning the favourites Poland went down 4-3. The game winner resulted on a power-play from Dampier's successful call for a Polish stick measurement. Three victories later and an emotional 4-3 defeat of the Dutch at Eindhoven were followed two days on by a 10-4 defeat of Romania. Britain was back at the top with a game to spare. For the first attempt at Pool 'A' in thirty-two years almost half of the squad had played at the Wembley finals two days prior to the opening encounter with Russia in Italy. The financial backing, preparation and class of the opposition proved too strong for even Dampier to counter. Before standing down he noted: 'Great Britain are a 'B' Pool nation. There's no way I'm carrying on if we're again given no time to prepare.' Nonetheless, to have got the team there at all was a major achievement, not even dreamt of five years earlier when he took on the role.

Born on 3 May 1951 at Nipigon, Ontario, he commenced hockey in earnest with Charlottetown Islanders of the Major Junior Hockey League at eighteen, taking two trips to the Memorial Cup play-offs. A year with Lakehead University Nor'Westers followed. His 1972/73 season spent in the Eastern Hockey League with Cape Cod produced 32 goals and 50 assists and preceded a season for Muskegon Mohawks in the IHL. Here he scored 12 goals and 16 assists in sixty-six games. The next four years were devoted to obtaining a degree in physical education back at Lakeland.

He left Britain to move back to Canada to settle there with his family, in the summer of 2004, after an absence of twenty-six years.

Competition Statistics	GP	G	A	Pts	PIM
Murrayfield Racers*	74	36	63	99	51
* Excludes 1978-80					

Coaching	GP	W	L	D	W%
Nottingham Panthers	506	247	226	33	48.8
Sheffield Steelers	204	149	39	16	73
Newcastle Riverkings	58	18	37	3	31
Great Britain Under-21	26	11	12	3	42.3
Great Britain – Senior	41	20	19	2	48.7

Gerry DAVEY

Inducted 1949

Gerry Davey got up from his sick bed, kitted up and skated onto the ice at the outdoor rink at Garmisch on a February day in 1936 to score the go-ahead goal in Great Britain's 2-1 Olympic victory over Canada. In doing so he went a long way to ensuring gold medals for Britain.

The fourth member to join the BIHHofF, and nearly sixty years later (July 2007) he still holds the record as the all-time leading British goalscorer, with forty-four, in the World, European and Olympic Championships.

Gerald John Davey was born on 5 September 1914 at West Ham, London. He told two journalists, including Phil Drackett, that he had been born in Barking, east London, which is just four miles from West Ham. He grew up in Port Arthur, Canada, having been taken there as a child. What is not in doubt is that he learnt to play ice hockey while in Canada with Elmwood Midgets. His mother returned to England with Gerry when he was sixteen. His father, who was from Devon, had been killed in the First World War. With the assistance of a London newspaper he found a hockey club, joining Princes for the 1931/32 season.

His talents were quickly recognised by the British selectors for the mid-March European Championships held in Berlin. Davey finished as Great Britain's top scorer with seven goals, netting four of five in the consolation pool win over Latvia. The following winter saw him playing five games for Zurich SC before returning to London to sign for Queens. Moving to Streatham the following autumn, he remained with the south London club for four seasons. Here he won English League and International Club tournament medals during 1934/35. With hockey staring to boom in Scotland he joined the first year Falkirk Lions in September 1938 as player-coach. The second winter ended with Scottish Points Tournament and Airlie Trophy silverware.

With the coming of war he spent four years in Canadian senior hockey with Geraldton Gold Miners, St Catherine Saints and Hamilton Majors. With the latter club he had a crack at the Allan Cup prior to joining the Canadian Navy. Here he turned out for Toronto Navy Bulldogs.

Back with Streatham by July 1946 – with his English wife Susie – for the resumption of the ENL in the autumn, Davey, who moved to defence, had not lost his touch. In 47 matches he scored 52 times. Early on the following season he switched to Wembley Lions, combining a maintenance job at the Empire Poll with playing. Here he added 32 goals then retired. But not completely from the ice game, he took up refereeing and managing a sports shop.

But it's that goal on 11 February 1936 which was, not surprisingly, Davey's most treasured hockey memory, 'Well, it just made me feel good,' he later recalled. Forty seconds from the opening face-off with Canada, the slightly built, 160lb curly haired right-winger collected the puck at centre-ice. With his right-handed wrist shot he sent it flying past Francis Moon, the Canadian netminder. The goal judge waved his flag (sic) into the cold late evening air, it was -2 degrees Celsius, and via the radio surprised listeners back home learnt that Britain were leading the World Champions.

Next day he netted again in the 1-1 tie with Germany and potted a trio in the final round 5-0 defeat of Czechoslovakia.

This was not the only goal Gerry scored against Canada in World play. The year before, the two nations had met at Davos and in the opening round he netted both goals in the 4-2 loss. He also scored in the 3-1 final round win by Canada at Prague in 1938.

Ten years later, in an attempt to retain the triple Olympic, World and European crown, Davey was recalled to the British colours. Although Great Britain finished sixth at St Moritz he contributed five goals.

Gerry Davey as a referee in the early 1950s. It was his exploits as a player that led to his induction into the Hall of Fame. He scored the winning goal against Canada at the 1936 Olympics and it remains his most-treasured hockey moment.

After retiring from Wembley Lions he made a brief return to London ice, turning out for the amateur Streatham Royals during 1949/50 before he and his family relocated to Canada.

Competition Statistics	GP	G	A	Pts	PIM
Streatham*	112	63	47	144	32
Falkirk Lions	---	68	42	99	---
Wembley Lions	46	32	9	41	22
Great Britain	45	44	5**	49	---

★ Also scored 15 goals & 4 assists in 1933/34

★★ 1937 & 1938 only

Norman de MESQUITA

Inducted 2002

Norman de Mesquita never played ice hockey, but has served the sport with distinction in many varied guises.

Taken to see his first game aged fourteen, as league hockey resumed at the Empire Pool, Wembley, in October 1946, he describes the experience as 'love at first sight.' He became an instant fan of the sport in general and of Wembley Lions.

By the late 1940s and early 1950s he held the franchise for sales of the weekly *IHW* tabloid-size paper at the three large capacity London arenas at Earls Court, Harringay and Wembley. During this period he made the acquaintance of many of the major personalities in hockey, including Ernie Leacock who was at that time assistant secretary of the BIHA and their referee-in-chief.

He started skating in 1948 and six years later decided to take up refereeing, so naturally he turned to Leacock for guidance. His first organised match was on a Sunday morning in January at Streatham, where Royals faced Southampton in a Southern Intermediate League fixture. He officiated in three further matches that season. Early in October 1955 he was on the ice at Southampton when Sweden took on the local Vikings. His experience broadened with trips to the Durham and Whitley Bay-based Northern Tournament. One of his few chances in the pro BNL occurred at Nottingham in 1958 when he deputised for the assigned official. The early to mid-1960s were particularly busy with matches most weekends. His last was where he first saw the sport, as Wembley Lions shut-out Paisley Mohawks 3-0 on 20 November 1968. Strangely his mentor Leacock's final match – three years earlier – also involved the Paisley team, in Brighton Tigers' last match on home ice. Norman commented on those years, 'I loved it, wouldn't have missed it for anything'.

In the early 1960s he was employed as an advertising production manager. A move into broadcasting stemmed from a friend he met at drama school. He worked as a commissioning producer for the BBC World Service news magazine where Mesquita contributed many reports, including cricket, his other sporting passion. This led into Radio London where he rose to become sports editor. Many older fans will recall his Sunday morning phone-in, when, not withstanding the topic under discussion, he always managed to turn the chat to ice hockey.

Ice hockey returned briefly to Wembley during 1973/74 with the Detroit Red Wings-backed London Lions. Norman was the PA announcer, as he was for numerous other sporting events at the Empire Pool since 1968, including boxing, tennis, five-a-side football and basketball.

When Heineken commenced to stage the season-ending British Championship weekend at Wembley from 1984 Norman was the man on the mike. During those years until the sponsorship ended in 1996, he became known to the fans, who flocked to the renamed Wembley Arena from virtually every rink in the country, as 'The Voice of Wembley'. His deep dulcet tones imparted information clearly and dispassionately. In an interview at that time, he told reporter Anthony Beer: 'I consider myself to be very fortunate… incredibly so because what with hockey in winter and cricket all summer I actually get paid to do things I would readily pay for.'

When the *Ice Hockey World* was revived as a glossy monthly magazine by Phil Drackett in 1984, Norman was one of the regular contributors. After it was discontinued nine years later he began his provocative 'From the Shoulder' column for the fortnightly *IHNR*. He also became ice hockey correspondent for *The Times* and chairman of the British Ice Hockey Writers' Association, holding both posts for fourteen years.

He was one of the first, if not the first person, to realise the attraction to British fans of an organised travel package to watch live NHL games. His first 'London Ice Hockey Nuts' trip started in 1979 when he took a small group of friends to New York. 'Nuts' lasted twenty-five years with visits to Boston, Philadelphia, Hartford, Pittsburgh, Washington, Edmonton, Calgary, Winnipeg, Ottawa, Anaheim and Los Angeles.

'The Voice of Wembley' – Norman de Mesquita, an ice hockey enthusiast whose love of the sport has never diminshed.

In 1999 a serious illness curtailed his activities on behalf of the sport. A lasting effect is a speech impediment which means his announcing days have sadly ended. He continued to cover the NHL for the weekly *Ice Hockey News* until its abrupt closure in 2002.

Norman de Mesquita still lives in the north London house at Cricklewood where he was born on 28 January 1932. Here he now spends many hours listening to his large collection of classical music CDs. Hockey these days is mainly confined to watching his beloved NHL via the NASN satellite TV channel.

However, few, if any, can claim to have been more active in spreading the ice hockey message around Britain in the past fifty years or so.

Frank DEMPSTER

Inducted 1992

Frank Dempster spent nearly fifty years in the sport in many capacities but he will be best remembered as an administrator; in his earlier days as an unpaid helper, moving into paid employment in the days of the HBL, through to Superleague of the late 1990s.

His interest in ice hockey started when he was a schoolboy watching Ayr Raiders of the SNL. He later married the niece of his favourite Raiders player – the Canadian-born Ernie Domenico. When they folded in 1955 he travelled to Paisley on Friday evenings to follow the Pirates.

Frank Dempster relaxing at a
Wembley Finals weekend.

During the 1956/57 season he became part of the newly formed junior team at his home rink at Beresford Terrace in what he described as 'inter-rink' games, an early form of recreational hockey. From there he joined a Glasgow-based pool of players in senior amateur hockey, and sometimes guested for Perth Blackhawks, Fife Flyers and Falkirk Lions, mainly at rinks in southern England, including Wembley. Working at the Ayr rink provided the chance, in 1961, of being involved in the formation of the short-lived Ayr Balmorals (named after a local café) and then the Rangers. Whilst with the latter team the Bruins were founded to provide opportunities for younger players. Dempster helped out with club affairs and started to coach as the new group developed into a senior league side. He commenced contributing articles on hockey at Ayr to magazines covering the sport.

He started out as a winger, moving to defence in 1967. By spring 1971 he had played 170 matches in NL competitions contributing 213 points with a measly twenty minutes in penalties. He hung up the skates the following year when the original Ayr rink closed. Concentrating on coaching Bruins, who now called Ayr's smaller Limekiln Road rink home, they won the Icy Smith Cup in spring 1974 and he was named an All-Star 'B' coach. Club secretary for six seasons, he also served as manager of Rangers and the Bruins from 1974. This administrative experience broadened to include taking on fixtures for the NIHA 1968-82 and later for the Scottish equivalent.

From 1974 onwards he commenced travelling to London as one of the Northern Association representatives at BIHA council meetings. Two years later he was a 'personal' member, effectively a directorship, of the British governing body as a Company Limited by Guarantee. He was elected president of the SIIHA when it was revived in 1979 and was chairman at the time of his death.

With the formation of the HBL he took over drawing up their fixtures from 1983 for the next eleven years. As the sport expanded so did the administrative task. The BIHA utilised Frank to oversee disciplinary player control, serve as a member of the Doping Control Panel and Premier Division administrator. Team liaison and BIHA delegate and Great Britain general manager at the 1969 Pool 'D' World Championships in Belgium and Committee chairman twice at World Junior C and Senior 'D' Pool events were some of the his other duties. He represented the BIHA at twelve European Cup group tournaments.

During the life of Ice Hockey Superleague Ltd he held the title of hockey manager (discipline). He was the first full-time salaried administrator with the BIHA since the mid-1950s. In an interview he gave in 1992 he said, 'Very few people get paid to work in a sport they love to be involved in. From my point of view it can be seven days a week, for months on end, with no time off. I knew what it was going to be like.' It's for that degree of commitment and dedication that he was elected to the Hall of Fame.

Frank Dempster was born in Ayr on 13 March 1937 and educated at Newton Academy. After leaving school he served an apprenticeship as a wall and floor tiler then joined the RAF Medical Services. He became a member of the maintenance staff at Ayr ice rink and from then on hockey prevailed.

He underwent a serious operation for stomach cancer in the early 1990s. After a long illness he died on 24 December 2004.

Phil DRACKETT

Inducted 2007

Philip Drackett was the doyen of British ice hockey journalists and a life-long professional writer whose first sporting love was ice hockey. He contributed on a weekly basis to the *Ice Hockey World*, compiled and later edited that publication's yearbooks and many years later authored the story of British ice hockey in *Flashing Blades* and several others on the sport.

Phil was born on 22 December 1922 at Finchley in north London. His love for hockey started as a thirteen year old when he and his brother Bill followed the exploits of Richmond Hawks and Earls Court Rangers via newspapers and magazines. He saw his first match, along with his brother, when their father took them to the newly opened Harringay Arena. They got skates at about the same time, his were goalies' double runners. He remembered watching Montreal Canadiens and Detroit Redwings at Earls Court in May 1938 during the first NHL tour outside North America.

His hockey writing career commenced just at the beginning of the Second World War with Bob Giddens' weekly *IHW* and continued until the mid-1950s. The first piece under his name appeared in the issue of 3 January 1940, recalling the Manchester Rapids team of three years earlier. He resumed in the pre-season pocket magazine of spring 1946, not on hockey but 'Show Business on Ice'. In the next issue he did get to write about his favourite sport again, under the heading 'The International Season'. From then on Drackett was a named contributor in almost every issue. He wrote match reports from Brighton and Harringay, various feature articles – including 'Know the boys as they are' and similar player profiles – described teams' road trips, reviewed clubs prospects, and met incoming Canadians off the ships at the dockside. His writing was always fluid, lucid and seamless with a dash of mid-Atlantic adjectives.

He compiled all nine of the *Ice Hockey World Annuals* first published in summer 1947, and added editor to his role for the last three. They set the standard and provide the model for all subsequent British yearbooks. In the days before computers and electronic calculators the compilation and checking of player statistics would be a time consuming task, requiring endless patience.

Phil Drackett was the leading British ice hockey journalist of his time.

During his early days with the *World* he was the practice netminder for the two Harringay teams and also organised and managed the occasional outings of the *IHW All-Stars* to various rinks in England.

By 1956, with decreasing revenues and increasing costs forcing the *World* to reduce the number of pages, he stepped off the 'Great Ice Way', as he put it in *Flashing Blades,* to take his trusty typewriter round the corner to a sports desk in Fleet Street. In fact he joined the Royal Automobile Club (RAC) as press officer. By the time he left twenty-three years later he held the post of director of Press and Public Relations and continued occasional work for them. He also held the post of secretary to the Segrave Trophy Committee 1956-2003 and acted as press officer to the Speedway Control Board.

He wrote several books on motorsport plus occasional articles on boxing and other sports for numerous newspapers and journals.

Phil returned to ice hockey as the sport grew in the early 1980s. Living in Norfolk since 1979, he produced a sixteen-page glossy monthly magazine, *Puck.* It ran for five issues, from October 1982 to the following February, backed by publisher Dick Lack. His next venture, also with Lack, was to revive *Ice Hockey World* in October 1984, but in a similar format and style as *Puck*, selling at 75p.

There was a one-season absence. It reappeared in spring 1987 with a new financial backer in Dennis Fill, a very successful British-born businessman based in the USA. In total it ran for forty-nine issues, the last one appearing in summer 1993. From an initial sixteen pages it varied between twenty and twenty-four pages, including numerous photos. As managing editor Drackett relied on correspondents for the majority of the contents, his writings were confined to an editorial and the occasional feature.

His return to hockey was best marked by four books commencing with the hardback *Flashing Blades* of 1987. This was followed five years later by *Vendetta on Ice,* a well-researched paperback about the 1936 Winter Olympics hockey won by Britain. His final two works were written in collaboration with Dennis Fill. *Champions On Ice*, a 158-page hardback, is a mix of memories and photos of the pre-1960 era and none the poorer for that. In 2005 *Hollywood On Ice*, a thin paperback, detailed the links between hockey and the silver screen.

A burly and jolly man, in 1994 he was made an honorary life member of the BIHWA, and was always helpful to his fellow scribes.

Phil Drackett died on 27 November 2006, aged eighty-three, at Mundesley, Norfolk.

Jack 'Jackie' DRYBURGH

Inducted 1991

Jack Dryburgh is another fine example of native Scottish ice hockey talent honed in the 1950s, who later carved out an illustrious career in ice rink management.

With his father employed as an engineer at the Kirkcaldy ice rink he was able to start skating at the remarkably early age of three. He was playing ice hockey by the time he was nine. This was again exceptional for that era, which showed later in his skating and stick control. As a centre-ice he moved through the 'midget' team and onto Kirkcaldy Flyers, a junior side.

In October 1955 his skills had developed sufficiently to try breaking into the semi-pro BNL with Nottingham. As an eighteen year old he still needed to find work outside of hockey, but was unable to find a suitable post to continue his apprenticeship as an aircraft fitter. During his five games with the Panthers he scored a goal and three assists before heading back to Scotland. The 1957/58 season saw him finish as top scorer with the undefeated Edinburgh Royals in the one-year North British League. That autumn the Murrayfield-based club once

Jackie Dryburgh as a Southampton Viking in 1961.

again tried pro hockey, with Dryburgh in the predominately Canadian line-up. He played in 17 of their 25 matches before the rink folded the team. Glasgow benefited from his services for the remainder of that winter, including the Flyers' Continental tour.

In October 1959 he came south again, this time to sign for Southampton, whose team – the Vikings – staged non-league 'home' tournaments. These consisted of entertaining the top amateur sides from England and Scotland. Those with the best goal difference returned to contest the final. He scored four goals in his first match, a 10-2 victory, over, coincidentally, the visiting Glasgow Flyers. He went on to score in every match, finishing as Southampton's leading scorer. He also found time to turn out twice for Nottingham Panthers. Having helped Vikings retain the Southern Cup and BIHA Southampton Tournament and completed his apprenticeship at nearby Portsmouth, he returned to Scotland.

After starting the next winter at Murrayfield he was persuaded to rejoin Vikings in January 1961. Again in his first outing he netted six times in a 17-7 thrashing of Streatham Royals. After a dispute the following autumn between the managements of the Southampton and Brighton clubs the BIHA ruled that Dryburgh was a Brighton player. His greatest years on ice followed as he spent four seasons on the Sussex coast. A tireless forechecker he was deadly around the net. He won the scoring championship for 1963 and 1965 and was second in the other two campaigns.

The Tigers swept the board winning their own tournament four times, collected three Cobley and Southern Cups and won the Southampton Tournament twice. Dryburgh was voted onto the 1962 All-Star 'B' team and gained an 'A' team place the next spring and again two years later.

After the cessation of the sport at Brighton in May 1965 he played with Liege in Belgium for several seasons. He also appeared at Wembley in early autumn and late spring guesting in challenge matches for the visitors, mainly Fife.

Selected for the 1961 World Championships for Great Britain, he scored in the Group 'B' 3-2 defeat of Poland in March. He represented Scotland in the annual series with England during 1961 and the next year, scoring four times.

By the late 1960s he had hung up the blades to become rink manager at Aviemore in the Scottish Highlands. He got ice hockey started there in 1969 and promoted an annual summer league. His next move was to the Solihull rink. Whilst there he also managed the Barons during 1977/78 when they won the Southern League and subsequent play-offs. Next year he was back at Aviemore. Two years later he was managing the rink in his home town. Here he sometimes acted as bench coach to the Flyers during the 1980s in the revived British League. During this period he was recruited by the BIHA, serving on their council representing the Scottish Rink Managers Association. He also sat on the sub-committees of coaching and junior development set up by the BIHA in late 1983.

Jack Dryburgh was born on 14 January 1939 at Kirkcaldy. In his youth he won the Scottish Amateur Tennis Championship and was capped in a junior football international. He was offered a trail with Glasgow Rangers.

Today he is the manager of the Dundee Ice Arena.

Competition Statistics	GP	G	A	Pts	PIM
Nottingham Panthers	7	1	3	4	0
Edinburgh Royals*	17	7	6	13	2
Glasgow Flyers	---	---	---	---	---
Southampton Vikings	26	77	32	109	20
Brighton Tigers	131	205	262	467	64
Great Britain	5	1	---	1	---

* Excludes 1957/58 & 1960/61

Sir Arthur ELVIN MBE

Inducted 1990

If it had not been for Sir Arthur Elvin, who died fifty years ago, there would not have been a thirteen-year run of Championship weekends at Wembley Arena from the mid-1980s. This end of season climax provided the sport with media focus and generated extensive TV coverage and is still discussed with awe by those who attended the atmospheric weekend festivals.

Born in Norwich on 5 July 1899, the son of a policeman, he left school at fourteen and tried numerous jobs. Two years later he moved to London to become a successful salesman. With the coming of war he volunteered and obtained a commission in the Royal Flying Corps. Shot down over France he spent two years as a prisoner of war. Back in London after the Armistice he was sent to France by the Ministry of Munitions in charge of dismantling ammunition dumps.

His association with Wembley started in 1924 as an assistant in a tobacco kiosk at the Empire Exhibition. He soon secured options on additional kiosks – ultimately eight – selling souvenirs. Following the exhibition's closure two years later he made his fortune in buying up derelict pavilions, demolishing and selling off the scrap materials or the abandoned structures for use elsewhere. When the football stadium went into liquidation, within a fortnight Elvin had raised sufficient backing to buy the complex. He sold out to the newly formed Wembley Stadiums Ltd, took his profit in shares and became the managing director, aged twenty-seven.

Having successfully introduced greyhound and speedway racing to the stadium he turned his attention to indoor sports. He persuaded his board that a multi-purpose indoor sports arena would compliment the adjacent outdoor activities. Work started in October 1933 on a design in ferro-concrete, by Sir Owen Williams, an innovative structural engineer, a building that served as a swimming pool in the summer and converted to an ice rink in the winter.

Sir Arthur Elvin MBE, a successful impresario, was responsible for raising the profile of ice hockey in Great Britain and masterminded the Championship weekends held at Wembley in the 1980s.

From autumn 1934 two teams of almost exclusively Canadians – the Lions and Canadians (renamed Monarchs two year later – played twice a week in the Empire Pool and Sports Arena. Slick presentation in comfortable surroundings, with plentiful off-ice facilities, supported by an informative multi-page programme changed the face of ice hockey in Britain. The example set by Elvin lead to the creation of the professional ENL and to several more purpose-built arenas. Within two years Earls Court and Harringay housed two pro teams apiece.

He was a demanding employer who required an all-out effort from his staff. He aimed for perfection and praised loyalty. Like many self-made men he failed to delegate responsibility to his executive staff. He was devoted to Wembley, almost working round the clock in his modest office within the stadium.

There were boom years for ice hockey either side of the Second World War with plenty of silverware entering Wembley's trophy cabinet, plus the staging of two World Championships. But as the 1950s dawned with increasing competition from car ownership and other attractions such as television, long-running ice shows in the middle of winter took the place of hockey. Monarchs were folded in 1950.

Awarded an MBE in 1945, Elvin was knighted a year later, and became chairman of Wembley in 1947. Elvin fought long and hard to sustain the Wembley complex, railing against entertainment tax. The struggle took its toll. He developed emphysema and in November 1956 suffered a partial stroke. He hoped a cruise to South Africa early the next year would restore his health. Regrettably he was struck down by a further stroke and died in his cabin on 4 February 1957. He was buried at sea.

Lions continued until the BNL collapsed in 1960. There was a three-year gap before the team returned for a further five years as an amateur side, playing mainly challenge encounters. Whether, if he had lived longer, he would have been able to ensure greater continuity for ice hockey at his beloved Wembley we shall never know.

Sir Arthur Elvin would certainly have been proud to know that his creation was dubbed 'the sport's spiritual home' during the Heineken Championship era and beyond, even if for only one weekend each year for a span of less than a decade and a half.

Carl ERHARDT

Inducted 1950

Carl Erhardt captained Great Britain to the 1936 Olympic, World and European gold medal triumph – the first time the triple crown fell to one nation.

A stay-at-home right-sided defender, who was difficult to get around, he anchored Great Britain's blue line in six of the seven matches. He sat out the 5-1 win over Hungary. Great Britain secured Olympic gold on the day of his thirty-ninth birthday, in the 0-0 triple overtime deadlock with the USA. He is the oldest player in Olympic history to have won a gold medal at ice hockey.

His international career with Great Britain began in February 1931 at the World Championships in Poland. Here he scored twice in the 11-0 thrashing of Romania. When next called up by Great Britain, for the 1934 World event in Milan, he scored singletons into the nets of Italy and Belgium. Twelve months on at Davos he was captain as Britain defeated the Czechs 2-1 in overtime for European silver and World bronze medals. Named on the 1937 British roster a knee injury forced him to stand down.

Carl was one of the last to progress to the higher levels of the sport in Britain who had learnt to skate whilst at school in Germany and Switzerland. Later on at winter sports holidays in Switzerland ice hockey matches were arranged for the guests at the various hotels. Back home he skated as much as possible when the Ice Club at Westminster opened in 1926, joining the revived Princes club there the next winter. In his 1937 book *Ice Hockey* he notes that 'ice hockey players were merely tolerated'. He told BBC commentator Bob Bowman that getting to the top rank was a very difficult task. When a team was organised in London any Englishman took a back seat if a Canadian was available. He said that these discouraging experiences helped him to work harder to play better. So that when hockey became a major sport he found a place on teams largely composed of Canadians.

In his speeches and writings he tried to direct the sport into a channel between going too far commercially and the need to avoid hindering the game from developing as a spectator sport. He foresaw before others, the dilemma of the small rinks versus the large multi-purpose

Carl Erhardt of Streatham in 1936.

arenas. As a player and a born leader from a more gentlemanly era he set an example of fair play and common sense, encouraging his Canadians to provide the game with style and class. He always claimed that Bowman was wrong when in his BBC rink-side broadcast of the Great Britain *v.* USA game at the Olympics he said that Erhardt had engaged in fisticuffs.

His first organised team was Princes in the original British League of 1929/30. He moved to Queens, playing out of the basement rink on Queensway in Bayswater, in autumn 1932. A year later he signed for Streatham, the south London club with whom his name is most often associated. He was not against the inclusion of Canadians and in fact invited George Shaw, 'Red' Stapleford and Bob Giddens to join Streatham direct from Canada at the beginning of the 1934/35 season. By next spring the team, captained by Erhardt, had won the English League and the four nation International Club Tournament.

Two years later, with his availability limited by business commitments, he dropped out of the by-now semi-pro National League. His final playing season of 1937/38 was with Streatham Royals, winners of the London Provincial League.

He did not lose touch with hockey as he coached Great Britain to sixth place at the 1948 Olympics and refereed two years later at the World Championships held in London. He served on the BIHA from the early 1930s, being made a vice-president in 1936 and continuing in that role until the late 1970s.

Carl Alfred Erhardt was born on 15 February 1897 at Beckenham, Kent, and educated in Austria, Germany and Switzerland. In business he was a director of a successful London-based engineering firm. His other sporting interests were skiing and tennis and he was also a founder and the first president of the British Water Ski Federation.

His six-bedroom home 'Sentosa' in Esher, Surrey, was specifically designed for him in 1935 by architect Howard Robertson. With a flat roof and large wrap-around windows looking out over the North Downs, with an acre of garden containing a swimming pool, it was highly regarded by 1930s society.

He died at Esher aged regular, on 3 May 1988.

Competition Statistics	GP	G	A	Pts	PIM
Princes/Queens	---	---	---	---	---
Streatham*	---	0	0	0	2
Streatham Royals	---	---	---	---	---
Great Britain	19	4	---	4	---

★ Excludes 1933–35

Jimmy FOSTER

Inducted 1950

Jimmy Foster – Britain's netminder at the 1936 Olympic Games – proved crucial in securing Olympic gold. If the British defence were the anchor then Foster was the bedrock on which victory was built. He shut-out the opposition four times and conceded just three goals in the seven games with an astonishing saves percentage of 98.7.

Of his performance in the unexpected 2–1 victory over Canada at the Olympics the *IHW*'s on-the-spot correspondent wrote in the hyperbole of the day: 'Foster rose to dizzy heights, outguessing the Canadian sharpshooters and turning away their bullet-like drives with the

Jimmy Foster, resplendent in his Harringay Greyhounds strip in autumn 1936. He is the outstanding netminder in Great British ice hockey's history.

coolness of an ice-man.' Earlier the Canadian hockey authorities claimed that Foster had not only left their jurisdiction without permission, but that he was deemed to have previously represented Canada because his club team had played a game in the USA. None of this hiatus disturbed the 5ft 8in-tall, blonde-haired, modest man with his calmness in the nets, instilling confidence in his teammates.

The only Scotsman in the Olympic squad, he returned to Britain in the autumn of 1935 with his reputation as a puck stopper well established. He arrived with two Allan Cup medals after a tryout the year before with Montreal Maroons of the NHL. Along with Percy Nicklin, his coach from his last two seasons in Canada with Moncton, he signed for Richmond Hawks. Back-stopping his new team to the runners-up slot in the ENL was recognised with an All-Star 'A' rating.

The following autumn, along with Nicklin, he moved north-east across London to join the Greyhounds at the newly opened 8,200-seat Harringay Arena. In his third of three winters there, Hounds won the ENL title and the London Cup, with Foster being named to the All-Star 'B' sextet. The previous season he topped the netminders averages in the National Tournament and London Cup and achieved 2.46 goals against per game percentage in all competitions.

But it's for his performances on the world stage that Foster was honoured. Twelve months after the miracle of Garmisch he again donned Great Britain garb, this time in London. Astonishingly he blanked the opposition in eight of the nine matches, but was forced to concede three goals to Canada, one in each period, in an emotional and tempestuous game on home ice at Harringay. Thanks to their goaltender, Britain retained the European gold. It was three in row on the open air ice in Prague, in mid-February 1938. Here he shut-out Germany and Norway on successive days in Pool 2 of the opening round. A third clean sheet came in the 1-0 win over the Czechs in the Final Pool for a World silver medal. With a change of policy bringing in more British-trained players, Foster racked up his last and sixteenth shut-out from thirty starts for Britain, at Zurich in front of 3,000 spectators on 5 February 1939.

Intending only to holiday back in Winnipeg that summer, the drums of impending war in Europe meant Jimmy decided to stay put, although he had an offer from Brighton Tigers for the next season. He never returned, although according to his daughter, hung on to his British passport for the remainder of his life.

James Foster was born on 13 September 1905 in Glasgow where he commenced his education at Hyde Park Public School. Along with his siblings his parents migrated to Canada in August 1912, settling in Winnipeg where Jimmy learnt to skate.

He first appears in the hockey records in 1922 with Argonauts of the local Junior League. Two years later with the University of Manitoba he competed for the Memorial Cup. Several years of senior hockey followed with various clubs in Winnipeg, including Elmwood Millionaires during 1929-31. That autumn he moved east to Moncton Hawks. Here his reputation soared with a stingy goal against average of 1.40 and six shut-outs in the 1931/32 regular season, followed by 1.10 and eleven clean sheets next winter. He topped this with consecutive Allan Cup finals triumphs in the spring of 1933 and 1934 and first team All-Star selection in the Maritime Senior League.

He hung up the catcher and pads in the spring of 1942 on a high, being named to the first All-Star team in the Cape Breton League and a career total of 55 shut-outs. Two years earlier at the Montreal Forum Foster he back-stopped an All-English League line-up to a 5-2 win over a combined Quebec Senior and Provincial Leagues team. After war work at an aircraft factory he became a travelling salesman in tea, coffee and spices.

He died of cancer after a short illness, on 4 January 1969 at a hospital in Winnipeg, aged sixty-three.

Competition Statistics	GP	W	L	D	GA	GAA	SO
Richmond Hawks	47	20	16	11	114	2.42	---
Harringay Greyhounds*	77	40	23	14	338	4.38	8
Great Britain	30	22	5	3	24	0.78	16

★ Excludes 1936/37

Robert 'Bobby' GIDDENS
Inducted 1986

Robert Giddens, affectionately known as 'Bobby', founded the World's first journal devoted to ice hockey to be published on a regular basis.

In October 1935, whilst player-coach and publicity manager to the recently formed Kensington Corinthians playing out of the newly opened Empress Stadium in west London, he produced his first weekly edition of *Ice Hockey World and Skating Review.* Not withstanding the latter portion of the title, which was in much smaller type-face, it was hockey that predominated from the first issue.

More of a newspaper than a conventional magazine, No.1, dated 9 October 1935, consisted of a four-page broadsheet selling at two pence. From this issue the mix of content was firmly established, consisting of detailed match reports, editorial comment, features, statistics and photos. Six pages were produced for No.30, the final copy for the inaugural season which appeared on 30 April. From autumn 1936 the *World* expanded to eight pages which then remained constant. Circulation steadily increased with weekly sales reaching 8,000 three years after being launched. For the first three seasons loose 'souvenir plates', which were team photos suitable for framing, were given away with each issue in the spring. In October 1938 Giddens produced a give-away pocket size *Who's Who* – the forerunner of the post-war annuals.

Features included a series of 'Potted Personalities', cartoons and the occasional article on the NHL plus readers' letters. It was Giddens who introduced to British hockey the concept of an end of season All-Star 'A' and 'B' team selection. The first such appeared in the *IHW* of 30 April 1936 and included six players now enshrined in the British Ice Hockey Hall of Fame. The inside back page usually held news on ice skating shows and there were also occasional fictional stories featuring hockey. As the sport grew in Scotland, coverage was given to hockey north of Hadrian's Wall and post-war a Scottish edition ran for some years.

The coming of the Second World War caused a reduction in page size to slightly smaller than a tabloid format, although the length remained at eight pages. Publication was suspended in early April 1940. Although he gave up as a player at the end of the *World*'s first season he briefly donned skates again in the autumn of 1939 to help out as a referee in the ENL.

With the ending of hostilities three pocket-size magazines were produced during the summer of 1946, although league hockey did not recommence until that autumn. The weekly *World* resumed on 14 September, with the mix as before and continued every winter until 1958. The price was now 4 pence, rising to 6 pence in February 1951. Page numbers occasionally reduced to four during periods of industrial unrest and national crises. Circulation climbed to 35,000, peaked at 50,000 per week and in total there were 542 issues. Amateur hockey was not forgotten with reports on matches at Liverpool, Blackpool, Durham and Southampton and other rinks. News from Europe started to be included as British-based Canadian players moved to clubs on the Continent.

In 1948 Giddens introduced the British Ice Hockey of Fame to his readers.

The first of nine consecutive *Ice Hockey World Annuals* appeared in summer 1947 covering the previous season's exploits. He was author of *Ice Hockey: The International Game* published in the Foyles Handbook series in 1950.

From the mid-1950s onwards Giddens struggled with rising costs and fewer rinks promoting the sport. Cutbacks were made, staff reduced. The closing of Harringay Arena and the consequent loss of a substantial sales outlet was the final straw. Reluctantly he discontinued the *IHW*. The final copy came out on 3 May 1958.

Informative, sometimes provocative, now a scarce source for the games of yesteryear, its value to followers of hockey for over twenty years cannot be over emphasised. Several sports writers and broadcasters learnt their trade contributing articles to the *World* including Gordon Ross – cricket correspondent to *The Times* – Howard Bass of the *Daily Telegraph* and Phil Drackett. Alan Weeks, Norman de Mesquita and Barry Davies all later broadcast for the BBC.

In October 1935, Bobby Giddens founded *Ice Hockey World*, a weekly newspaper, and quickly gave up playing in order to concentrate on the full-time editing and publishing of what was an excellent journal. Between 1938 and the mid-1950s, the circulation of *Ice Hockey World* rose from 8,000 to a staggering 35,000. Over 500 editions were published.

Robert 'Bobby' Giddens was born on 15 March 1906 at Ottawa. Playing at right-wing, he was the first Canadian to captain the Harvard University hockey team. The year he graduated he was voted onto the All-American 1929/30 team. He spent 1933/34 with Stade Francais in Paris, moving to Streatham as player-coach that autumn. He guided the south London team to the English League title. Pre-war he spent the summers at Perkins in Quebec.

Bobby was a truly outstanding pioneer and evangelist for British ice hockey with his *Ice Hockey World* and companion *Annuals*. He worked constantly to promote the sport he loved and at times his health suffered.

He died in London on 12 October 1963, aged fifty-seven, after a long illness.

Bill GLENNIE

Inducted 1951

Bill Glennie was among the fourth annual selection to the Hall of Fame. Forever associated with Harringay Arena, he is one of the few Canadians to be unanimously ranked with the greatest right-wingers between 1946 and 1958 with over 1,000 points.

He was virtually a one-club man in his dozen years in the English and then British National Leagues. The rookie season was spent with Harringay Greyhounds and in autumn 1947 he moved to their rink-mates the Racers, until Harringay Arena closed to ice sports in spring 1958.

From his first winter at Harringay to his last he stood out, collecting an All-Star 'B' rating as Hounds won the London Cup in 1946/47. Awarded five further 'Bs', including a successive trio in his last three years on the ice, the experts upped this to 'A's for 1948-50 and 1953/54. During those years his scoring prowess helped the Racers to the ENL title in 1949 and three Autumn Cups. From 1954/55 the English and Scottish Leagues merged and the Racers won both the inaugural league and Autumn Cup titles with Glennie as their player-coach. *IHW* selected him as their 'Player of the Year'. This was his most productive winter with 113 (48+65) points from 60 matches, twice before he reached 99. Although he never won a scoring title, he was hardly ever out of the top ten. Second highest points scorer in the ENL and Autumn Cup during 1948/49 and for the Autumn Cup in his final campaign was the nearest to a title.

Further career highlights were being a member of the 'England' team, composed almost entirely of ENL Canadians, which defeated Canada and the USA to win the Churchill Cup. He led Racers to a 5-3 victory at Harringay over Canada, the newly crowned 1955 World Champions. Racers were also the first hockey team from the west to visit Moscow, playing their opening fixture at one end of the open-air Dynamo football stadium. Frostbite set-in before the national anthems were finished. The Soviets were also fascinated by Glennie's contact lenses.

At 6ft tall and weighing 175lbs he was a tough competitor and a hard-working back-checker, often circling round behind his own defensive pair to take out an unsuspecting attacker. If he or a fellow defender were caught out of position Bill would skate across the ice at full tilt, putting on the brakes just before he checked the puck carrier. To many onlookers this appeared to be charging, but not to the referees.

Away from the rinks Glennie was a modest and friendly man who liked to play the piano. With golf as a favourite recreation, he played from scratch, partnering the British Ryder Cup captain – Dai Rees – on several occasions in foursomes.

William 'Bill' John Glennie was born on 14 March 1924 at Portage La Prairie, Manitoba, where he played minor and junior hockey. Leaving school at barely seventeen years of age, he volunteered for the Canadian Army, spending four years of the Second World War with the 17th Field Artillery in England, Italy, Belgium, France and Germany. After demobilisation, with his Hampshire-born wife, whom he married just before the army took him to Italy, he moved to Canada and signed for Washington Lions of the US Eastern League.

Bill Glennie spent the 1947/48 season with the Harringay Racers.

The Lions were owned by the legendary Eddie Shore. He learnt more about hockey there in a week than he would have in years elsewhere. He already worked for the GRA, the owners of Harringay Arena, before retiring as a player with the demise of the Racers. The GRA appointed him to an executive position. For a while he was assistant manger of White City Stadium in west London. Eventually they moved him to Edinburgh as general manager of the Powderhall Stadium.

He died on 11 March 2005, three days before his eightieth birthday, at his home in Longniddry, Scotland.

Competition Statistics	GP	G	A	Pts	PIM
Harringay Greyhounds	39	37	34	71	14
Harringay Racers	574	479	493	972	524

Alec GOLDSTONE

Inducted 1992

Alec Goldstone was a successful team manager with three clubs in London during the late 1970s and throughout the 1980s.

His first involvement with ice hockey was when Tony, his thirteen-year-old son, started playing at south London's Streatham ice rink in 1974. This was the first time he had seen ice hockey and went along out of curiosity. He soon became a convert and was totally committed, getting roped in to provide help when and where it was needed, initially with the juniors. As a parent he paid for equipment and took players to away games. Hockey took over the family.

His career in team management started when a second senior side – the Hawks – entered the Southern 'A' League in autumn 1976, to provide experience at a higher level for the many youngsters emerging from Streatham's youth development programme. He was one of the organising committee for the June 1977 Silver Jubilee trophy for junior teams at Streatham. By early January the following year the Redskins match night programmes were listing Alec as team manager, a role he continued to fulfil for the next ten years.

That first season the Redskins won the finals of 'home' tournaments held at their own rink, Solihull and Southampton. League titles followed with the ICL senior crown for the next year and 1980/81 plus the play-offs; and for 1981/82 along with that winter's one-year ENL. Redskins were also runners-up in the British championship final to Dundee Rockets.

Tony Goldstone was a successful team manager with three London clubs, including Streatham Redskins who appeared in their only Wembley finals under his stewardship.

Then, in the spring of 1984, they lost out on penalty shots as the score was deadlocked at 6-6 after sixty minutes.

The high point during Goldstone's stewardship came in spring 1985, the only time the Redskins appeared in the end of season Wembley finals. To get there involved fifth-placed Redskins inflicting a shock 9-2 defeat upon Durham, the Premier Division champions, on the Wasps' home ice. In the return the following weekend at Streatham, one point from the 5-5 tie was sufficient. The semi-final on 6 May was an anti-climax as Fife won 12-3. For Alec and his boys being there was reward enough.

Streatham struggled to stay at the highest level without a substantial sponsor. Two years earlier it had cost £33,000 to run the club. In spring 1988 Alec resigned in protest when the club committee sacked coach Mark Didcot, and briefly moved to a similar role with Medway Bears. The following autumn he was reunited with Didcot at Richmond. Juggling players and recruiting several dissatisfied Redskins enabled the Flyers to retain their place in Division One. He then moved to Lee Valley to pull off the same escape act, not once but twice, as a struggling Lions won four straight games in the relegation play-offs in spring 1991.

Described as a man with many opponents and no enemies, he more than made up for his late discovery of the 'fastest game in the world' by the dedication, good humour and the sound common sense he applied during his seventeen years with the sport.

In 1990 he and his wife Kathy, who supported him as the club secretary, timekeeper, chauffeur and in many other roles, were jointly presented with the BIHWA Special Services to British Ice Hockey award.

Pat Marsh, a consultant to the BIHA said of him: 'he would do anything to help hockey.' Norman de Mesquita commented: 'He was the roughest of cockney diamonds with a keen sense of humour. He always greeted you with a smile.'

Alex Goldstone was born on 18 August 1938 in Clapham, London. He owned and operated his own tiling business. He died suddenly, as a result of a heart attack, at his home in Brixton, London, on the evening of 15 July 1991, aged fifty-two.

Ice hockey had lost a real character and a tireless worker for the sport.

Roy HALPIN
Inducted 1986

Roy Halpin was the first of the quality Canadian imports to enter the British game since the end of the semi-pro National League in 1960. A 5ft 8in-tall centre-ice/right-wing he set modern era records for most goals in a season at 128, most assists at 106 and most goals in a game at 14.

He first came to these shores in spring 1980 with Concordia University Stingers to compete in an international tournament at Dundee. The Dundee rink had been without league hockey for six years, so in September 1981, club owner Tom Stewart needed the Rockets to make an instant impact to attract fans. He signed three Canadians from the Concordia team including Halpin, who had spent the previous season in Japan with Snowbrand Sapporo.

In his second match he scored three times in the Rockets' 19-3 league win at Aviemore. In the twenty-four games of the major competitions of the Northern and Scottish Leagues and the British Championships, all won by Dundee, he scored 82 goals for a total of 139 points. The Rockets also collected the Spring and Icy Smith Cups. In the final of the British Championships, held at Streatham in front of Thames TV cameras, Halpin scored the game-tying goal at 51.43 as the Rockets powered to a 3-2 victory. Three weeks earlier at Durham he set a record, smashing 14 goals into the back of the Wasps' net in Dundee's 24-1 Spring Cup semi-final triumph. Being named to the All-Star 'A' team was no surprise.

The next season the Rockets were the first champions of the new British League and went on to win the end of season finals at Streatham, sponsored for the first time by Heineken. Halpin increased

Roy Halpin set the modern records for most goals in a season – 128 – most assists – 106 – and most goals in a match – 14.

his points total to 162 and a first-team All-Star place followed. He also contributed two assists for the British Select in their 14-6 victory over their Belgian counterparts at Solihull on 3 March 1983. Fourteen months on and the Rockets, with Halpin in their line-up, won the first British Championships held at Wembley by defeating Murrayfield by the odd goal in nine. He finished as top scorer in the inaugural Premier Division with 175 points and with a third consecutive All-Star first team selection. He was named 'Player of the Year' by the journalists association.

In the first round of the European Cup in early October Halpin scored three times. A series of injuries giving rise to back problems forced his retirement from the ice at the age of twenty-nine. In his final match, on 12 January 1985 at Nottingham with BBC Television present, he contributed a goal and an assist. Without his scoring prowess the Rockets failed to hold on to any of their titles. After a back operation he stayed to successfully organise the second Sport Goofy junior international tournament at Dundee. The club held a testimonial match for him in April, during which his No.9 sweater was retired.

With a friendly, outgoing personality allied with on-ice skills not seen in Britain for many a long year, he was credited by some as being responsible for hockey's revival in the early 1980s. Roy was more realistic and told the Dundee Press: 'If I've been able to do something to improve the standard of play in Britain, I'm more than satisfied.'

Roy Andrew Halpin, born on 18 October 1955 at Quebec City, started to play hockey at the age of four. He progressed to Major Junior 'A' with Quebec Remparts. During 1975-1978 he scored 32 goals for the Blue Eagles whilst at Moncton University. Named 'Rookie of the Year' for 1976, two years later he was voted onto the second All-Star team. Graduating with a degree in economic geography he gained a Masters in urban planning at Toronto University and a further Masters' degree, this time in sports administration, at Concordia in Montreal. At both he continued to play hockey including eight games for Canada's national team.

An accomplished golfer in his youth, he finished second in the Quebec Province Tournament and when first in Scotland returned 81 on the Old Course at St Andrew's.

Upon his return to Canada he took a job as tournament organiser with Tennis Canada. He is now at Stade Uniprix – a tennis centre in suburban Montréal. In his early years back home he played a bit of old-timers hockey but his back problems soon caused him to quit.

Competition Statistics	GP	G	A	Pts	PIM
Dundee Rockets	120	340	293	633	157

Art HODGINS
Inducted 1989

Art Hodgins, a defenceman, was probably the only Canadian in the pre 1960 British Leagues who could have made it to the NHL. He was Scotland's 1947 'Rookie of the Year' and England's two years later.

Although Detroit Red Wings were keen to get him under contract, with Scottish parents he declined, and instead crossed the Atlantic Ocean in the autumn of 1946 to join Paisley Pirates. Lou Bates, who witnessed the three-day August try-outs in Toronto, reported that Hodgins would be a sensation. He was right. In that first winter at the East Lane rink, Art helped the Pirates win the new Scottish Autumn Cup and the established Scottish Cup. This earned him the first of his six annual All-Star 'A' accolades. The second came twelve months later.

Streatham's coach 'Red' Stapleford persuaded Art to try the ENL and this brought him his third successive 'A' plus a second 'Rookie of the Year' award in spring 1949. The latter was presented by Red's daughter Sally, who years later made a name for herself in international figure skating. Strangely, although in the next campaign Streatham carried off the ENL and National Tournament titles, Hodgins did not feature in the end-of-season All-Stars. He did twelve months on with a fourth 'A'. With his team winning the 1951 Autumn Cup he picked up his first of three 'Bs'. More silverware joined the south London club's trophy cabinet the following winter with the ENL crown and a second 'B' for Art. He missed out for the 1953/54 season although the club won the Autumn and London Cups.

With the advent of the Scottish and English clubs joining forces, Streatham decided to drop hockey, so Hodgins moved across London to sign for Harringay Racers. He was just as effective on the blue line for his new club, gaining recognition with an All-Star 'A' as Racers decisively swept the opposition aside to lift both the Autumn Cup and British League titles.

Sinus trouble causing breathing difficulties forced him out of the game for eighteen months. He made a comeback with Brighton Tigers assisting them to the league crown, although he was far from fit. For the final winter of that era's BNL he moved north, signing for Nottingham. Here, back to his previous form, he helped the Panthers win the British League's first play-offs. The experts placed him on the All-Star 'B' sextet, alongside his defensive partner Lorne Smith.

In February 1961 Art joined the newly formed Altrincham Aces as player-coach, guiding them to a 10-5 victory over Paisley Mohawks in their 'home' tournament final. He left next January for Milan. Here he was dubbed '*Il Leone*' (the Lion) after collecting a broken nose from an errant stick and returning to the ice five minutes later. Back in England he signed for the revived Wembley Lions in October 1963, assisting in the capture of the one year London Tournament and Spring Cup staged at the Empire Pool. Here he gained his final All-Star rating, an 'A' in 1964. Thereafter the team mainly played challenge games. His on-ice career ended when the Lions were folded four years later.

At 5ft 11in tall and weighing 198lbs he was acknowledged as being one of the very finest defenders ever seen in Britain, with a clean body-check, striking up great understanding with

Art Hodgins on Streatham ice during 1951/52.

his line-mates. Never a prolific scorer, with few up-ice rushes, nonetheless he possessed a devastatingly accurate left-hand shot from the blue line.

Arthur Stanley Hodgins was born on 17 November 1927 at Timmins, Ontario, one of six siblings. Educated at the Central Public School and Timmins High School where he played on the left-wing, he was on defence for the first time in juvenile hockey with Timmins Lions. He joined the Canadian Army underage at seventeen, was found out and discharged to work in a gold mine for a few months. The winter prior to moving to Scotland he helped the South Porcupine Red Wings win the Kenning Cup.

In the 1960s he settled with his family in Nottingham where he was employed as a works manager for a soap manufacturer and then at Boots the chemists in their local factory.

Suffering declining health, he died of lung cancer on 11 March 1988 at Nottingham, aged sixty.

Competition Statistics	GP	G	A	Pts	PIM
Paisley Pirates	61*	25	57	82	191
Streatham	321	34	74	108	325
Harringay Racers	90	7	19	26	38
Nottingham Panthers	51	4	7	11	14
Altrincham Aces	16	3	8	11	0
Wembley Lions**	29	5	8	13	8

* Excludes GP 1946/47.

** 1963–65 only.

Shannon HOPE

Inducted 1999

In his prime Shannon Hope was the most difficult defenceman to skate around, although given the opportunity he liked to carry the puck up ice. Eleven years with Cardiff Devils yielded numerous medals including five league titles. He captained Great Britain at four World Championships and an Olympic qualifying tournament.

His first experience of Britain was at Peterborough in the 1984/85 season where he was probably the best player in Division One of the British League. He finished eighth in points scoring as the Pirates lost just once to clinch the title and promotion. Hope said "I can't begin to tell you how good it has been to play for the Pirates this season. It is great to be part of a winning club with such a fanatical and loyal support.'

He returned to Canada and took a job as a pilot for a mining company for the next two years. He had obtained his licence as a seventeen year old.

With the one-year-old Cardiff Devils gaining a place in Division One of the HBL, coach John Lawless contacted his previous clubmate from Peterborough. Thus began eleven years on Cardiff ice for Hope. Twenty-five points from the defenceman assisted in the winning of the Autumn Trophy. The next winter the Devils retained that trophy then proceeded to win the Division One title and the promotion play-off. All-Star recognition followed for Shannon, the first of three such successive awards. The rise of the Devils continued as twelve months later the Premier title and the first of three British Championships at Wembley were secured.

By spring 1993 the Devils had achieved the Grand Slam, winning the B&H Autumn Cup, League and play-off titles and Southern Cup. Hope scored in the very last game to be sponsored by Heineken, as the Devils defeated Humberside 7-4 at Wembley on 25 April 1993. Next year he collected a third Wembley finals medal. Strangely he accumulated his largest number of assists at 73 in 1995 when the best the Devils could achieve were runners-up in the B&H Autumn Cup and the play-offs. The following winter he made his 500th appearance in the Devils' colours.

With the advent of the Superleague and its vastly increased number of imports Hope retained his place, although nearing the veteran stage, as the Devils claimed the inaugural title. During his last campaign he provided an assist at a crucial time in the B&H Autumn Cup final at Sheffield which Cardiff eventually lost 2-1. His points total also increased compared with the year before.

With a British passport by spring 1992, he was a natural for the national team hosting Pool 'C' of the World Championships at Hull. Britain gained promotion conceding a measly 10 goals. Next year he was part of the squad in Holland in the triumphant promotion to the top level. Two years later he was made captain, a role he performed for a further three World Championships and the 1995/96 Olympic qualification tournament. In total he was a valued member of Great Britain's defensive core for nine IIHF competitions.

In the spring of 1998 he announced his retirement. He had been given a testimonial game the previous November. His No.35 sweater was also retired.

His coach Paul Heavey said, 'Shannon has been tremendous over so many seasons – he has been with the club through the best of moments.' 'I must be full Welsh now,' claimed Hope.

He had, as co-owner, opened a sports shop in Swansea in October 1991 and more recently had been successfully running his own business – Shine-Dog – designing and manufacturing player shirts and selling sports and leisurewear. He also took on the role of the Devils' commercial manager.

With Peterborough in financial difficulties in early 2000, Shannon, at the age of thirty-seven, dusted off his skates and briefly came out of retirement for expenses only. In eleven games he contributed 6+6 as the Pirates finished fifth in the BNL.

Shannon Hope as a
Cardiff Devil.

   Never one to back down, he stood 6ft tall and weighed 189lbs, his cut eye at Telford in his
first campaign for Cardiff led to the team skating off the ice and being heavily fined. Four
years on Hope was initially suspended for eleven games for fighting with Chris Kelland after
a post-game handshake. As an offensive defender he was usually among the top four or five
Devils in scoring, as evidenced by a total of 605 assists. As a natural born leader his motivational
skills inspired those around him.

   Shannon Hope was born on 25 November 1962 at Peterborough, Ontario, Canada. The year
before coming to England he was with Acadia University Axemen where he contributed 19
points. Until spring 2006 he had been director of hockey for the Devils. He sold his company
Shine-Dog a couple of years ago and these days is employed as a sponsorship manager with
Cardiff City Council, dealing mainly with music and sports.

Competition Statistics	GP	G	A	Pts	Pl
Peterborough Pirates	42	78	105	183	130
Cardiff Devils	550	234	605	839	1216
Great Britain	53	1	9	10	66

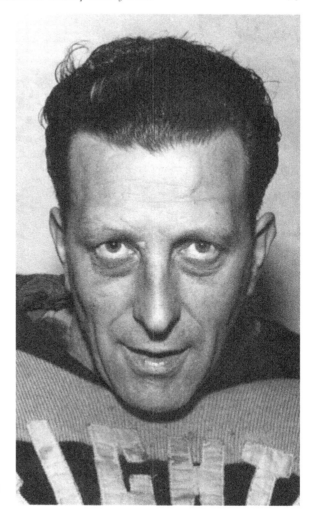

Gib Hutchinson as a Brighton
Tiger in 1947/48.

Gib HUTCHINSON

Inducted 1951

Gib Hutchinson backstopped Brighton Tigers to the ENL title in 1947 and repeated the feat the following year. He was a permanent fixture in English hockey for seventeen years, with five All-Star 'A' ratings and the only post-war pre-1960 netminder in the Hall of Fame.

He first arrived here from Canada in autumn 1936 to join Earls Court Royals in west London. The team conceded 232 goals in their forty games and were not heard of again. His future as a netminder did not look promising, so he fell back onto his trade as a carpenter, working at the nearby exhibition building.

Hutchinson was sought out and signed by Earls Court in late March 1938 as Rangers' regular keeper suffered a fractured nose. Initially sharing netminding duties, it was not until early the following February that he made the job his own. Although the team did not win any trophies the experts placed him on the All-Star 'A' team. He was the most consistent and the best clearer of pucks. With Empress Hall not staging league hockey, he moved to Streatham for the only wartime ENL campaign. Although the south London club finished last in the league and National Tournament, Gib was good enough to retain his 'A' rating at the end of season All-Star vote.

During the war years he worked at the Hawker aircraft factory with the occasional game of hockey. Representing Earls Court at Brighton the puck beat him once, whilst at the other end of the ice, Tuck Broda was guarding the nets for Sussex Tigers and conceded six. Previously Broda had spent 359 games in goal for Toronto Maple Leafs. On 31 January 1946 at Wembley Gib's opposite number in the RCAF nets was Johnny Mowers of the NHL Detroit Redwings. They were considered equally impressive in the 4-4 tie.

Organised hockey recommenced in autumn 1946 with Hutchinson in Wembley Monarchs cage. At the end of the inaugural Autumn Cup schedule, won by Brighton with Monarchs second, he transferred to the south-coast team at his request, to be with his long-time friend Bobby Lee. Here he shone as the Tigers swept to victory in the ENL and National Tournament. Gib topped the averages in both competitions and gained his third consecutive All-Star 'A' with thirty-four out of a maximum of forty votes. Next season the Tigers retained the league title, Gib gained a fourth 'A' and he topped the goalies' averages in all three competitions.

By the close of 1950 the Tigers had won the Autumn Cup and although Hutchinson was third in the goalies' averages he moved up a place in the league campaign. If these two averages are combined he tops the overall averages for that season. This gained him a well-deserved All-Star 'A' accolade, although it was his last. He retired twelve months later.

Gordon 'Gib' Gibson Hutchinson was born in 1912 at Calgary, Alberta, Canada and grew up at Swift Current, Saskatchewan. He spent 1930-32 with Regina Canadians of that city's Junior League and first moved to senior hockey for Regina Victorias in late 1932. The following three winters he guarded the nets for Prince Albert Mintos in the South Saskatchewan League, which included a trip to the play-offs for the Allan Cup. He secured seven shut-outs during this period.

Described pre-war by Bob Giddens as 'walking with the outdoor slouch of a tired cowboy coming in from the round-up,' this curly haired 5ft 6in-tall, slow-talking netminder was no slouch at puck stopping. He cleared the puck up to the red line with decisiveness and studied the attempted scoring methods of his opposing attackers to good effect. Gib once explained that in his day, that is without helmets and face cages, 'we played on beer and guts.'

He had married the daughter of Bombardier Billy Wells, Britain's heavyweight boxing champion for many years and the first winner of the Londsdale Belt. After hanging up the pads and catcher Gib became stage manager for Tom Arnold's ice shows at Brighton and then a publican.

He died in his sleep on 30 December 1996, aged eighty-four, at home in the Mile End Inn at Portslade, Sussex.

Competition Statistics	GP	GA	SoG	GAA	SO
Earls Court Royals	---	---	---	---	---
Earls Court Rangers*	5	12	---	2.40	0
Streatham	36	167	---	4.63	1
Wembley Monarchs	12	45	420	3.75	0
Brighton Tigers	381	1701	11475	4.46	6

* Excludes 1938/39

Thomas 'Red' IMRIE

Inducted 1987

'Red' Imrie was another of Scotland's classy players who emerged soon after the Second World War, with a spell in pro hockey before its collapse in 1960. He was the first Great Britain member to be named by the IIHF as an 'outstanding' player and later became a successful coach.

Red Imrie relaxing at home, *c.*1986.

He commenced the sport as a twelve year old in his native Falkirk. In organised hockey, initially as a forward, he spent a year with the Juveniles at thirteen then moved to the Juniors a year later before, at sixteen, breaking into the senior semi-pro Lions in their last year in the SNL. That winter Falkirk Lions were second in the SNL and went on to win the play-offs for the Anderson Trophy and also collected the Scottish Cup. 'Red', played in forty of those matches at either centre or right-wing, contributing 12 goals and 21 assists.

With the Scottish and English leagues combined for the next campaign the Lions were runners-up in the twelve-team Autumn Cup and finished fourth in the BNL just behind Paisley. Scottish correspondent Eddie Blane, in an issue of that season's *IHW* said of Imrie: 'I was seeing a kid who could be as great as any of them, another Stu Robertson...' (a star Canadian). He continued, 'I've never seen a teenager with so much potential.' In spite of tougher opposition Red increased his points production to 51. He credits Lions' coach George McNeil as being largely responsible for his development.

With all the Scottish teams, except Paisley, pulling out of pro hockey a replacement amateur set-up failed before the end of the following season. So he had a year away from the rinks to play football. He moved to Murrayfield for 1957/58. Whilst with Royals, who won the short lived North British League, Red travelled to Paris with a Scottish Select in the autumn of that season and in January went to Switzerland to spend six weeks with Champery. Edinburgh re-entered the pro circuit and were only two points off winning the 1958 British Autumn Cup. The Royals lacked crowd support and Red again found himself out of regular hockey. He was soon picked up by Paisley to help the Pirates win the BNL title.

Being called up for National Service and posted to Colchester in Essex provided an opportunity for Red to continue on skates. He spent 1959/60 on defence for Streatham who had returned to the BNL. The south London team were virtually unbeatable carrying off the Autumn Cup and league title. Imrie missed just once match, he had a very understanding CO.

He was also considered to be the most consistent defenceman in the league and was voted Best British Player.

For the next five years, apart from a couple of months back with Edinburgh in early spring 1961, he stared with Brighton Tigers. In the absence of league hockey the competitions were 'home' tournaments. Here he picked up All-Star awards, three at 'A' and a 'B' for 1963/64. The April 1962 edition of *The Hockey Fan* commented, 'Since joining the Tigers… his performance has been nothing short of spectacular'. In the half decade he helped the south coast club to win the Brighton and Southern Cups, the Altrincham Tournament, Southampton Tournament and Cobley Cup twice and the Brighton Tournament three times.

It was whilst with Brighton that Imrie's international career blossomed. First selected for Scotland in February 1961 he scored on his debut at Southampton and next day at Brighton netted with five seconds remaining to provide the 3-3 tie with England.

He was a natural choice as Great Britain re-entered the World Championships after an interval of eight years. He netted in three of Great Britain's five matches in Pool 'B', including the 3-3 deadlock with Italy at Geneva. Next year in the USA he was one of the few stars in the side, scoring against Finland in Britain's only Pool 'A' win. His next and final World appearance was in 1966 in Yugoslavia. Here back in Pool B he was named by the IIHF as the Best Defenceman from among all the blue liners of the eight nations. The first Brit to be so honoured.

With the Brighton rink closing in spring 1965 Imrie joined Wembley late that autumn. For the next four years Lions played almost exclusively challenge matches at the Empire Pool until they too were disbanded.

Now living in south London he returned to the sport to coach Streatham Redskins for five years from autumn 1977 and then mentored the second team Bruins from 1983 for a couple of seasons. He led the Reds to three consecutive ICL titles from 1979-82 with Imrie named All-Star 'A' coach. Two of those campaigns were topped with play-off triumphs. During his reign Redskins also collected a fistful of 'home' tournament silverware.

After stepping off the bench he remained with the club for a while as a general hockey consultant to return as coach for one more season. He guided Redskins to their only Wembley finals appearance in spring 1985 after they twice defeated the all powerful Durham Wasps in the quarter-finals.

He first became part of the BBC TV broadcast team for the Autumn Cup final of November 1986. The BBC regularly featured ice hockey in the late 1980s and early 1990s in their transmissions from the Wembley and the monthly game on *Grandstand*. Red was the 'colour' man to Barry Davies's running commentary.

As a player he was a fine stick handler, difficult to dispossess and made few trips to the penalty box and is one of the friendliest of men off the ice.

Thomas 'Red' Imrie was born on 15 July 1937 at Falkirk. A motor mechanic by trade in his early years, he was also a fanatical golfer with a handicap of ten by the age of twenty. Five years later this was down to six. Prior to retiring from the world of work he was employed by an insurance company as a motor assessor.

Competition Statistics	GP	G	A	Pts	PIM
Falkirk Lions	98	30	54	84	14
Edinburgh Royals*	25	2	20	22	12
Paisley Pirates	11	1	3	4	8
Streatham	57	9	21	30	10
Brighton Tigers	129	63	116	179	33
Wembley Lions	5**	7	4	11	---
Great Britain	19	6	5	11	2

* 1958/59 Autumn Cup only

** British Cup

Pete 'Jonker' JOHNSON

Inducted 1989

Pete Johnson was a stalwart for twenty-four years with Durham Wasps during the days of the Northern League and beyond. He captained them at the first Wembley Championships and later coached Humberside to the Heineken Championship finals.

He started playing ice hockey at the age of twelve at the nearby Durham rink, gaining experience with Durham Leopards in the North-East League (1962-64). He made his debut with the senior Bees under coach Bill Booth at Southampton on 27 October 1962, aged sixteen. The following season, he and the team now called The Wasps moved to Whitley Bay for a year, with Pete making rapid progress as a regular member on the right wing. At Brighton in the Cobley Cup he scored the winning goal in a rink-length rush on his first shift, to inflict a rare defeat on Tigers. That winter he played 28 times to contribute 15 points. He featured in the 'Know Your Players' article in the May 1965 edition of *The Hockey Fan*. This was a rare distinction for a nineteen year old.

Soon back at the Durham rink, Wasps did not enjoy great success in the sixteen years of the Northern League. Johnson was eighth overall in points for NL competitions for 1967/68 and fifth two years later when he gained the first of three consecutive All-Star 'B' ratings. He missed 1975/76 and most of the next winter due to suspensions. He then went to work in Saudi Arabia for a while. He returned to hockey in earnest in 1980.

He maintained his competitive edge and his points production in the three import era. The Wasps rose to fourth in the final NL campaign and topped the 'B' Section of the newly formed British League the next winter. They were runners-up at the conclusion of the inaugural Premier Division in spring 1984. The following winter, with Johnson as captain, Wasps won the Autumn Cup and Premier titles, as his points total increased to 54. For his last two seasons on the ice he had the enormous satisfaction of his two sons Anthony and Stephen playing alongside him in the Durham strip. He said after a game at Billingham, 'that was special the first time we had a goal scored by Johnson, assisted Johnson and Johnson, it was a very good feeling.'

Retiring from playing he took over as coach. Durham retained the league crown and continued onto the 1986 Wembley semi-finals. They also recorded the best performance by a British team in the European Cup. Johnson was named HBL P 'Coach of the Year'. He stepped down from the bench early next autumn due to pressure of work.

He returned to coaching with Humberside Seahawks, guiding them to the 1990/91 HBL D1 crown and play-off promotion to the Premier league. The brilliance of the campaign, which drew increasing crowds to Hull, was recognised with a divisional 'Coach of the Year' title.

His sons Anthony and Stephen were joined on Hawks' roster by Shaun, a third sibling. Twelve months later he steered the team through the play-off group to a Wembley final after overcoming Nottingham by 5-4 the previous evening. It was the best of the three games, with Johnson commenting: 'Nobody gave us a chance that helped us to lift our game.' He remained as coach until summer 1996.

He scored for England on his debut against Scotland in 1969 and made several more appearances opposing the 'auld enemy', captaining the team in 1974. Twice selected for Great Britain in Pool 'C' World Championships, both were held in Holland, in 1971 and 1973.

But that was not the end of his international involvement. Having previously coached the Durham Mosquitoes to an English Junior title he was appointed, in 1984, to co-coach the first England Under-16 team and be assistant coach of the Great Britain bronze-medal-winning Pool 'C' Under-21s three years later. By 1990 he was assistant to Alex Dampier with the British senior squad. Two years on Great Britain won Pool 'C' at Hull and the following year in Holland gained promotion to the top group. As a fiery motivator Pete played no small part in this outstanding achievement. Dampier said of him: 'We worked together for six years with the juniors.

Pete Johnson worked as coach to Humberside Seahawks in 1991.

He is a tremendous motivator.' A year later, along with Dampier he retired from the Great Britain programme.

As a player he was a hard-nosed competitor often indulging in what he referred to as 'old-time hockey'. Off the ice he is friendly and extrovert, good with youngsters, and has a font of larger-than-life hockey stories. Jonker is one of the few true characters of the sport.

Peter Johnson was born at Langley Park, Co. Durham on 14 April 1946. He started his working life as a coalminer and later worked on oil rigs in the Arabian Gulf.

At a ceremony before a Newcastle Riverkings contest in November 1998 he was made a founder member of north-east England's Wall of Fame.

He is, and has been for many years, employed by the local authority at Kingston as ice sports development officer at their Hull rink.

Competition Statistics	GP	G	A	Pts	PIM
Durham Wasps*	443	504	424	928	923
Great Britain	14	3	5	8	2

* Excludes 1965/66

Chris KELLAND

Inducted 2002

Chris Kelland, a defenceman, arrived in Britain from his native Canada in 1980 to play at the highest possible level for eighteen years, including captaining his adopted country's rise from the depths of Pool 'D' to face the might of Canada and Russia four years later.

He signed for Murrayfield Racers, coached by Alex Dampier, in the near all-amateur Northern League. On Saturday 2 November he made his debut in Racers 7-2 home win over Fife Flyers. His impact was immediate as he was named the next spring as joint Overseas 'Rookie of the Year'. He was also voted onto the All-Star 'A' team, a feat repeated for the next two seasons.

During his eleven years in the Scottish capital he normally logged around fifty minutes of ice time a game. His efforts were a major factor in Racers capturing the NL title plus the Autumn and Icy Smith Cups in his first year, and retaining the league crown the next season, as well as adding the revived Scottish League. Although losing finalists in the first Heineken-sponsored Wembley finals in 1984, Chris, now captain of Racers, collected a British Championship medal in 1986, followed by consecutive British League titles. Silver was gained in the nail-biting penalty shoot out loss to Cardiff at Wembley in 1990. All-Star 'A' accolades were gained in 1985, two years later and again for 1988.

Although initially used as a 'policeman' – he collected 175 penalty minutes in his first two seasons at Murrayfield – he stayed loyal to the club for eleven years. In January 1989 he told *Ice Hockey Today* that the club '… treated him well. We get ice time from 1-2 p.m. in the afternoon.' This was a major consideration at a time when most teams usually practiced around midnight only a couple of times a week. By March 1989 under the prevailing rule of a maximum of three imports he had resided in Britain long enough, to be reclassified as a 'non-import'. During his time in Edinburgh he featured on a Lyon's tea quiz card wearing his familiar No.21 shirt.

He claimed that Dampier was the biggest influence on his career, it was therefore no surprise when, in the summer of 1991, he followed his mentor to Nottingham. He helped Panthers to win the Norwich Union-sponsored Autumn Cup, a league runners-up position and to the final at the Wembley Championships. He missed the play-offs the following year due to injury and that summer moved to Sheffield, now coached by Dampier. Staying for five years he collected further winner's medals, including consecutive HBL P and championship play-offs, commencing in 1995. The B&H Autumn Cup joined the collection the next season.

Immediately upon obtaining his dual citizenship he was recruited to the Great Britain team in time for the 1990 Pool 'D' World Championships at Cardiff and named captain. He continued in that role for five glorious years as Great Britain rose from the 'D' to the 'A' Pool in Italy in 1994. The IIHF named him the competition's Best Defenceman in 1991 and again twelve months later. Although relegated after facing the might of Canada and Russia, Kelland performed his task with honour and commitment.

He remained at the highest level with the coming of the Superleague and its mass of imports, for two further campaigns at Sheffield. The first ended at Manchester Arena with a championship medal. Although intending to retire he was persuaded to stay with Steelers for a fifth year. But with the sacking of Dampier in 1998 he left as he now held down a full-time job.

Even that could not keep him away from the ice. Dropping two levels he helped Solihull Blaze to an English League Premier Division and play-off double. The following winter, the fact he stayed kept in shape with the amateur Sheffield Scimitars, of the English League Division One, persuaded Hull Thunder to sign him in January 2000 as emergency cover. His last competitive matches were at the new Coventry rink during 2000/01 where he assisted Blaze on five occasions.

Chris Kelland, captain of Great Britain's 1990 World Championship Pool 'D' winning team, celebrates with the trophy.

Christopher Kelland was born on 22 December 1957 at Sault Ste Marie, Ontario. His earliest memories are of skating outdoors, later he spent five years playing college hockey.

At 5ft 9in tall and weighing 185 pounds he took great care to look after his body and was always super fit. For many years he returned to Canada for three months each summer to work as a lumberjack. This all contributed to his longevity on the ice.

In 1998, aged forty and looking for security he fulfilled a long-held ambition by being accepted into the Yorkshire Fire Service.

Competition Statistics	GP	G	A	Pts	PIM
Murrayfield Racers	410	282	585	867	1469
Nottingham Panthers	92	25	114	139	256
Sheffield Steelers	295	45	173	218	432
Solihull Blaze	30	12	45	57	50
Hull Thunder	12	0	7	7	32
Coventry Blaze	5	0	1	1	2
Great Britain	31	10	8	18	41

Thorold McDiarmid 'Doc' KELLOUGH M.D.

Inducted 1950

Thorold McDiarmid Kellough was one of the small band of Canadian-born pioneers of English ice hockey who helped establish the sport here in the late 1920s and into the following decade.

His original *IHW* citation stated he '… did much to help young players and spread the gospel of hockey.'

Doc Kellough M.D., *c.*1950.

He was a founder member of the short-lived Hammersmith club in west London which formed almost as soon as the rink opened in December 1929; he was on the ice at Hammersmith as they lost 4-1 to Princes II in March 1930 in a British League Division Two knockout round. Bournemouth's first hockey match also featured Hammersmith with Kellough on defence, in the 10-6 win over Westover in December of the same year.

From there he moved to the basement-level rink at the Grosvenor House hotel on Park Lane. He captained the aptly named Canadians during their first season of 1931/32 when they ended as runners-up in the English League. Kellough was in GH Canadians line-up for the first game at the Purley rink on 16 March 1932 when they defeated Princes & Queens 3-1.

He moved to Queens for his last EL campaign during 1934/35. With rising standards and the increasing number of imported paid-to-play Canadians 'Doc's' on-ice hockey tailed off with a few 'recreational-type' games. From now on he organised. A November 1936 edition of the weekly *IHW* reported that, using his own money, he was holding practices at the Queens rink for the 'Forgotten Men.' In other words those veteran Canadians and younger English lads unable to break into semi-pro league hockey. He planned to take a team to the Continent over Christmas. A year later he took the two non-league teams of Queens and London Canadians to Blackpool to stage the first hockey match on the newly opened Lancashire rink. This was one of many such trips around the lesser rinks of England.

With the opening of Wembley to pro hockey in October 1934 Kellough became the honorary medical advisor to the teams based there. Next season he transferred his skills to Empress Stadium/Hall until the outbreak of war in 1939. He then moved west, back to Wembley, before hostilities closed down league hockey for the next six years.

'Doc' as he was affectionately known was short, stout and sturdy, with a husky voice. He was a font of hockey folklore and a ready conversationalist.

His place in the Hall of Fame is assured for his role as a father figure to many of the young impecunious Canadians who found their way to London during the depression years of the 1930s. Bob Giddens said that Kellough:

> … was Santa Claus to every stray Canadian hockey player in England and even in faraway out-of-the-way places in the woodlands and wilds of Canada any hockey player about to board a freight,

then a tramp steamer for Europe would be in possession of the tip – See Doc if you get to London and feel dazed and don't know which corner to take.

Following the Second World War he practised as a GP from his surgery in Holland Park. Doc Kellough died during the winter of 1956/57.

Willie KERR Snr

Inducted 1990

William Kerr was affectionately known as 'The Old Man' within the Murrayfield ice rink which he managed from 1959 until his untimely death twenty-four years later. For many years he was the managing director and during that time he acquired a vast knowledge and experience in all aspects of ice sports, especially ice hockey.

During the lean years of the early 1960s many Scottish hockey clubs were denied ice time or at the very least experienced difficulty in obtaining practice ice at their own rinks. Willie came to their rescue generously offering ice time at Murrayfield to a group of players from Falkirk, Kirkcaldy, Glasgow Flyers and Perth Blackhawks as well as a couple of other teams who all benefited from his gesture. This was the era of the 1962-65 Scottish League. A few years later Dundee Rockets were also assisted with some ice time.

He did much to keep hockey going through this period, playing a major role in the formation of a Scottish Committee of the BIHA in May 1962 and the Northern League four years later.

As the Murrayfield Royals faded from the scene by 1965 due to retirements and defections, Kerr encouraged youngsters to form the Racers, initially as a reserve side with the veteran ex-pro Johnny Carlyle as coach. Early products were the Reilly brothers, Derek and Glen, Freddie Wood and Lawrie Lovell.

This policy ensured the strength and hold that Racers had on the latter days of the NL and through into the era of the HBL of the 1980s. The team won the Northern League seven times between 1970 and 1981, and were nine-time winners of the Icy Smith Cup – emblematic of the British Championship.

A keen advocate of local talent he did much to encourage youngsters in the Edinburgh area to get involved with hockey. For instance, Murrayfield Ravens

Willie Kerr Snr was manager of Murrayfield ice rink, which he managed until his untimely death in 1983.

joined the NIHA Junior League for the Under-17s in its second season of 1976/77. From finishing in the basement in their rookie campaign they emerged as champions a year later and again in spring 1980.

The Kerr family were among the purchasers of the Murrayfield Ice Rink in the summer of 1957 and remain part owners to this day. He also had a business interest in the assembly Rooms at Leith.

Willie Kerr was born on 29 January 1912 at his parents' house in Ayr. In his twenties he was employed as a cashier in an estate agent's and, soon after the Second World War, as a commercial cashier. During the war he served as a corporal in the Royal Scots. He died on 10 August 1983, aged seventy-one, at Edinburgh's Royal Infirmary, from a heart attack.

Keith KEWLEY

Inducted 2005

Keith Kewley was the driving force in the winning of major trophies at three different clubs in Scotland in the 1940s and 1950s – as captain, then coach to Dunfermline and as coach at Ayr and Paisley.

He came to Scotland from Canada in the autumn of 1946 as a twenty-one year old, to be made captain of Dunfermline Vikings in the first post-war campaign of the revived SNL. At 5ft 8in tall and weighing in at 150lbs, he contributed 36 points at left-wing on the second line. Kewley's interest was towards coaching rather than continuing his playing career. Encouraged by Scottish-born head coach 'Scotty' Cameron he was a major influence in Vikings winning the Scottish League Flag, Canada Cup and play-offs for the Anderson Trophy. Asked by rink manager Bill Creasey to take over as coach the following season he guided Dunfermline to the Simpson Trophy.

For the next two years he remained in Canada with his Scottish wife before he was approached in the summer of 1950 by the manager of the Ayr rink to coach the Raiders. Here he guided the team to the Autumn Cup in his first season and its retention the next year plus capturing the Scottish League title.

The opportunity to again work with Bill Creasey, now rink manager at Paisley, saw Kewley coaching Pirates from 1952 for four outstanding years. In the final winter of independent Scottish competitions Paisley won the

The son of Toronto sports journalist Claude Kewley, Keith was one of four brothers to play successfully in Scotland.

Autumn and Canada Cups and the league title for 1953/54. Next season Pirates' third place at the higher standard of the rookie British Autumn Cup and National League earned Kewley a coaching All-Star 'A'. A second successive accolade came twelve months later as Paisley finished as Autumn Cup runners-up.

In these years he particularly enjoyed the luxury of almost unlimited practice ice time at East Lane as training had been restricted at Dunfermline and Ayr by the more lucrative demands of the curling fraternity. His mix of the all-Scottish contingent of the Syme brothers on defence, with Ferguson, the Billy's – Brennan and Crawford – up front, supported by Joe Brown made a significant contribution to Paisley's success. He had realised that to be cost effective the small rosters of around twelve Canadian imports, reducing to ten by the early 1950s, in a schedule of around sixty games a season, needed boosting to win titles. Putting time and effort into coaching potentially talented local youngsters up to the required standard provided an answer and a legacy that lasted well into the 1960s.

Keith Kewley was born on 10 July 1926 at Stratford, Ontario, Canada, grew up in Kitchener and was educated at the local Victoria School before the family moved to Toronto. Here he played for the OHA Junior 'B' champions – Toronto Victory Aircraft, along with his brother Herb, an All-Star defenceman at Dunfermline and from 1950-54 at Ayr.

Brennan, in remembering his first experience of Kewley's coaching, said of him: 'I learnt more in that hour than I had picked up in the previous four years.' In the summer of 1956 he returned to settle in his homeland with his family at St Thomas, Ontario. Here he worked in industry management before moving into real estate brokerage.

His involvement with hockey continued as coach to the local senior 'A' Royals for a couple of years. For seven years from 1961 he developed youngsters in Junior 'B' with St Thomas Barons and then at Midget level for several seasons.

Kewley always preferred to take a low profile, allowing the players to take the credit for their on-ice success and consequent silverware. Now a widower and in retirement, he regularly plays golf and heads south to Florida in winter.

Competition Statistics	GP	G	A	Pts	PIM
Dunfermline Vikings	---	22	14	36	37

Coaching	GP	W	L	D	W%
Dunfermline Vikings	56	27	24	5	48.2
Ayr Raiders	120	66	43	11	55
Paisley Pirates	234	132	76	26	56.4

Marsh KEY
Inducted 2007

Marsh Key is regarded as the outstanding forward produced in Britain during the first era of professional leagues. Tony Allen, instigator of the revived Hall of Fame, watched Key over fifty years ago. He told author David Gordon: 'I have to smile… every time… somebody describes Tony Hand (a certain future Hall of Famer) as the best British player ever. They obviously never saw Marsh Key.'

He learnt to skate as a thirteen year old at his local rink in Dundee. Spotted by pre-war player George McNeil at a public skating session he was invited to attend a hockey practice. Key made rapid progress as a centre-ice with a left-hand shot, moving from the pee-wee Cubs to the junior Rockets in 1947. He made his senior debut with Tigers in the Scottish National League at the age of sixteen during the 1948/49 season.

A happy-looking Marsh Key at Harringay in 1956.

The following winter Tigers' Canadian coach Walt McDonald used Key to centre the second forward line on a regular basis although National Service in the RAF restricted his games during 1950/51.He was to remain a permanent and valued fixture on Tigers roster until pro hockey ended at the Kingsway rink in spring 1955. Two years running he finished as Dundee's third highest points scorer, dropping to fourth for 1953/54 to regain third spot the following season. A remarkable achievement for a Scottish boy at that time of twelve-man rosters, nine of which were invariably imported and paid Canadians.

Following a winter with Perth Panthers in the short-lived Scottish Amateur League he had a brief mid-season stint during 1956/57 as player-coach in Switzerland with Crans-sur-Sierre during the run of the ice show at Harringay Arena. He had signed for Racers as their second mandatory British-trained player with fellow Scot Johnny Carlyle. At the end of the next campaign, Harringay's last, his 56 points total placed him seventh in the BNL points scoring table, higher than many seasoned Canadians. Key was his team's second-highest scorer. He lay just six points behind veteran Bill Glennie who had been voted into the Hall of Fame seven years earlier. The weekly *IHW* for 3 May reported: 'Marsh Key ran away with the readers' votes for the best British boy of the season.'

He came back to Scotland to sign for the reformed Edinburgh Royals, but by Christmas Murrayfield's old problem of lack of crowd support forced the management to pull the team out of pro hockey. Key contributed the most points at 51, six ahead of Ted McCaskill, who nine years later played thirty games in the NHL for Minnesota North Stars. In the new year one game with Paisley was sufficient for him to secure a contact for the 1959/60 season with Pirates, along with McCaskill.

Marsh continued in hockey after the collapse of the BNL in spring 1960, first at Murrayfield but a back injury suffered early in the second period at Brighton on 29 January 1961, after contributing a goal and two assists, forced him out of the sport for two and half years.

Returning to hockey following recovery from spinal fusion during 1963/64, he assisted Perth Black Hawks in six games at Ayr, Kirkcaldy and Whitley Bay.

The following winter he was back at Murrayfield with Royals in a total of nineteen games, including thirteen in the Scottish League and at the 'home' tournaments at Brighton and challenge matches at Wembley. He also helped the Glasgow club on a couple of occasions.

Although he was first capped for Scotland in 1950 for the annual clash with England and again in 1962, it was not until March 1965 that he represented Great Britain in his only trip to the World Championships. At Group 'B', held in Finland, he scored on successive days in losses to Germany and Austria. Previously his RAF commanding officer, a club owner and then injury had prevented his release.

That spring he left hockey for a second time only to be enticed back four years later as player-coach when Dundee Rockets moved up from the NIHA Reserve League to the senior set-up. A fifth-place league finish was followed by third place in the 1970 Autumn Cup. Unfortunately, Rockets were then excluded from the NL due to a dispute between the company claiming ownership of the club and the league authorities. Dundee's correspondent in that year's *Ice Hockey Herald Annual* paid Key this compliment: '…the bulk of the club's success to date has been directly attributable to Marsh.'

He retired from hockey in March 1971 to concentrate on golf, his other sporting passion, as a member of the Carnoustie club, with at one time a handicap of three. His place in hockey was recognised by his home town in 2000 as he was asked to open the new Dundee ice rink, where a function suite is named in his honour.

Marshall Whitton Key was born on 18 June 1932 in Dundee and educated at the local Morgan Academy. On leaving school he worked for a while in newspaper circulation with the *Daily Mail*. After full-time hockey he took over his father's newsagent and tobacconist shop in Dundee and expanded the business to include a snack bar and public house. Later he was the landlord at the Invergowrie Inn in the village where he and his wife now live in retirement.

These days Marsh enjoys the links with a couple of old hockey chums and during winter enjoys golfing breaks at his villa in Florida, USA.

Competition Statistics	GP	G	A	Pts	PIM
Dundee Tigers	337	130	186	316	143
Perth Panthers*	---	---	---	---	---
Harringay Racers	107	53	81	134	14
Edinburgh Royals	25	20	31	51	6
Paisley Pirates	32	14	31	45	4
Murrayfield Royals**	19	24	20	44	22
Perth Black Hawks	6	5	2	7	26
Glasgow Flyers	2	0	1	1	0
Dundee Rockets	19	15	26	41	16
Great Britain	6	2	4	6	0

★ Statistics unavailable

★★ Excludes 1960/61

Jack KILPATRICK

Inducted in 1993 as a member of the Great Britain 1936 Olympic and World Champions

Jack Kilpatrick is the youngest Briton, at eighteen, to have won an Olympic gold medal at the Winter Games.

He made just one appearance, in his usual left-wing position, in the opening match at Garmisch on 7 February, in which Great Britain shut-out Sweden 1-0. Soon after Britain went ahead early in the first period Kilpatrick almost put his team two goals in front, 'but the play was called back for offside.' He was not selected for the remaining six encounters. Nonetheless, the gold medal was his.

Prior to returning to England in the autumn of 1935 straight from school, he had only played Juvenile hockey for St Mark's at Prince Albert. The team won a championship headed by Kilpatrick as their leading scorer. He was spotted by the Scottish-born netminder Ronald 'Scotty' Milne who wrote to Wembley Lions saying that he was the most promising English born youngster playing in Canada.

Signed as the seventh and reserve forward and therefore the tenth man – as nine was the usual game night line-up of that decade – he saw little action at the Empire Pool. Used as a checking forward or filling in for an injured player, which occurred more frequently in his second and final winter in the ENL, provided the majority of his ice time. Bearing in mind the low scores of that period and the limited opportunities afforded him, a total of ten points is not unreasonable. He was described at the time as quiet and unassuming, popular and an expert cook at the flat he shared with teammates Tony and Albert Lemay.

Jack Kilpatrick was born on 7 July 1917 at Millom in Cumberland, a small town on the southern fringes of the Lake District. His birth is registered over the county border at Bootle in Lancashire. He moved at the age of four to St Albert, a township in Saskatchewan with a population of around 10,000.

Going back to Canada in the summer of 1937 he spent the next four winters with Nelson Maple Leafs in the Kooteny Senior League accumulating 55 goals. According to the 1942 NHL Guide he turned pro the previous September with Chicago Black Hawks, although it was reported much later that he said 'the offer was not good enough.' He spent 1941/42 with Victoria Bapcos in the professional Pacific Coast League totalling 46 points from thirty-one

Jack Kilpatrick on Wembley ice during the 1935/36 season.

matches. The last year of the Second World War was spent in the military, followed by seven seasons back in Nelson with the Maple Leafs. His career was ended by a hip injury in making a sharp turn to avoid a body-check.

Looking back in 1984 on his time at the Olympics he said: 'It seems so long ago now and it is hard to imagine it happened, and yet golden days for an eighteen year old lad.' He retired from the British Columbia Telephone Co. in 1982 and died five years later aged seventy-two, on 18 December 1989.

Competition Statistics	GP	G	A	Pts	PIM
Wembley Lions	---	6	4	10	4
Great Britain	1	0	0	0	---

Charles J. KNOTT Jnr

Inducted 2004

Charles Knott Jnr, known affectionately as 'CJ', was a keen advocate of the home-grown player, and managing director of the Southampton ice rink and the Vikings team from 1952-63. During this period he presented amateur ice hockey at Southampton in a showman-like professional manner, publicising the city as 'The Heart of English Ice Hockey'.

CJ took over the running of the newly rebuilt Southampton rink when it opened in March 1952. He immediately arranged for the Sussex team – mainly English lads who played their fixtures behind closed doors at Brighton – to move west along the coast to continue playing in the Southern Intermediate League (SIL) as Vikings. Instant success followed with capacity crowds and the league title by the close of the inaugural season. Triumphs over the next few years included winning five BIHA Cup tournaments and the Southern Cup on three occasions as well as the Liverpool Tournament.

He elevated the status of the SIL, whose members mainly played late at night, devoid of spectators in their local rinks. His expertise maintained crowd levels as fans were treated to visits from England, Scotland, Sweden, the USA and Czechoslovakia plus foreign club sides.

By 1959 Knott was assisting the sport's governing body as a selector for England, with appointment to the BIHA Council coming a year later in recognition of his efforts on behalf of home-grown talent. Two of whom – Mike Madine and Pete Murray, later went on to play for Great Britain at World Championship level. By then almost half the Vikings consisted of locally trained players. In the absence of any organised youth leagues a junior section had been in existence for five years, ultimately with two age groups.

Great Britain returned to the World Championships in 1961, after an interval of eight years, with CJ travelling to Switzerland as the BIHA representative.

In the summer of 1963 the Knott family sold their adjoining sports facilities, along with the rink to

Charles J. Knott, *c*.1957.

Rank. It took thirteen years before Rank realised that ice hockey attracted paying customers. CJ made a return to the sport to head up the club management committee for the second season of Vikings' revival.

Always approachable and immaculately attired in an evening suit CJ was never one to shut himself away in his rinkside office. He could often be seen talking to his patrons and young aspiring players. Rink rats never misbehaved when CJ was around. Roy Saunders, one of the few surviving Vikings of the early 1950s, recently recalled him as the finest gentleman he ever met.

Charles Knott was born in Southampton on 26 November 1914 and following his education at the local Taunton grammar school joined his father – Charles senior – in the family fishmonger's business. In 1939 Charles Snr purchased the original ice rink located adjacent to the speedway and greyhound stadium he founded some years earlier. That rink was destroyed eighteen months later during an air raid.

Cricket was CJ's other sporting love, he was a successful and immensely popular amateur bowler between 1938 and 1954 with Hampshire County Cricket Club. He took 676 wickets in 173 first-class matches and strongly disliked the class-ridden attitudes of that period, which decreed separate changing rooms for amateurs. Serving as club chairman for twenty-one years, he retired in 1989.

He died aged eighty-seven, on 27 February 2003. A road in a housing estate adjacent to the site of the ice rink, demolished in 1988, is named in tribute to father and son as Charles Knott Gardens.

Gordon LATTO

Inducted 1998

Gordon Latto was virtually a one-club man, spending nearly all his twenty-six years in ice hockey helping his home town Fife Flyers to win titles.

He started skating as a five year old at the Kirkcaldy rink when his dad took him and his brother Doug to the Sunday morning public sessions. Three years later he commenced playing hockey under the guidance of Harold 'Pep' Young and Bert Smith. He worked his way up from the Pee-Wees into the second team Kestrels. His debut for the senior Flyers came as a fourteen-year-old centre-ice during the 1972/73 NL campaign in a match opposing Glasgow Dynamos. Four weeks later he scored his first goal for the blue and gold against Durham Wasps. Some weekends he would turn out for the Pee-Wees, Kestrels and Flyers. He continued to gain experience helping the Kestrels retain the Second League title in 1974/75, to be named 'Player of the Year'.

After impressing the instructors at a hockey school for Swedish youngsters held in the Highlands at the Aviemore rink, Latto was invited to spend the winter in Gothenburg. Commenting on his time with Vastra Frolunda's Under-19 league outfit Latto told Dundee's *Sporting Post*: 'Training three hours a day brought my game on a ton.'

He returned to Scotland to dominate the NL scene. In twenty-four games he scored 44 goals and assisted on a further 40. He was a shoo-in that season for Great Britain's 1976 Pool 'C' venture to Poland, where he iced in four of the matches at Katowice. His prowess coincided with Flyers' triumphs. Whilst Gordon was named Northern League 'Player of the Year' three times in succession (1977-79) his team won the NL Grand Slam for 1976/77 and retained the NL crown and Icy Smith Cup the following season. Named a centre-ice 'A'-team All-Star in 1978 he moved to right-wing to gain the same accolade at that position next year and again in 1980. A prolific scorer he topped the Autumn Cup points chart in 1979 and went on to win the Earl Carlson trophy as leading scorer in all NIHA competitions that winter.

During 1982/83 he was briefly enticed away to Tom Stewart's Dundee Rockets, to soon return to the Kingdom of Fife. Autumn saw the introduction of the British divisional league and the use of better quality paid-to-play Canadians. Flyers were no exception to this trend and set the standard for 1984/85 with three, including Ron Plumb – the first player from the NHL to ply his trade in Britain for over twenty-five years. Flyers swept their play-off group 4-0 to proceed to the finals at Wembley Arena. On 4 May, Latto, now captain, netted the opening goal at 3.59 in the 12-3 semi-final crushing of Streatham. Next day it was a proud skipper who held the trophy aloft after the defeat of Murrayfield. It was Flyers' first silverware in seven years. Defeated coach Jim Lynch described Latto 'as probably the best guy in the team.'

Five years on and the return to the Wembley finals weekend in April 1990 was not as fruitful second time around. Latto could not urge his men past Cardiff in the first semi-

Gordon Latto was a highly respected defencemen in the Heineken League era.

final. Now a family man and disappointed by relegation from the Premier Division he retired for a brief period in 1991 but returned in time for the promotion play-offs won by Fife.

During 1994/95 Latto defied his veteran status by reverting to a wingman alongside ex-NHL player Mark Morrison. In the spring, deemed the sport's most gentlemanly player, the BIHA presented him with the Ernest Ramus medal.

The collapse of the fourteen-year-old British League with the founding of the Superleague for 1996/97 forced Fife and Latto into the newly established Northern Premier League which they duly won along with the play-offs. In his final season Flyers retained their Premier title and also contested the revived BNL. Latto played a full slate of forty-seven games.

He announced his retirement, at the age of thirty-nine, at the testimonial match held in his honour at Kirkcaldy on 30 March 1998. At the same time, in front of 3,200 fans, Flyers retired his No.16 shirt. In addition the BIHA awarded him their Ahearne medal.

After a third trip to the World Championships in China in 1981, Britain and Latto did not participate again until 1989 in Belgium. He said this was the 'lowest point in my career' as he was one of several players deemed to have failed a drugs test. It took many months before the

IIHF admitted mistakes in the testing regime and Gordon gained belated clearance of taking anabolic steroids. His justified pithy comment was: 'It was just a farce.'

Like many before him Latto, at 5ft 10in in height and weighing 168lbs, was a fitness fanatic who hated to lose and extended his career by moving back to defence. The taste of Swedish hockey left a long-lasting preference for the European style of the game. Statistics point to a playmaker rather than an outright scorer, who avoided the sin bin.

Gordon Latto was born in Kirkcaldy on 18 August 1958. He works as an optical engineer, lives in the Kingdom of Fife and still enjoys the occasional game of recreational hockey as well as being a fine golfer.

Competition Statistics	GP	G	A	Pts	PIM
Fife Flyers	921	405	723	1128	555
Dundee Rockets	5	4	2	6	6
Great Britain	21	2	2	4	10

Tommy LAUDER
Inducted 1951

Tommy Lauder, the outstanding Scottish-born player of his era, skated in every post-war season of the predominantly Canadian-staffed semi-pro SNL.

Lauder was a defenceman who spent his early years in Lachine, Quebec where he picked up the rudiments of ice hockey and graduated through the ranks of youth teams. Some of the Canadians of the burgeoning SNL in the late 1930s remained during the years of the Second World War. They helped develop the local lads and occasionally banded together as the Scottish Select, which included Lauder, to take on Canadian Armed Forces teams at rinks around Scotland not requisitioned by the government. Lauder was in the Scottish Select line-up beaten 8-5 by Sweden at Paisley on 19 March 1946.

This all helped Lauder hone his skills to the point where, with the resumption of league hockey in the autumn of 1946, he was signed as player-coach by Paisley Pirates. His 27 points helped Pirates gain the Scottish Cup although he stood down from coaching before the season finished. Next season his points production increased by twenty-four as Pirates clinched the Autumn Cup. His last trophy with Paisley came two years later with another Scottish Cup victory.

Tommy Lauder – the outstanding Scottish-born player of his era.

For the next six campaigns he moved north-east to skate for Perth. At the end of his second season Panthers ended as play-off finalists in the Anderson Trophy. His third Scottish Cup medal was secured during 1953/54 – the last for the Scottish NL competitions. Lauder contributed 10+37 from the blue line. The following autumn Perth were a member of the twelve-team BNL. Eight months on and all the Scottish teams, bar Paisley, withdrew. Lauder retired from pro hockey to coach Perth from the bench in the short-lived Scottish Amateur League.

Ice Hockey World's original 1951 issue read: 'Tommy Lauder is another heady Scottish defenceman and in the opinion of the "World" is the best Scottish-born player yet produced.' However, he was overlooked by selectors for Great Britain's 1948 Olympic squad and the

World Championships held in London two years later. Perhaps by the early 1950s he was considered to be at the veteran stage of his career.

Lauder was a big rearguard and whilst never an All-Star, was steady and dependable with few visits to the penalty box. In his day considered one of the 'gentleman' of the sport, his playing style bore comparison with Wembley's defender Sonny Rost.

Away from the rinks he worked as a journeyman iron turner and like so many other hockey players, golf provided a second sporting outlet. When he played for Paisley he could be found at the Elderside course where, in his younger years, he enjoyed a low handicap.

Thomas 'Tommy' Lauder was born on 7 January 1918 at Johnstone, Renfrewshire. It is considered likely that he migrated to Canada after hockey finished at Perth.

Competition Statistics	GP	G	A	Pts	PIM
Paisley Pirates	178*	69	121	190	72
Perth Panthers	298	32	116	148	40

* Excludes 1946/47.

John LAWLESS
Inducted 1997

John Lawless first came to Britain from his native Canada in the autumn of 1982 to join the newly formed Peterborough Pirates. He carved out an outstanding career as a player, coach and team manager over the next sixteen years.

As a centre-ice he led the Pirates to second place in the southern section of Division Two of the British League, scoring six or more goals in a game eight times to finish with 100 goals and 71 assists in 18 matches. Over the next three seasons Lawless inspired Pirates to the Division One title and promotion to the Premier Division, accumulating 713 points in the process from league and cup games. He had won the Division One scoring title for 1984/85. Two years later he assisted Oxford Stars in a couple of league matches.

Whilst living in East Anglia he joined the managerial ladder, initially as assistant rink manager. He moved to a similar position when he masterminded the setting up of Cardiff Devils when the Wales National Ice Rink opened for business in November 1986. As player-manager the rookie Devils were an instant success, drawing fans to pack the building as the team won their section of Division Two and were finalists in the end of season play-offs staged in the Welsh capital.

Moving up a division, Cardiff won the league crown and the play-offs for promotion to the Premier Division at their second attempt. Audacious signings of quality imports and top class British players alike stamped Lawless as a bold judge of talent and player chemistry. He was highly criticised by longer established clubs for signing the Cooper brothers – Ian and Stephen – in 1988, and was accused of cheque-book hockey. Two years later he led his team onto the Wembley ice for the first of their five appearances in six years in the British Championship finals, which they won in a dramatic penalty shoot-out. Stepping up onto the bench for most games, Lawless coached Devils to the Premier Division and Championships again in 1993, adding the B&H Autumn Cup for the grand slam. Donning skates he assisted Devils to retain the league and Wembley crowns the following spring which gained Lawless his second consecutive 'Coach of the Year' title. He announced his retirement from the playing side.

In the summer of 1995 he took on fresh challenge, the daunting task of manager-coach for Manchester Storm at the new 17,000-plus-seat Manchester Nynex Arena. Sweeping the Division One title with two defeats in fifty-two matches delivered a third 'Coach of the Year'

As Cardiff Devils' manager-coach John Lawless presided over a team that was nigh-on unbeatable. The zenith came in the 1992/93 season where the club won the British League, and play-off trophies, as well as the Benson & Hedges Autumn Cup. Here John can be seen showing of the fruits of these triumphs.

trophy and membership of the Superleague for Storm. This time he stayed in the office and on the bench for a difficult year. Manchester escaped the cellar by four points and ended bottom in their play-off group. Honest John said, 'I underestimated the standard and I hold my hands up.-' He paid the price, being relieved of his duties a month after receiving his Hall of Fame certificate on the ice at the championship finals in Manchester.

A phone call from the Telford management early in November 1997 brought Lawless back across the Atlantic. With infectious enthusiasm he injected professionalism into the struggling

Tigers as they moved up the BNL table ending as runners-up. He donned the skates again for six of the play-off contests, with the team making the semi-finals at Hull.

It all went sour next autumn after Lawless steered Telford to the B&H Plate final. Funding mysteriously dried up and by spring Lawless reckoned he was owed around £9,500. As one would expect, he remained loyal to the club, staying into the play-offs, having kitted-up in a total of twenty-four matches. It did not embitter the memories of his time in Britain. Philosophically he noted: 'No way. I'm not going to beat myself up about it.'

By 1990 and eligible for the British national side he played at the World Championships that year and the following winter. Whilst with Cardiff he was involved in six European Cup attempts. At the third in 1994, Devils defeated two clubs from the former Soviet Union.

Always intensely competitive he was also refreshingly honest in acknowledging responsibility for his coaching and management decisions. At 5ft 5in in height and weighing around 145lbs his stature belies his achievements, as his record proves he was no lightweight in making a major contribution to the sport in Britain.

John Lawless was born on 8 January 1961 at Orillia, Ontario, Canada. After leaving school he qualified in civil engineering at Centennial College in Toronto. He returned to Canada with his English wife, Debbie, and their children in the summer of 1999, to settle in his home town of Orillia. John worked on the designing and drafting side with Aimicon, a company that fitted out and remodelled ice rinks and sports halls. He also found time to coach the Junior 'A' Huntsville Wildcats.

Competition Statistics	GP	G	A	Pts	PIM
Peterborough Pirates	118	351	362	713	181
Cardiff Devils	289	406	508	914	268
Oxford City Stars	2	6	4	10	0
Manchester Storm	27	29	30	59	54
Telford Tigers	34	10	18	28	26
Great Britain	12	5	10	15	22

Coaching	GP	W	L	D	W%
Cardiff Devils	15*	11	2	2	73.3
Manchester Storm	122	73	43	6	59.8
Telford Tigers	48	27	17	4	56.2

★ 1993 & 1995 play-offs only

Ernest 'Ernie' LEACOCK

Inducted 1987

'Ernie' Leacock was the principal referee in Britain for thirty years from the mid-1930s until 1965. He officiated in over 2,000 senior matches including the Olympics and World Championships.

Leacock returned to England in September 1934, having written from Canada in July for a trial with the newly formed Wembley Lions. He was transferred to Richmond Hawks. Selected as a forward for Great Britain's attempt at the World Championships in Switzerland in February his amateur eligibility was challenged. Representatives of Canada's governing body for hockey the CAHA, travelling with their national side, pointed out that he had played pro hockey in the USA. In the days of sham amateurism the BIHA had no option but to withdraw him. Leacock was also barred from continuing for Richmond. He would have needed to be out of the game for three years to regain amateur status.

He promptly retired to take up the whistle on behalf of his chosen sport with the formation of the ENL the following autumn. He also coached around 200 youngsters

at Richmond. From the autumn of 1938 the normal two-man refereeing system was discontinued in favour of a single official on the ice, usually Leacock. He worked several of the five exhibition matches between Detroit Red Wings and Montreal Canadiens held at Brighton and London's Earls Court stadium in spring 1938, often being surrounded by argumentative players.

Employed full-time as assistant secretary by the BIHA in the early 1950s, he was in charge of both intermediate (the real amateur leagues and competitions) and junior hockey. In London in February 1950 he became the first professional referee to be selected to work the World Championships. He went on to officiate at the event the next year in Paris and at the 1952 Olympics held in Oslo.

The final match at the Brighton Sports Stadium in May 1965 was also Ernie's last refereeing assignment. He never got to wear the now familiar black and white vertically striped top. In his day a white shirt under a dark blue jersey (white pre-1940) and a

Ernie Leacock, a Hall of Fame member for his services to refereeing: he officiated in over 2,000 senior matches.

BIHA tie were the norm. Firm and standing for no nonsense, Ernie always gave any benefit of doubt to the player and helped many a novice whistler gain confidence in his presence. An aircraft fitter by trade he worked for many years in a local factory.

Ernest Sidney Leacock, the son of a Freeman of the City of London, was born in the capital on 22 March 1906 at New Southgate. His family emigrated to Banff in Alberta when he was two years old. He developed as a hockey player in this winter sports resort and played as an amateur in Portland, Oregon.

A 6ft-tall slightly built defenceman at 155lb, equally at home on right-wing, he turned professional in 1928 with Victoria Cubs of the Pacific Coast League. Here he skated in select company as several of his teammates went on to the NHL, including Ossie Asmundson and Gene Carrigan for New York Rangers plus Earl Robertson, who later kept goal for New York Americans. He then played for Vancouver Lions, Saskatoon Crescents and Portland Buckaroos which were all pro outfits.

Ernie Leacock died at Whitton in Middlesex in the summer of 1977, aged seventy-one.

Benny LEE

Inducted 1995

Benny Lee was a sportsman in his early days but best known as the general-manager of the Brighton Sports Stadium from the mid 1950s, showing great faith in ice hockey following the collapse of the semi-pro British League in 1960.

He became manager at Streatham in 1939 and after war time service in the RAF returned to the south London rink until 1951. The impresario and entrepreneur Tom Arnold, a director of the Brighton rink, engaged Lee to manage the Sports Stadium. Six years later he was made a director. One of the facility's main attractions was the Brighton Tigers, members of the English/British Leagues since 1935. Tigers won the BNL for 1957/58 and the Autumn Cup the next season. They closed that era of pro hockey in clinching the experimental British Championships.

From losing around £900 a week, Lee soon had the Sports Stadium making a handsome profit. To maximise the potential at a time of increasing affluence and competition for the leisure pound he staged many attractions, including ice shows, basketball (the Harlem Globetrotters), boxing, wrestling, tennis, snooker and five-a-side football. Always immaculately dressed in a mohair suit with his trademark Havana cigar he recognised what the public wanted. His flair for such a varied mix fully justified the marketing claim of the Sports Stadium as the 'Sports and Entertainment Centre of the South Coast'.

With the ending of the BNL, Nottingham, Paisley, Streatham and Wembley folded their teams and left the sport for some years. Only Benny Lee of Brighton had the faith and courage to continue and trust that the public would turn up in sufficient numbers to watch a team consisting of more home-grown players than Canadians, playing in non-league 'home' tournaments. Two

Benny Lee in his office at the Brighton Sports Stadium.

thousand turned up at opening night on 9 October 1960. A month later the stadium was running at capacity. And so it continued most hockey nights for five years, with Tigers winning trophies galore. Lee also found ice time to bring on local youngsters in Brighton Tiger-Cubs and for them to progress to the older Brighton Ambassadors.

For being proved right when many people considered he was crazy to take the risk, he takes his place in the Hall of Fame along Sir Arthur Elvin, Willie Kerr, Charles Knott Jnr and Icy Smith as one of the great builders of the sport in Britain.

Benny Lee was born at Notting Hill, London, in 1904 into a sporting family. His father Harry was a boxing promoter at the Royal Albert Hall, his older brother a speed skater. His younger sibling Sydney was a billiards and snooker champion.

In the 1920s and 1930s Benny became a champion speed skater, first on rollers and then on ice. He was a member of the Great Britain squad which beat France and Belgium in the fifteen-mile roller-skate races of 1924 and 1925. On ice, outdoors at Rickmansworth Lido in 1933, he won the London Professional title at one-and-a-half miles.

After the Sports Stadium closed Benny Lee worked in retail clothing. He died in Brighton in May 1990, aged eighty-six.

Bobby LEE

Inducted 1949

Bobby Lee was the most admired and respected player of all the Brighton Tigers from the day he first stepped onto the ice at the Sports Stadium until the day he retired.

In the summer of 1936 Brighton's coach Don Penniston, who had played with Lee when both were with Montreal Royals, asked him to join Tigers. The twenty-two-year-old 5ft 10in-tall Canadian centre-ice, with a right-hand shot was an instant hit, getting the puck into the net and assisting others to do likewise. At the close of the forty-game schedule he had accumulated 53 points which included 32 goals, placing him seventh in ENL scoring.

The new management team at Empress Hall in Earls Court enticed Bobby to the capital the next winter as pivot on the second line, then switched to left-wing for the remainder of the winter. Here he was voted onto the second All-Star team at season's end – a feat he repeated twelve months later as Rangers moved up the table to finish third, as they did in the London Cup.

When war was declared he was back in Canada. He spent 1939/40 with Quebec Aces, who were back-stopped by Great Britain's 1936 Olympic-winning netminder Jimmy Foster. Next year Lee moved to Quebec Royal Rifles followed by two seasons with Aces back in the Quebec Senior League, including a trip to the Eastern Canada Allan Cup finals in spring 1942. The following winter, whilst with Montreal Royals, he was called up by Canadians for one game in the NHL. Service in the RCAF permitted hockey in Montreal, Scotland and in England at Brighton and Wembley, where he coached the RCAF HQ Meteors to the Canadian Services League title.

Had hockey resumed at Earls Court immediately after the war he would have coached Rangers. Instead he returned to Brighton, whose rink had not been requisitioned, as player-coach and his greatest triumphs. He masterminded Tigers to the first post-war ENL crown, the National Tournament and the inaugural Autumn Cup. The league title was retained the following year as Lee became the first player in British hockey to reach and pass the 200-goal mark. He had topped the points chart for the second year in succession, earning two consecutive All-Star 'A' ratings to go alongside his two similar coaching accolades. *Ice Hockey World* named him 'Player of the Year'. Two more 'A's came his way for 1950/51 as Tigers gained a second Autumn Cup and Lee his third for coaching. For the first three post-war years at Brighton he was Tigers' leading scorer and second highest for the next two.

Having spent more time behind the bench and a little less on the ice during the two previous winters he was back with a vengeance for his last season as an active player. At the age of forty-three he finished third overall in the scoring race with 113 points to gain his last All-Star 'A' rating at centre-ice at the close of the 1954/54 campaign. Bobby was presented with a testimonial at Tigers' final game of the season.

Bobby was the best centre of all the Canadians seen in Britain pre-1960 and the first to reach the 300-goal plateau in English hockey. Brighton gained publicity from the Lee-led all-conquering Tigers that would have cost thousands of pounds by conventional methods. As a man with charm and charisma, allied with a great sense of humour, he became a local legend in his own lifetime.

Bobby Lee on the ice during his first season for the Brighton Tigers in 1935/36. It is hard to argue the case for anyone else to be recognised as the most-admired and respected Tiger ever.

Robert 'Bobby' Lee was born on 28 December 1911 at Verdun, Quebec. He first appears in the hockey records during 1929/30 with Queen's University of the Senior Ontario Association. The following winter he was listed for Columbus of the Montreal City League and then spent another two years with Queen's University. After eighteen months with Montreal Lafontaine he moved to faster company in the USA, signing for Baltimore Orioles of the Eastern Amateur League. In 1936 the John Carlin Trophy was awarded to Lee as the EAHL's top scorer with 49 points.

After hanging up his skates he made a new career as a publican in Sussex, first at the Oak Inn in Portslade and then for thirteen years at the Windmill Inn, Southwick.

Bobby Lee died on 31 December 1974, aged sixty-four, after being taken ill with pneumonia on Christmas Eve.

Since March 2004 Brighton and Hove Bus & Coach Co. have run a bus serving their Metro Line 1 emblazoned with the words 'Bobby Lee' between the front headlights.

Competition Statistics	GP	G	A	Pts	PIM
Brighton Tigers	494	430	397	827	247
Earls Court Rangers	---	43	39	82	17*

* Excludes 1938/39

Lawrie LOVELL
Inducted 1992

Scotsman Lawrie Lovell was in the topscorers' list for many years from the mid-1960s, an All-Star coach at club level, a regular for Great Britain at the World Championships and for over a decade the coach to the Under-18 national side.

Son of Canadian hockey player Les Snr, who arrived in Scotland in the late 1930s, Lawrie unsurprisingly commenced skating at Murrayfield at the age of three. Progressing rapidly

An incredibly clean player, Lawrie Lovell spent all of his club career in Scotland.

through the club's youth programme, he first came to prominence with Royals, the senior side, during the inaugural campaign of the revived Scottish League during 1962/63. A natural centre-ice he contributed 8 goals and assisted on a further 10 in twelve matches, pivoting the second line before injury intervened. Moving to Kirkcaldy the following winter, as Royals had folded, he shone with the extra ice time, finishing the season on 44 points. He was named 'Best Young British Player of the Year'. Flyers won Section 'A' of the 1964/65 Scottish League and were finalists in the play-offs and competed in 'home' tournaments with Lawrie scoring 19 goals.

With the Racers now the senior team in the Scottish capital he returned to his home club, to be selected for Great Britain at the 1966 Pool 'B' World Championships in Zagreb. The advent of the Northern League that autumn saw Lovell finish second, never to drop lower than seventh during the next twelve seasons. In his seven seasons with Racers he was either first or second (excluding his first winter) in overall points for NIHA competitions. Racers held the league title for three straight years and achieved the Grand Slam' for 1970 and 1971, collecting all four pieces of silverware. Lawrie gained an All-Star 'A' in 1970 and again two years later plus the Earl Carlson Trophy as leading marksman. During this period the lanky playmaker, flanked by Derek Reilly and Willie Kerr Jnr, progressively increased his points production from 62 to 168 by the close of the 1971/72 season.

Fife Flyers gained his services from the autumn of 1972 where he remained for eight years. In his first winter at Rosslyn Street Flyers won the Autumn Cup. The next one came along three years later. Lovell was now the player-coach, collecting All-Star 'A's as coach and at centre, plus the Earl Carlson Trophy as the Northern Association's leading scorer. These were feats he repeated the next season as Flyers won the league, Icy Smith and Autumn Cups. The league and Icy Smith were retained for 1977/78 and Lovell was voted onto the All-Star 'B' sextet as Flyers hung onto the Autumn Cup the next season. He turned out a few times for Aviemore Blackhawks towards the end of 1979/80. Back at Kirkcaldy next autumn he was relieved of his coaching duties after six games.

He returned to his original club now coached by Alec Dampier, as Murrayfield completed the Grand Slam of NL, Autumn and Icy Smith Cups. The following autumn saw the introduction of the British League, albeit with the top division divided into three regional groups. Lovell's 30 points helped Racers as far as the Scottish semi-final. Coinciding with the advent of a reorganised league from autumn 1983, he retired prior to the play-offs after twenty-two years at the highest level the sport offered in Britain.

At international level he missed just one year with Scotland between 1969 and 1980 and was selected for Britain at a further four World Championships following his debut in Yugoslavia. His next opportunity, in 1971 in Holland was his most productive as he contributed 4 goals and 7 assists to the national cause. He was back in the Netherlands two years later, Poland in 1976 and Spain in 1979, all Pool 'C' tournaments.

Three years before taking off a Racers shirt for the last time Lovell was appointed coach of Great Britain's team that had been competing in the European Junior Championships since 1979. Among his charges in 1982 were fourteen-year-old Tony Hand and Stephen Cooper who was voted the Best Defenceman of the tournament .At his sixth attempt in Pool 'C 'Britain finished above their two rivals to take home gold medals. Lack of funding inhibited adequate preparation so after two years at the higher level in Romania and France his boys were back in the 'C' Pool. He persevered until a second gold medal triumph at Sofia in March 1991.

During his playing days Lawrie was a remarkably clean player, especially in the rumbustious days of the Northern League. His total of penalty minutes must be one of the lowest on record. It is unfortunate that his year-on-year statistics are incomplete, although there are indications that in NIHA competitions he totalled 1,451 points.

Lawrence Lovell was born on 14 August 1944 at Kirkcaldy. Away from the rinks his working life was spent in electrical sales.

Competition Statistics	GP	G	A	Pts	PIM
Murrayfield Royals	12	8	10	18	---
Fife Flyers**	164	271	318	589	38
Murrayfield Racers*	232	343	367	710	67
Great Britain	31	11	9	20	6

* Excludes 1965/66

** Excludes 1974/75 and includes unknown number of games with Aviermore Blackhawks during 1979/80.

Jim LYNCH

Inducted 2001

Jim Lynch is a successful player and coach, with awards from both aspects of a career in Britain stretching over twenty years. He holds the unique achievement of coaching play-off championship winners in the HBL and Seconda Superleague, with the subsequent award of 'Coach of the Year' on both occasions.

In his first championship triumph he led Murrayfield Racers to victory in April 1986, having already lifted the NU AC the previous autumn in his first spell as a player-coach. In the Wembley final he scored the insurance goal in the 4-2 victory over Dundee Rockets, on assists from Tony Hand and Paul Heavy. Lynch had assisted Racers first two markers in front of an attendance of 7,657.

He first came into contact with William J. Barr in January 1992, after a season and a half playing at Hull for Humberside Hawks. He moved behind the bench to coach Ayr Raiders playing out of the now defunct Summit Centre in Glasgow. Handicapped by inadequate finances and travelling thirty miles to all their home games, it was only the intervention of Barr Construction quickly followed by the appointment of Lynch that kept Raiders afloat.

Renewing his connection with Fife for three years he took Flyers to a runners-up place in the Premier Division of the British League in 1994 and to a Wembley semi-final. The next autumn Flyers won all eight contests in their group of the B&H Autumn Cup to progress to the quarter-finals. A year later Lynch surprisingly moved with his assistant, the late Milan Figala, to coach Dumfries. Here he guided Border Vikings to the Autumn Trophy and a fifth place finish in Division One of the British League.

With the advent of the Superleague the next season he rejoined Barr, owner of the Ayr Scottish Eagles, the only new club in the rookie out-and-out professional league. Astute recruiting of a mix of Canadians and Czechs immediately paid off with an unbeaten run of eleven matches, although they lost out in the final of the B&H Autumn Cup. A respectable

Jim Lynch watches intetnly from the sidelines in 2001.

third place in the league and a play-off semi-final appearance gained Jim the 'Coach of the Year' award.

The following winter saw his greatest coaching triumph with the 'grand-slam' of B&H Autumn Cup, *The Express Cup*, the Superleague title and an overtime play-off victory. A second successive 'Coach of the Year' accolade acknowledged the skills of hockey's 'quiet man'. Eagles' success gained entry to the European League with outstanding home and away wins over Russian champions AK Bars Kazan, by 4-2 and 3-1, in October 1998.

His coaching career ending prematurely at the age of forty-seven after Ayr's B&H Autumn Cup quarter-final game on 7 October 2000 at Newcastle. An old back injury proved too painful to allow him to pace the bench area during games. Lynch said, 'I'm not able to stand for any length of time or go on buses or skate. I've been on a lot of painkillers, it's really a sort of hockey-related problem over the last twenty years that has caught up with me.'

He tried a short-lived comeback with Paisley Pirates of the BNL in the autumn of 2001 but left before winter set in after a seven-game winning streak. He now works as a taxi driver in Ayr.

James Lynch was born on 6 June 1953 in Toronto, Canada. From hockey with the local junior Markham Waxers he moved to the Inter-Collegiate League. His first taste of European hockey was an unhappy six weeks in the German Bundesliga.

He came to Scotland in September 1980 to join Fife Flyers. In his first outing he scored three times in a 14-3 Northern League win at Aviemore. By the close of his first campaign he was, along with Alex Dampier, joint winner of the Northern Association's Overseas 'Rookie of the Year' and an All-Star 'A'. Third best scorer in the SNL and NL the next winter earned Jim a second successive All-Star 'A' rating.

Returning from a holiday in Canada in the summer of 1983, to find he had been replaced at Kirkcaldy prompted a call to Dampier, then coach at Murrayfield. He stayed in the Scottish capital for three seasons, taking over as player-coach two years later.

After a long, but finally fruitful battle with the BIHA to be reclassified as a non-import player, the ambitious Solihull Barons made an approach for his services for their 1989/90 campaign. Always his own man, he quit before the season commenced citing management interference, to sign for Humberside where his on-ice performance assisted Seahawks to the Autumn Cup final.

His move to Ayr in January 1992 ended his playing days as he moved behind the bench. Whilst admitting to not being the greatest skater, he was blessed with all-round on-ice vision enabling him to put up respectable numbers during a twelve-year career.

As a coach he had the knack of recruiting and moulding a winning team and he was never afraid to speak his mind. His 60 per cent win percentage in the Superleague era speaks for itself.

Competition Statistics	GP	G	A	Pts	PIM
Fife Flyers	154	174	178	352	247
Murrayfield Racers	143	166	171	337	210
Kirkcaldy Kestrals	30	52	49	101	34
Solihull Barons	44	32	40	72	20
Humberside Seahawks	83	28	45	73	36

Coaching	GP	W	L	D	W%
Ayr Raiders	15	3	9	3	20
Fife Flyers	165	81	73	11	49
Dumfries Vikings	58	36	20	2	62
Ayr Scottish Eagles	258	155	82	21	60
Paisley Pirates	16	7	9	0	43.7

Pat MARSH

Inducted 1988

Pat Marsh has been at the heart of ice hockey in Britain over half a century since her future husband Geoff, a netminder with Streatham Royals, took her to the rink to watch her first game in 1950.

Three years later she successfully applied for the post of secretary to Bunny Ahearne – secretary of the BIHA and director of his own travel agency – after seeing an advert in *IHW*. For many years she served a dual role for both organisations. Full time for the first year and then part-time until 1969, she originally shared an office with Ernie Leacock.

When Ahearne became president of the IIHF in 1957 her workload increased as she was also effectively secretary to the IIHF president for the next eighteen years. The knowledge and contacts gained stood her in good stead when in 1972 she became secretary of the BIHA. That year, as the BIHA delegate, she attended her first annual congress of the IIHF held in Prague and returned there in 1992. She was also present at congresses during 1986 at Colorado Springs in the USA and four years later in Paris. She admits to finding these events a bit daunting as well as exciting and educational.

Pat Marsh was secretary for the BIHA and travelled abroad with the British junior teams. She proudly cites the Great Britain Under-19s gold medal triumph in Barcelona as one of her proudest ice hockey moments.

Ten years after taking over the role on a part-time basis the sport had expanded, requiring Pat to work full-time as BIHA secretary. Her home became the governing body's base during the early 'Heineken years' until she retired on 30 September 1987. The following spring she stood on the ice at Wembley to be presented with the Ahearne Medal. However, her long years of detailed experience and knowledge of most aspects of ice hockey – both domestically and at international level – were much in demand. She immediately became the BIHA's first special consultant and a 'personal member' of the BIHA from August 1988, regularly attending meetings and rinks around the country. She was helped by husband Geoff, whose working life in the travel industry was invaluable in assisting Britain's Under-19 team with behind-the-scenes tasks. On several occasions he was able to accompany Pat, one of the highlights being the youngsters' gold medal win in Barcelona in 1986. She was the BIHA delegate to the Women's Pool 'B' European Championships in 1990 and again two years later. Overseeing the sport's doping control programme was another of her duties. She finally retired from the BIHA in February 1999, five months prior to that body's demise. For a few more years she provided the Superleague with advice and guidance and was to be seen at the season-ending finals in Nottingham.

Her calm efficiency earned her the admiration of players, officials, administrators and media alike for her ready accessibility and willingness to tackle any task. In March 2002 the IIHF honoured Pat with the annual Paul Loicq Award for administrative services. She is first Briton to receive the prestigious award, named after a previous president (1922-47) of the sport's world governing body.

Patricia Marian Marsh (née Griffiths) was born on 12 February 1934 at Brixton in south London and educated at Loughborough Central. Widowed from her husband and helpmate in 2003 she lives in well-deserved full retirement at her home in Croydon, Surrey. Her immediate family and travelling are now her main interests.

Terry MATTHEWS

Inducted 1987

Terry Matthews was an English player, then coach, who brought intensity and enthusiasm in equal measure to both roles from the late 1950s through to the early 1990s.

He began playing ice hockey soon after the Whitley Bay rink opened opposite his home. At the age of seventeen he was a member of the newly formed Whitley Bees, runners-up in the North British League in spring 1958. Alternating between defence and wearing No.3 and No.12 as a forward, Matthews and his team outplayed local rivals Durham Wasps to win the play-off for the Northern Tournament in 1959 and 1960. As Bees had folded, autumn 1961 saw him move to Altrincham Aces for their inaugural local 'home' tournament. He was joined by many former Bees and Wasps. Wearing No.5 he played on defence as Aces defeated Paisley Mohawks 10-5 to win their own tournaments and travelled south to beat Southampton in the Southern Cup. As first reserve Matthews gained his first trip with Great Britain, at Pool 'A' in the USA in March 1962 when one of the veterans had to drop out. Later that spring he was voted Most Promising Young Player. the following season Aces were not quite as successful, he also turned out a couple of times for Brighton.

The following autumn lack of crowd support at Devonshire Road forced Aces to curtail the season. He headed back to the north-east to join The Durham Wasps, reformed at the Whitley Bay rink, where they competed in the Scottish League and the Northern Tournament which they won. From his thirty games Matthews totalled 45 points. By spring 1965 his skills were recognised with an All-Star 'B' rating in spite of missing a few games due to a broken foot.

Whitley Bees were founder members of the Northern League in autumn 1996 and for the next eight campaigns Matthews, in Warriors first line of attack, was one of the top-ten NL scorers.

As well as being inducted in to the British Hall of Fame, Terry Matthews was one of the five original North East Wall of Famers.

He gained All-Star awards for all three forward positions: an 'A' at left-wing in 1968, a 'B' for centre-ice twelve months later, again in 1972 and finally an 'A' in his last year with Warriors as a right-winger during 1975/76. In addition, coaching recognition came his way with a 'B' in the spring of 1971. At the end of the next campaign he was named by the NIHA as 'Player of the Year' as Warriors won the Icy Smith and Autumn Cups. Matthews totalled 74 goals and 55 assists, his best-ever points haul. Whitley continued to collect major trophies during the next four winters with league titles for 1974 and 1975.

A year away from the sport renewed his energy and enthusiasm. He made a spectacular comeback in November 1978 as player-coach with Billingham Bombers who had moved up from the Second League. A NL fourth place, followed by reaching the play-off final gained a coaching All-Star 'A'. Shedding his coaching responsibilities, Matthews' last season on the ice provided 40 goals and 65 assists, to combine in total points for runner-up for the 1980 Earl Carlson Trophy.

Throughout his playing career Matthews was a constant when ever England took on Scotland or Great Britain entered World play. The most productive of his six British campaigns came in Holland in 1971 where he scored 8 goals for a total of 11 points.

In March 1977, twelve months after his last appearance in a Great Britain shirt he was back; this time behind the bench in civvies for the World Championship attempt on Pool 'C' in Denmark.

His second venture as a coach at national level occurred the winter before he hung up the blades. He took charge of the British Under-19 team during their first attempts at the European Championships and again a year later in Denmark.

At domestic level he became Warriors bench-coach mid-way though the 1985/86 season and head coach the following autumn. The next two years he steered Warriors to their first end-of-season finals at Wembley. A month prior to his second Heineken championships Matthews was in charge in Belgium when Britain returned to the World Championships after an eight-year absence.

The last time behind the bench was a twelve month part two season spell at Billingham in 1993. A few days after taking over, Bombers defeated Durham for the first time in forty-six attempts and scrambled into the quarter-final round of the play-offs. Starting the following autumn with the prefix Teesside replacing Billingham, their coach had to depart at year's end as his business required undivided attention.

In November 1998 at a ceremony in Newcastle Arena Terry was one of the five original inductees into the North East England Ice Hockey Wall of Fame. He said: 'I enjoyed the sport immensely throughout it all and that's why I kept going as long as I did.'

Terrance Matthews was born on 18 February 1940 at Whitley Bay. His early working life was spent as a coalminer. During the 1990s he owned and ran a sports equipment shop in his home town. Now retired, Terry is seen at the occasional game at the Hillshead Road rink.

Competition Statistics	GP	G	A	Pts	PIM
Whitley Bees	---	---	---	---	---
Altrincham Aces*	18	9	9	18	4
Brighton Tigers	2	2	0	2	2
The Wasps	46	42	41	83	75
Whitley Warriors**	196	418	289	707	215
Billingham Bombers	63	110	110	220	42
Great Britain	35	13	6	19	30

* 1961/62 only

** Excludes 1974/75

Coaching	GP	W	L	D	W%
Whitley Warriors	95	55	35	5	57.9
Billingham/Teesside Bombers	59	16	42	1	27.1
Great Britain	10	2	7	1	20
Great Britain Under-19	8	1	7	0	12.5

George McNEIL

Inducted 1951

George McNeil originally hailed from Canada and was an outstanding coach in Scotland in the decade after the end of the Second World War.

The lanky 6ft, 165lb, ginger-haired utility player, could skate equally well as a defender or as a forward. He first arrived in Britain in the autumn of 1936 to join Richmond Hawks of the ENL. One commentator claimed that, 'on arrival [he] hailed as the greatest defenceman seen here' and was 'an artist at body-checking'. McNeil moved from the blue line to the right-wing whilst with Richmond and finished the season with Brighton in the spring Coronation Cup series. For the next winter he signed for Earls Court where Rangers had a poor season, just missing the cellar in all three competitions.

Moving to Scotland in 1938 to play for Dundee, where Tigers won the league Tournament for the Canada Cup and Mitchell Trophy in their rookie season, he also stayed on the next winter.

In both campaigns he finished among the SNL's top points scorers. During 1941/42 he turned out for his Canadian army unit stationed in Scotland.

With the return of peace McNeil rejoined Dundee in 1946 as coach, staying for two years, winning the Arlie Trophy at the first attempt and the play-offs for the Anderson Trophy

twelve months on. For this feat he won the All-Star 'A' team coaching vote. Falkirk next engaged his services, adding the manager's role, with the Scottish and Canada Cups entering the trophy cabinet in his first season. Although Lions did not win the Scottish League crown, he did win the Anderson Trophy in his first two years and again in 1953/54. His methods were so highly regarded that a run of four consecutive 'B' All-Star selections followed, only broken by a year spent as senior referee of the Scottish circuit at the request of the sport's governing body in Scotland.

The first year of the BNL, commencing in autumn 1954, was his last as coach. He guided Falkirk to an Autumn Cup runners-up position and a fourth spot in the league for another 'B' coaching accolade.

His work with Scottish youth cannot be too highly commended as he recognised and developed many into pro players including Tommy Paton, Bill Sneddon, Marsh Key and Joe McIntosh. He was a proud man when two of his Falkirk Cubs Red Imrie and Johnny Carlyle joined him in the Hall of Fame.

George McNeil,
photographed in 1954.

A spell as manager of the Falkirk rink ended as the McNeils (George married Eveline, a Dundee lass) moved to America at the end of 1956. He continued to follow hockey being a charter member of the NHL Philadelphia Flyers.

George McNeil was born in 1913 at Lourdes, Nova Scotia, and brought up from his early teens by the Beaton family. As an eighteen year old he spent a year with New Glasgow Tigers in the Nova Scotia Eastern League. From 1932-1936 he moved around within the NS Antigonish-Pictou County League with New Glasgow teams and Stellarton High-Toppers.

His nickname in this era was 'Gummy', presumably because, like many players, he lost teeth at an early age. Also an outstanding baseball player in his youth, he coached the English team in the late 1930s.

George spent his later years at Norristown, Pennsylvania. He died there in 1997 at the age of eighty-three.

Competition Statistics	GP	G	A	Pts	PIM
Richmond Hawks	---	8	3	11	20
Brighton Tigers	4	0	0	0	0
Earls Court Rangers	---	2	2	4	6
Dundee Tigers	---	44	44	88	25

Coaching	GP	W	L	D	W%
Dundee Tigers	120	66	41	13	55
Falkirk Lions	432	239	147	46	55.3

Frederick MEREDITH

Inducted 2003

Frederick Meredith's major achievement during his seventeen-year reign as president of the now defunct BIHA, was the securing of three major blue-chip sponsors and a BBC Television contract. Both raised credibility and public and media awareness of the sport to levels never seen before, or since.

Following the successful end-of-season experimental sponsorship by Heineken of the British Championship weekend at Streatham rink in south London in April 1983, shown on Thames TV, they dramatically expanded their involvement from the next autumn. Via their parent company's promotional agency – The Wight Company – Heineken sponsored the entire British League, culminating in the first Championship weekend at the 8,000-seat Wembley Arena. The increased marketing of the sport saw average attendances over the previous winter increased by 37.5 per cent.

This brought in nationwide BBC Television coverage of many matches during the following seasons and live transmissions of the finals on the afternoon *Grandstand* programme. The greatly increased profile of domestic ice hockey was enhanced on the small screen by the effort put into 'dressing' the rinks prior to the television games, plus a far greater public relations emphasis. A clause in the sponsorship contract provided for modest financial contributions to the clubs in the Premier and Division One to assist with away travel costs.

These arrangements continued until the spring of 1993, with Meredith saying '…the dramatic growth of the sport in this country would not have been possible without Heineken's backing.'

Norwich Union took up sponsoring the traditional season-opening Autumn Cup, for six years from 1985, to be succeeded after a twelve-month gap by Benson & Hedges. Their input was considered by some to be the most beneficial. A hands-on presence was evident at every game, and continued beyond the cessation of the BIHA.

Frederick William Louis Meredith was born on 24 November 1937 in Montreal of a British father and a Canadian mother. During his early school days, when he learnt to skate, he played both ice hockey and cricket as a wicketkeeper. This position explains why later at Bishops College he converted to a netminder.

A move to England at a the age of eighteen to Trinity College, Cambridge, saw him immediately welcomed into the Light Blues hockey team, then perennial losers to their Oxford University rivals. By his third year the previous annual defeats of 1-11 and 2-5 were crowned by a 6-1 victory. Upon graduation with degrees in law and economics, he coached the Varsity to two further successive triumphs in a run of four wins in five years behind the bench.

Both the Oxbridge captains had an automatic place on the BIHA Council of the national governing body for the sport, a hangover from the 1920s. Meredith became Cambridge's representative. His abilities must have impressed the long-established members as in 1960 he was elected as a 'personal' member of council, effectively a directorship. Two years later he went to the USA with the British World Championship team as the BIHA representative.

He served the BIHA as secretary between 1971-73 until his career as a management consultant with IBM curtailed his activities at a time of grass roots revival of ice hockey in Britain. He had retained his place at the BIHA table and took over in 1982 as president upon the retirement of Bunny Ahearne.

In an interview given to *Puck* magazine at the time he was asked how he would differ from his predecessor. He replied, 'I am not an autocrat, but I do not believe the sport can be run on completely democratic lines. The BIHA must take the lead in setting the games objectives.' Five years on he became a member of the British Olympic Committee, with election to the executive board in 1991 and membership of several working parties. This involvement showed

President of the BIHA for seventeen years, Frank Meredith's major
achievement was securing major blue-chip sponsors and BBC television
coverage for ice hockey in Great Britain.

in April of that year when he admitted to *IHNR* the need for an Olympic place would be
paramount in raising hockey to the next level. 'I will not compromise on that one. Olympic
status would give us a tremendous boost'.

In 1989 a Great Britain senior team was revived and from then on competed annually in
the World Championships. In the mid-1990s he was chairman of the short-lived Great Britain
Board set-up to control the national team's development programme.

Like most people involved with the running of the sport at that time in Britain the
voluntary hours Meredith put into hockey away from his day job ate into family time and
holidays – a sacrifice he was prepared to make.

A year after joining the BOC he gained a place on the IIHF Rules Committee. In 1994, having left IBM to act as a consultant, he became a council member of the world governing body for ice hockey. Very soon he was chairman of the Medical Committee and serving on several others.

With his resignation from the BIHA's presidency and that body's demise in 1999 Meredith has since expended his energies on the international stage. For many years chairman of the IIHF Legal and Statutes & Bylaws Committees he more recently added chair of the Insurance Committee to his workload.

He again became involved, albeit briefly, with British hockey during 2003. In representing the IIHF he endeavoured to assist in resolving the bitter dispute between the new Elite League and the established British National League.

Frederick Meredith resides near Maidenhead, Berkshire.

Alfie MILLER

Inducted 1989

Alfie Miller was a high-scoring centre-ice for twenty-one years with Whitley Warriors, his only club, and was selected to represent Great Britain in four successive World Championships.

Taking up skating at the age of twelve the first organised game he took part in was between periods of a senior match at the Whitley Bay rink. He was soon challenging for a place at the top level. In 1969/70 Whitley entered two teams in the senior NL which opened up places for youngsters from the Braves, a team in the Second League. Alfie got his chance and iced in twenty matches for the senior Warriors scoring 16 points, equally divided between goals and assists in twenty matches. He was awarded the Montford Trophy as 'Rookie of the Year'. The following winter he could old manage thirteen games due to a hockey-related injury.

He came into his own in his third NIHA campaign as Warriors captured the Autumn Cup with Miller tenth in points total, improving three places in league play. Unfortunately statistics are missing for his next two campaigns. By the end of season 1976/77 he had contributed 88 points, including first place in scoring in the Autumn Cup. He gained his first of four All-Star accolades, being top NL scorer for the next two winters brought a 'B' followed by an 'A' at the end-of-season All-Star voting. Although his 1980/81 points total was not his highest ever, his

Alfie Miller, a high-scoring one-club man with Whitley Warriors and Great Britain.

sparkling play gained recognition as 'Player of the Year' plus his third 'A' All-Star.

Having played for England many times from the age of sixteen, he was selected for the next four of Great Britain's successive Pool 'C' World Championships entries. In 1976 he travelled to Poland, the following year saw the team in Denmark. Two years later Great Britain went to Barcelona where Miller contributed 3 points. Again Britain skipped a tournament before flying east to China. In Peking attendances averaged 10,000, a record at this level of World play. Alfie commented: 'It was the toughest World Championships I've played in.' His zero penalty minutes helped Great Britain gain the Fair Play Cup as they did at his first British appearance five years earlier.

When the Northern Association competitions ceased in spring 1982 it is likely that Miller was ranked fifth on their all-time scorers list. Through the transition of the sport with the coming of paid imports and the absorption of the regional leagues into a two-division British League sponsored by Heineken from 1983, his points production continued unabated with 98 in 1984, his only season as coach, to go one point better three years later.

By now he had been made captain and led Warriors to their first Wembley weekend in April 1988. Here he announced his retirement at the age of thirty-four. The BIHA presented him with a silver salver to mark his nineteen years on the ice. A year later he served as assistant non-playing coach as Britain returned to the senior World Championships in Belgium.

However he got bored with sitting on the sidelines and laced up the skates again halfway through Warriors' 1990/91 league schedule. He reinvigorated the second line where Paul Towns and the sixteen-year-old Simon Leach benefited as Warriors gained 22 points from seventeen post-Christmas matches.

Twelve months on history was repeated as Warriors, with Miller in the line-up, made a second Wembley play-off appearance, again as losing semi-finalists, this time to local rivals Durham. Retiring a second time, with no further comebacks planned he said: 'I couldn't have found a better place to finish.' In the forty matches he added 12 goals and 20 assists to his career totals. Five years later Alfie reflected: 'I wanted to prove to myself that I could still do it after a couple of seasons away. However that eighteen months got it out of my system'.

At 5ft 6in and weighing 147lbs, he more than made up for his lack of height with skating and stick handling. A skilful playmaker, who was never averse to the rough and tumble, and disliked the tag 'the Gent', his meagre penalty minutes total provides the reason. Fellow teammate and one-time coach Terry Matthews described Miller as 'the thinker on the team'.

In November 1999 at Newcastle Arena his name was added to the North East Ice Hockey Wall of Fame.

Alfred Miller was born on 13 April 1954 at Whitley Bay and educated locally. He is now a successful businessman owning and managing Miller Motors at Ashington, a few miles to the north of Whitley Bay.

Competition Statistics	GP	G	A	Pts	PIM
Whitley Warriors*	522	484	667	1,151	184
Great Britain	24	3	3	6	14

★ Excludes 1973–75.

Wally 'Pop' MONSON

Inducted 1955

Wally Monson, a bald-headed centre-ice, came to these shores in the autumn of 1936 to join Harringay Racers from their formation until spring 1940. During his four years here he captained the north London team to the ENL title for 1937/38 and twice as runners-up.

In his (and Racers) rookie season they won the London Cup final 9-4 on aggregate from Wembley Monarchs. In the final group of the Coronation Cup, Racers defeated all three opponents. Wally was named to the All-Star 'B' sextet with 18 goals plus 24 assists in league play.

The following winter the main prize of the league title fell to Racers by a 13 point margin over Monarchs. Monson weighed in with 7 goals and 10 assists. He and his teammates were also second in the London Cup and finalists in the National Tournament. In the last peacetime campaign Racers just missed out on silverware as runners-up in the London Cup and National Tournament.

Racers recaptured the capital's Cup during 1939/40, Monson's final winter this side of the Atlantic Ocean. Wembley Lions went down 4-1 and 8-1 in the home and away play-off. In the eight-match series he contributed six points.

With natural ability, allied with determination, loyalty and finesse he was well liked and whilst with the Harringay club acted as assistant coach to the famous Percy Nicklin. The knowledge gained was put to good use when he hung up the blades.

Walter 'Pop' Monson was born on 29 November 1909 at Winnipeg, Manitoba, Canada. At 5ft 9in and weighing 170lbs this left-shooting forward worked his way up, via Midget, Juvenile and Junior League hockey to the senior Elmwood Millionaires, including trips to the Memorial and Allan Cup play-offs.

Willy 'Pop' Monson on the ice for Harringay Racers during the 1937/38 season.

Transferring to the Winnipeg Winnipegs (sic) he again saw action in the Allan Cup finals and led Canada's 1932 Olympics gold medal winning team in scoring seven goals and four assists. This was followed by spells with Selkirk Fishermen, Saint John Beavers and the Pittsburgh Yellowjackets of the Eastern League the winter prior to coming to London. In his youth he also won several championship cups at soccer.

He ended his playing career in 1942 after two seasons with Glace Bay Miners. Turning to coaching for the next fifteen years he took Winnipeg Monarchs to the 1946 Memorial Cup victory and ended 1951/52 winning the league and play-offs.

After the Second World War he recruited many players for English hockey including Ron Barr, Mike Daski, Gordie Fashoway and Milt Swindlehurst.

Walter Monson died aged seventy-eight on 9 January 1988.

Competition Statistics	GP	G	A	Pts	PIM
Harringay Racers	---	56	85	141	66*

★ Excludes 1938-40

Johnny MURRAY
Inducted 1996

Johnny Murray has been involved in the British game as player, coach and administrator at club and then national level for most of his life.

He began skating at the age of eleven the year after the Empire Pool & Sports Arena opened in 1934 at Wembley, just west of London. He soon joined the junior hockey scheme run initially by ex-NHL Ottawa and Montreal netminder Clint Benedict, now in the Toronto Hall of Fame and later by Lou Bates. By November 1936 he had gained a regular place with the Cubs in the four-team Wembley 'house league'. Games were usually played as a curtain-raiser to the senior Monarchs and Lions matches. In March 1938 he scored in Cubs' 2-1 victory over Princes for the Hunter Cup.

The following winter John, a centre-ice, moved up to the adult Wembley Colts who won the eleven-member London Provincial League. During the 1939/40 season he enjoyed a handful of games for the senior Lions, registering an assist, before war interrupted his budding hockey career.

Wembley's 1946 summer series gave him the opportunity to shake the rust off his skates as a reserve for Royals. From that October he became a regular member of Wembley Lions, netting a hat-trick against Streatham in his first game in the Autumn Cup. As more Canadian players became available his ice time as the seventh and spare forward in the twelve-man rosters became limited. He did not get a single game during the 1949-51 seasons and for some others only a handful. The final season of semi-pro hockey was his most productive with 12 goals and 11 assists from forty-eight games during 1959/60. In his ten seasons of life with the Lions he kitted up 326 times to score 26 goals with an additional 37 assists for a mere 7 minor penalties.

Sometimes he managed to get away with the team on the tours of the Continent during the long Christmas/New Year breaks at the Empire Pool to accommodate the annual ice show. Usually used by Lions as a winger, he centred the second line to net 15 goals on Wembley's December 1957 Scandinavian tour, only Canadian Les Strongman scored more.

When not required by the senior team he played a prominent role with the Terriers, serving as captain then coach. During the seven years (1949-1955) of the Southern Intermediate League he was never out of the top-ten scorers' list, twice finishing second and winning the title in 1951 with 13 goals and 24 assists. Only the RAF team in 1950 and Southampton three years later wrested the league title from Terriers perennial grip.

Johnny Murray of the Southampton Vikings on the ice during the 1961/62 season.

Murray's international streak commenced in 1947 with selection for England and continued until his last appearance for Great Britain in 1962 at the age of thirty-eight. Representing Great Britain at the 1948 Olympics in Switzerland he went on to play in three further Pool 'A' World Championships and three in Pool 'B'. He was captain, coach and manager of the England team which won the Pool 'B' tournament at Liege, Belgium in 1952, retaining the triple role the following year. Britain returned to the World Championships in 1961 and the next year in the USA, with Murray back as player-manager.

When Wembley closed down the Lions Murray joined Southampton Vikings for three years of amateur 'home' tournaments. It was during this time that he was elected to the BIHA Council.

With Rank buying the Southampton rink in the summer of 1963 to show ice hockey the door, most of the Vikings became the new Wembley Lions thus enabling the sport to return to the Empire Pool. He served as player-coach, with most games of the challenge variety, until his retirement in April 1968. Lions folded eight months later.

Predominately a playmaker and always an exponent of clean hockey with few penalty minutes in such a lengthy career, he has also been a strong advocate for the native produced British player.

From 1982 until the BIHA ceased in 1999 he was one of their two vice-presidents and also spent a short time on the International Olympic Committee.

John Murray was born on 27 January 1924 at Hampstead, London. Educated at Harrow Technical College he volunteered for the RAF in 1941. Two years later he was transferred to the Royal Engineers as he possessed a degree in physics, seeing service in the Middle East and reached the rank of captain by the time of his demobilisation.

By the early 1960s he managed his own confectionary and tobacconist business then held directorships in garages. By the mid-1990s he was a managing director in the oil industry and now lives in Hertfordshire.

Competition Statistics	GP	G	A	Pts	PIM
Wembley Colts	---	---	---	---	---
Wembley Lions*	371	58	86	144	12
Wembley Terriers	67	81	100	181	16
Southampton Vikings	64	72	83	155	6
Great Britain**	25	8	3	11	0

* Excludes 1939/40
** Assists missing 1952 & 1961, PIM missing 1952, 1953 & 1962

Scott NEIL

Inducted 2007

Scott Neil was a skilled forward for Murrayfield Racers, Sheffield Steelers and Great Britain for twenty-one years before becoming player then owner/sometime coach and manager of Edinburgh Capitals. In recent years he has worked hard to raise funds to maintain the sport at the highest level in the Scottish capital.

Learning to skate at the part-family-owned Murrayfield rink he took up ice hockey at the age of fourteen, initially on defence. Quickly moving up from the junior Ravens and the second team Raiders, he scored his first goal for the senior Racers two years later at Billingham in April 1979 in the Icy Smith Cup final against Streatham Redskins.

The following winter he was sixty-fifth in overhaul points scoring in NIHA competitions. Twelve months later he had moved up to twenty-ninth with a haul of 39. That spring Alex Dampier, his coach and now in charge of Great Britain, took Scott to Pool 'C' of the World Championships in China, his first of seven such trips.

Two years earlier at the Under-19 European Championships in Bulgaria he enjoyed his first taste of the game at international level. Twelve months on he captained the Great Britain Under-19s in Denmark where he slammed five goals past the Belgium goaltender in the 8-7 win in Denmark.

For the next four years Scott skated on Canadian ice. Via a contact of Dampier's he spent four years at the University of Prince Edward Island on a business course. Although training with the varsity his hockey in his last two years was mainly confined to inter-squad games. In years three and four he also played football for UPEI Panthers and was named MVP in the 1984 Atlantic University Championship.

He returned to find hockey in Britain much changed, and for the better, with the Heineken-sponsored divisional British League providing improved competition and media exposure. Seven seasons with the Racers of Murrayfield followed. The following spring he was at Wembley to score at 11.46 in the second period as Racers defeated Dundee 4-2 in front of 7,657 spectators for the British Heineken championship. Three further matches at Wembley followed including 1991 where Neil scored twice in the 6-6 deadlock with Cardiff. Twenty-four penalty shots were needed for Devils to win. As a 5ft 10in-tall centre/right-winger, weighing 185lbs he totalled over 100 points in six of the seven campaigns and was voted a Premier Division British All-Star for 1988.

After an eight-year gap Britain returned to the World Championships in 1989. Neil was an automatic choice, as he was for the next four years, culminating in the 1993 Olympic

Scott Neil in action
with the Sheffield
Steelers.

qualifying tournament at Sheffield. After consecutive nine, then two eight-point totals he increased production to 10 (6+4) at the 1992 'C' Pool triumph at Hull.

After missing out on a Wembley appearance in 1992 a consortium took over hockey at Murrayfield. Neil was released and at the age of thirty moved south to sign for Sheffield Steelers at their year-old 8,500-seat arena and be reunited with Dampier. In his first year Steelers gained promotion to the Premier Division, and although injury forced Scott to miss the play-offs, he accumulated 55 goals and 61 assists. Twelve months later he scored the only goal for Steelers in their first Wembley final appearance, to record his second successive 100-point-plus season for Sheffield.

The next year Steelers won the league and cup double as Scott netted the second goal in the 4-3 play-off final at Wembley. Sheffield went one better in 1995/96 by adding the Autumn Cup. Reflecting on those years he said: '… I've no doubt that I made the right decision, because I had a great time at Sheffield. We had a very successful team.'

With the coming of the Superleague and reduced ice time Neil returned to Murrayfield in autumn 1997. He captained the new one-term Royals in the reformed BNL. Relabelled as Edinburgh Capitals he spent his last winter on the ice as a player and a club director.

Scott Neil was born on 1 August 1962 at Edinburgh and educated at the Royal High School. He played a lot of sport as a youth, mainly football and rugby as a stand-off or centre for Edinburgh Schools. After leaving school he worked for the Civil Service before college in Canada.

These days he lives with his family about ten minutes from the Murryfield rink. As sole owner of Capitals he works tirelessly to maintain his team in the Elite League. Being very much aware of the need to economise he was one of the first to appreciate the enhanced value provided by recruiting East European players.

For a bit of relaxation he coaches the local Under-12s and occasionally plays a round of golf.

Competition Statistics	GP	G	A	Pts	PIM
Murrayfield Racers*	386	544	400	944	211
Sheffield Steelers	272	149	185	334	92
Murrayfield Royals	48	39	49	88	22
Edinburgh Capitals	59	10	21	31	30
Great Britain Under-19**	3	5	0	5	0
Great Britain	37	23	12	35	18

* Excludes 1978/79
** Excludes 1979

Percy NICKLIN

Inducted 1988

Percy Nicklin's greatest claim to fame this side of the Atlantic Ocean is as coach and master tactician to the British gold medal winning Olympic team of 1936.

His reputation was well established in the land of his birth, coaching Moncton Hawks, of the Maritime 'Big Four' League to Allan Cup victories in 1933 and again twelve months later with an identical roster. He once referred to the Hawks as 'the highest paid amateurs to ever chase a puck'.

He came to England in the autumn of 1935 to coach another Hawks side, this one based at Richmond in west London. Here he adopted the tactic of using his weaker second line of forwards to drop back on defence, leaving the pair of defencemen to skate through onto the opposing goal. His efforts drew almost immediate recognition with appointment to the British national team. Over nine days in February, at Garmisch in southern Germany, Britain defeated Sweden, Japan, Canada, Hungary and Czechoslovakia, tying with Germany and the USA to win the triple crown of Olympic, World and European titles.

A strict but fair disciplinarian, Nicklin selected players with complimentary styles. His teams were based around sound goalkeeping (Jimmy Foster was with him in Moncton, Richmond, Harringay and, of course, Great Britain) and back-checking forwards. Unusually in an era of smaller rosters, he constantly switched lines to prevent fatigue, and to match opposing combinations. The day after Britain's 2–1 victory over Canada, team manager Bunny Ahearne told the *Southern Daily Echo*:

> We won the game on tactics. It was psychology that did it. We knew we were not within five goals as good as the Canadians. So instead of trying to out play them in skill we wanted to take advantage of any opportunity that offered themselves. They did so and we took them and won.'

In his book *Ice Hockey,* published later that year Peter Patton said of the Great Britain coach: 'His tactics, especially in our match against Canada, after we had gained the lead for the second time, constituted strategy of the highest order.'

Under Nicklin's guidance Great Britain retained the European title in London in 1937 and the following year in Prague plus World silver medals. By the last World title tilt before war

Percy Nicklin, the coach and master tactician, who led Great Britain to the Olympic and World Championship titles in 1936. He is seen here a year later. His teams were based around sound goalkeeping and back-checking forwards.

engulfed Europe, the BIHA had replaced many of the Canadian trained Brits with home-grown talent.

In the ENL he steered Richmond to joint first place by spring 1936 with 33 points, losing out on goal difference to Wembley Lions. Six months later he commenced his long association with the newly opened 10,000-capacity Harringay Arena in north London. Right up to March 1940, when league hockey ceased for six years, the Harringay programmes listed Nicklin as coach to both the Racers and Greyhounds, even in games when they faced each other!

Racers and Greyhounds finished second and third in the ENL in their rookie campaign, Racers also carried off the London and Coronation Cups.

For the next three years Racers, then Greyhounds, twice lifted the league title, with Hounds gaining the London Cup in 1938/39 and the National Tournament the following season. Nicklin moved into management in 1938 to combine the role of rink manager, and then arena manager the next year with coaching. He also found time to return to Canada every summer, scouting recruits for the next season.

When hockey returned to Harringay in 1946 he became general manager of the arena until the sport ceased there in 1958. His influence showed in the shrewd choice of coaches. Racers won the league in 1949 after finishing as runners-up the previous two seasons, and took the Autumn Cup in 1947, 1950 and 1953. Success continued with the introduction of the BNL as Racers won the inaugural 1954/55 title and the AC, in which they were second in their final two campaigns.

E. Percy Nicklin was born and grew up in Fort William, Ontario, during the closing years of the nineteenth century. His first recorded hockey was on defence in 1911/12 with Fort William GTB in the Thunder Bay Senior Hockey League. During the next five years he continued in the same league including two games in the Allan Cup in 1916. Then came spells with Winnipeg, Eveleth, in the USA, and Fort Frances from 1926-30. He had started coaching ten years earlier and was full-time behind the bench when he won the Memorial Cup with Elmwood Millionaires in 1931. Moving to Moncton next autumn he immediately took them to three league titles and two Allan Cups.

He was devastated by the death of his only son Jeff, killed in action in Germany in March 1945, who was Lieutenant-Colonel of the 1st Canadian Parachute Battalion, and never really recovered from the loss. He died in the early 1970s.

Nicklin was inducted into the New Brunswick Hall of Fame in 1970 as a member of the Allan Cup-winning Moncton Hawks of 1933 and 1934.

Coaching Statistics	GP	W	L	D	W%
Richmond Hawks	47	21	17	9	44.9
Great Britain	29	21	5	3	72.5

Bethune Minet 'Peter' PATTON

Inducted 1950

'Peter' Patton holds the distinction, along with the Canadian George Meager, of introducing ice hockey to Britain. As a founding pioneer, he assisted in spreading the sport to mainland Europe.

Educated in public schools at Winchester and Wellington, he no doubt learnt to skate at winter sports holidays in Switzerland. Patton started a form of ice hockey early in 1897 on the 210 x 52 feet ice at the recently opened Princes rink in London's fashionable Knightsbridge district.

In 1902, through the assistance of Canadian students, military personnel and businessmen resident in the London area he helped establish a more recognisable version of the sport, using a puck in place of a ball and long-handled flat-bladed sticks. A year later he acted as president to a five-team league, the first such in Britain and Europe. This was the first real ice hockey in Europe which he subsequently took to the Continent, with the first match in Lyon on 25 January 1904 where Princes defeated the local club 2-0.

Peter Patton as netminder at a
Swiss open-air rink, c.1926.

Captain of Princes in the first European tournament in Berlin in October 1908, he fulfilled the same role as his club represented a victorious Great Britain at the inaugural European Championships two years later in Switzerland. He also captained England in the first of the annual England *v.* Scotland clashes at Glasgow in December 1910. He led Princes to innumerable European tournaments either side of the Second World War, including runners-up in the third annual LIHG club championship in 1913 at St Moritz.

With advancing years Patton moved from defence to goal, acting as reserve netminder for Great Britain at the 1924 Olympics at Chamonix in France. He was the only native-born member of the Great Britain team in the 14-1 defeat by Montreal Victorias. Held in London in January 1927 he kept goal for the third period. On 4 April 1930 he made his final appearance for England at fifty-four years of age, in a 2-2 tie with France at the Golders Green rink in north London. A year later, on 13 October, he finally hung up the pads in Paris following London's 4-0 defeat.

Founding president of the BIHA in 1914, a post he held until 1934, he was instrumental in the formation of the first world governing body – the LIHG – he served as vice-president 1910/11, 1913/14 and 1923/24 and briefly in 1914 as president.

Patton was elected vice-president of the London-based clubs at Streatham and then Wembley in 1934 and president of the short-lived Public Schools IHC. He presented trophies in his name for the newly instigated semi-professional ENL and the annual Varsity match between Cambridge and Oxford. His book *Ice Hockey*, chronicling the early days of the sport in Britain, the only such volume, appeared in October 1936.

He won prizes for ice dancing and held over 300 awards for canoeing and punting during a twenty year span, the last in 1928, mainly on the River Thames at Cookham where he lived for many years. A keen skier he was also one of the founders in 1923 of the International Bobsleigh Association.

Bethune Minet 'Peter' Patton was born into a military family in London on 5 March 1876. As his first name was his father's third name and Minet his German-born mother's maiden name, it's not surprising that he was generally known as 'Peter'.

He joined his father's regiment, who had been a brigadier-general and served in the 3rd Somerset Regiment, rising to the rank of major. He saw duty in France during the First World War from September 1914 until May 1916, and then with the Serbian Army, being awarded their Order of the White Eagle. Upon returning home in July 1919 he worked at the Historical Records of Motor Units attached to the Serbs, retiring from the Army in 1921.

For his pioneering role and his service to the sport he loved over many years he was dubbed 'The Father of British Ice Hockey' when first inducted into the British Ice Hockey Hall of Fame.

'Peter' Patton died aged sixty-four, in March 1939 at Tiverton, England.

Bert PEER

Inducted 1955

The *Ice Hockey World* citation at Bert Peer's induction to the Hall of Fame stated that he was 'possibly the greatest right-winger in the history of senior amateur (sic) hockey… if he had taken his hockey more seriously in North America there is no doubt he would have made the NHL.'

Peer crossed the Atlantic to join the newly formed Harringay Racers in October 1936. He made a remarkable impact at the north London arena, ending next spring as the ENL's third-highest scorer with 60 points (38+22). He was named to the All-Star 'A' team as Racers finished as runners-up and won the knock-out London Cup and the one-off Coronation Cup.

He refused to turn professional in the North American leagues meaning he was free to return to Harringay for the next campaign. Although missing several weeks due to injury he

Bert Peer played the 1937/38 season as a committed member of Harringay Racers.

helped Racers win the league title by 13 points from Wembley Monarchs. He contributed 8 goals and 5 assists to retain his All-Star rating, only this time it was on the 'B' sextet. Racers were also runners-up to Wembley Lions in the London Cup and National Tournament where Peer totalled 12 goals.

From autumn 1938 this 5ft 11in, 180lb tricky right-winger, who shot right and whose deceptive changes of pace and swerve baffled opposing players, displayed his craft exclusively in North America. A season with Valleyfield Braves in the pro Quebec League was followed by a winter split between Ottawa Senators and Omaha Knights of the AHL, sandwiching one game in the NHL for Detroit Red Wings. In 1941 he moved to Fort Worth Rangers gaining an All-Star 'B' before a year with Toronto Navy and then two years of military service. The 1945/46 season was divided between Tulsa Oilers of the US League and Valleyfield. He bowed out of hockey with two winters of senior hockey for Hamilton Tigers including trips to the Allan Cup play-offs.

Herbert 'Bert' John Peer was born on 12 November 1910 at Port Credit, Ontario, Canada. As a young man he graduated from a commercial college course. His first recorded hockey is eleven games during 1932/33 for Toronto Bell Telephone in the Toronto Metropolitan League.

Bert died aged eighty-one on 19 July 1992 at Mississauga, Ontario.

Competition Statistics	GP	G	A	Pts	PIM
Harringay Racers	---	58	29	87	82

Allan and Annette Petrie in their Great Britain tops at Basingstoke in November 2006.

Allan and Annette PETRIE

Inducted 2005

Home Counties-based husband and wife Allan and Annette Petrie are the founders and organising force of the Great Britain Supporters Club (GBSC). This unique group is the world's only supporters club for a national ice hockey team.

It all started in March 1991 when the young pair, who first met whilst working for the same firm, arranged a trip for around twelve fans to Copenhagen to watch the Great Britain seniors who had moved up to Pool 'C' of the World Championships for the first time in ten years.

Two years later, with Britain having gained promotion to the 'B' Pool at Eindhoven in Holland, they again made the travel arrangements. As numbers had increased to twenty-five so did the complexity of the tasks that had to be undertaken. Whilst in Eindhoven they discovered that groups of fans had paid a lot more for their journey and hotels.

The Petries knew from these two trips that strength in numbers provided greater negotiating power when dealing with transport operators and hotel owners. These factors provided the germ of an idea and the impetus for the formation of a formal structure for a recognisable supporters club. The ideal occasion arose later that year as the Great Britain team and Sheffield Arena played host to an Olympic Qualifying tournament. The BIHA were contacted by

Annette and Allan who gave permission to use their logo and blessing to the creation of an official club. The Great Britain Supporters Club was therefore duly launched in late August 1993.

Since then arrangements have been successfully completed for visits to cheer on the national team at Bolzano in Italy and to the annual Pool 'B', now Division One, tournament, in many countries including Holland, Slovenia, Denmark, Poland, Hungary, France and Slovakia. Membership grew as the workload increased, needing the occasional trip to make contacts and inspect potential hotels.

During the summer they each spend two to three hours a week on the affairs of GBSC, during early winter this rises to between five and six hours and from January to April to fifteen hours. This is all in addition to the couples' day-jobs. Allan works at European internal sales while Annette is employed as a document controller.

The main objectives of GBSC are to arrange transport and accommodation for the fans to the World Championships and to raise funds to assist the Great Britain national team programmes for which over £45,000 has been raised since its formation. In 2005 £5,000 was paid over for a training camp prior to the Championships in Hungary. The youth teams at Under-20 and Under-18 and the Women's team also benefit from GBSC financial support and arrangements for their fans to travel to places like Croatia and Lithuania.

Annette, born in the Southampton suburb of Bitterne on 2 December 1967 is the chairperson of GBSC and Allan, who was born at Paddington, London on 26 October 1964, is the vice-chair. They are helped by a five-strong committee plus a representative from most of the clubs in the UK, all elected annually.

Wherever British teams go the fans follow, enjoying facilities equal to or better than the players, thanks to Annette and Allan's hard work and superb organising abilities.

Gordie POIRIER

Inducted 1948

Gordie Poirier's citation to the Hall of Fame reads: 'Claimed by many as the most clever player in British puck history.' The 1950 *Ice Hockey World Annual* continued, 'a good forward pre-war, he turned into a brilliant defenceman after the war, playing a big part in Brighton's two successive title wins'.

The 5ft 10in-tall, 158lb Canadian centre-ice with a left-hand shot joined Brighton Tigers of the ENL in October 1936 for their second campaign. He scored in their first game. In spite of an injury to his chin later that year, which turned so septic that doctors gave him just five hours to live, he survived to score 25 league goals that season. He stayed with the seasiders until the outbreak of the Second World War, although the highest position Tigers reached in any competition was third in the 1938/39 National Tournament. Gordie was seventh-best scorer with 8+4 to include his pre-war total of 117 points. His dark, dashing good looks had the fans screaming whenever he burst up ice to score a goal at the Sports Stadium on West Street.

Back home thirty-six games with St Hyacinthe Gaulois of the Quebec pro league yielded 80 points. On 14 February 1940 he was signed as a free agent by Montreal Canadiens to spend ten matches in the NHL. Two winters with Ottawa Senators followed with a second team All-Star in spring 1942. Joining the army, where he rose to the rank of captain in the CASC, provided two seasons with Ottawa Commandos including the winning goal for an Allan Cup medal. A year away from hockey included landing in France in 1944 on D-Day plus 17. A return to 'civvy street' in 1946 saw him on the ice again with Senators before an invitation to rejoin Brighton was accepted.

A move to the blue line did little to reduce his offensive power as Tigers won the inaugural Autumn Cup, the league and the National Tournament. Poirier was Brighton's third-highest

Gordie Poirier of Brighton
Tigers, 1947/48.

scorer, his 75 points being rewarded with a place on the All-Star 'A' team. His all-round vision
and positional play from defence enabled him to repeat his feats of the previous winter with
31+31 as Tigers retained the ENL crown.

Brighton did not win any titles in the third post-war campaign but he ended his time on
the south coast as his team's second-best points scorer. After a year away from the rinks he was
back in 1950 for a final winter, signing for Harringay Racers two games into the season. In
the forty matches he contributed two goals and 12 assists.

Gordon 'Gordie' Arthur Poirier was born on 27 October 1914 at Maple Creek,
Saskatchewan. The French-Canadian progressed to the 1931/32 Montreal Columbus in the
city's junior league, moving onto St Francis Xavier. At nineteen he broke into Canadiens of
Montreal's senior league for two seasons. Having had a brief taste of Italian hockey during
1933/34 and then Swiss hockey, he returned to Italy in the winter of 1935/36 to captain and
coach Diavoli Rosso Neri Milan. At Davos he netted 5 goals as Milan won the Spengler Cup
and also trained the Italian team before they went to the Olympics.

In his youth he was a scratch golfer and champion canoeist. An electrician by trade, upon
returning to Canada in the early 1950s he became a restaurant owner and import businessman.

He died of a heart attack aged fifty-seven, in the Montreal suburb of Beaconsfield on 25 May 1972.

Competition Statistics	GP	G	A	Pts	PIM
Brighton Tigers	140*	170	155	325	204**
Harringay Racers	40	2	12	14	20

★ Excludes 1936-39
★★ Excludes 1938/39

Derek 'Pecker' REILLY

Inducted 1987

Derek Reilly spent twenty years as an outstanding forward for Murrayfield, he also served his club as coach, Public Relations Officer and part owner in his native city.

He started skating at the age of four and then began playing hockey with the Murrayfield junior team, graduating to the seniors as a seventeen year old during the 1964/65 season with Royals in Section 'A' of the Scottish League. He also enjoyed a trip to the English south coast in May for a Brighton Tournament match.

With the advent of the NIHA from October 1966 ice time improved, with thirty-one games in all competitions that season providing 20 goals. From now on a prodigious scorer, he won the NL scoring title the next winter with 22 goals and 7 assists and repeated the feat in 1976. This time he scored 39 times and added 14 assists. He was not out of the top ten until 1977 and after that one-year hiatus was back at second, dropping to fifth in 1979 and then eighth two years later as age and the increasing number of Canadian imports rose. He was almost as successful in the season-opening Autumn Cup, usually being among the top ten pointsmen. In 1978 the Earl Carlson Trophy came Reilly's way for most goals and assists in the four official NIHA competitions.

It was during these years that he was chosen to represent Great Britain at the Pool 'C' World Championships for 1971 in Holland, again two years later in the same country and in 1977 in Denmark, for a total of 15 points.

During his twenty-two years in a Racers uniform the Murrayfield team hoisted the Icy Smith Cup aloft eleven times. They won the NL title on seven occasions, the Spring Cup – awarded as NL play-off champions – and the Autumn Cup were displayed in Racers' trophy cabinet over six summers. All four went in at once in spring 1971 and on five further occasions three pieces of silverware needed a summer polish. Derek's contribution to these successes was recognised with four consecutive All-Star selections at right-wing from 1968 to 1971; three 'As' and one 'B'.

In the year of the revived SNL during 1981/82, dominated by Dundee's three class imports, he ended seventh on 13+10 as Racers finished runners-up. The advent of the three-region British League Division One the following autumn pulled in more imports who took eight of the ten All-Star places with Derek seventh in points for his club. Autumn 1983 saw the creation of the Premier Division to the HBL.

Murrayfield suffered one of their worst-ever league campaigns and then peaked at the right time for the play-off quarter-final group. Winning three from four took them to the first Wembley championship weekend. Coming from behind Racers slid past Ayr to confront Dundee in the final on the afternoon of 6 May 1984 in front of a 5,500 crowd. Derek crowned his glittering on-ice career by assisting Jim Lynch to the go-ahead goal at 15.04 in the second period and then scoring the 'insurance' marker forty-six seconds later. Unfortunately for the Murrayfield fans Rockets blasted off in the third period with three unanswered goals. 'I'd rather have a winner's medal than a goal,' he said afterwards.

A joyful Pecker
Reilly at Wembley
Arena in April
1937.

He promptly retired at the age of thirty-seven to fill the role of Racer's Public Relations
Officer which suited his easy-going manner with the public.

His tally of 882 goals was the highest ever recorded by a British player. Johnny Carlyle and
Alex Dampier are the coaches that he rated the best during his years with Racers, with the
nickname of 'Pecker' arising from his distinctive 'bobbing head' skating style.

Having passed over the public-relations job to Tony Hand at the start of 1986/87, Reilly was
free to take over as Murrayfield coach for the remainder of the campaign. Racers stormed to
the HBL title, through their play-off group and onto Wembley. After a draining 9-6 semi-final
victory over Dundee they faced Durham in front of *Grandstand* cameras and a full house of
7,900. Even Reilly could not lift them past a hungry Durham.

His final involvement with Racers was sadly not a happy experience. In the summer of
1992 he and his brother-in-law – local businessman Robert Adams – bought the club from
the Murrayfield rink owners. With Adams as chairman and Reilly as general-manager, Racers
ended as HBL runners-up and Wembley semi-finalists. 'We achieved what we set out to do…'
he said. Late the next winter a bitter dispute between club and rink on rentals ended with
Adams and Reilly suspended from running hockey by the BIHA over alleged debts.

None of this detracts from Derek's dedication and loyalty to one club and his record point-
scoring mark.

Derek Reilly was born on 24 December 1946 in Edinburgh. Most of his working life has
been spent in sales, with golf and squash as leisure activities.

Competition Statistics	GP	G	A	Pts	PIM
Murrayfield Royals*	6	1	0	1	2
Murrayfield Racers	525	882	398	1,280	384
Great Britain	19	10	5	15	18

★ Excludes 1965/66

Clarence 'Sonny' ROST

Inducted 1955

Longevity and loyalty are the hallmarks of 'Sonny' Rost's career in British ice hockey. He is the only player whose record stretches the whole length of professional league hockey at Wembley from 1934 until 1960.

He first crossed the Atlantic, which took a fortnight on the liner *Ascania*, in September 1934 to join Wembley Canadians, one of two newly formed teams at the Empire Pool and Sports Arena in Middlesex. Alternating between left-wing and left-defence he helped his team to second in the English League and to lift the London Cup. Many years later he recalled his first season: 'For a lad fresh out of Winnipeg, coming to play ice hockey at the Empire Pool when it opened in 1934 was like some fantastic dream come true.' A mediocre season followed for the team in the inaugural ENL, although they did manage to defeat Kensington Corinthians in the consolation Channel Cup.

Canadians were renamed Monarchs in the autumn of 1936. A year later Rost transferred to their rink mates the Lions, where he stayed until 1940. Lions won the National Tournament in Sonny's first two years with them, adding the London Cup in 1937/38 and again two years later. A clever stick handler, with the ability to lay a pass up ice to his wingers, his low goals and assists count of 11+24 from 1935-40 derive from an era when defenders rarely skated beyond the mid point.

After war work as a fitter in an aircraft factory he was back on Wembley ice with Lions, in a series of challenge matches, when hockey returned in December 1946.

When the ENL resumed the next autumn Rost rejoined Monarchs as captain and was voted onto the season end All-Star 'B' team. Autumn Cup and National Tournament trophies were won during 1948/49 aided by his 20 assists. Named as player-coach from spring 1949, he added the managerial role the next winter in Monarchs' final campaign.

With the end of Monarchs in spring 1950 he moved across to Wembley Lions where he remained loyal to that club for the entire decade. In his second winter, Lions won the ENL title as Sonny played the entire league and Autumn Cup slate of sixty matches. On 4 December 1952 he, along with all the Lions, was presented to the Duke of Edinburgh after the specially arranged charity match with London All-Stars, and given a commemorative medal.

He returned to coaching in 1954 for the first season of the BNL, whilst retaining his defenceman slot to continue in the dual role until the spring of 1960. He often took to masterminding from behind the bench as winter gave way to spring, achieving the league title for 1956/57. Nine months later the Autumn Cup was captured as the number of games in which he donned skates jumped from the previous season's 31 to 54. His retirement from pro hockey was forced upon him at the age of forty-six after his and the Lions' last match on Wembley ice on 23 April 1960, a 10-1 thrashing of champions Streatham. The professional British League ceased to exist the next month.

His final appearances in hockey uniform were with the amateur Streatham Royals and Richmond Ambassadors in a handful of games between 1960 and 1962 at various 'home' tournaments.

Clarence 'Sonny' Rost was born on 9 March 1914 in Winnipeg, Manitoba, Canada. As a nine year old he was playing in the Public Parks League, progressing from St Paul's College at Midget level via the Juveniles of Elmwood Maple Leafs for 1931/32. A year each with Winnipeg Monarchs and Kenora Thistles of the Manitoba Junior League followed, before taking ship to England.

He was, for many years, to be frequently seen at the Slough ice rink in Berkshire where son John and grandson Warren, maintain hockey connections. He celebrated his ninetieth birthday there after a Jets game, at a gathering with family, friends, hockey players and teammates from the 1950s including John Murray and Roy Shepherd who are also members of the Hall.

Sonny Rost of the Wembley
Lions takes to the ice during the
1950/51 season.

Regrettably Sonny, who lives near Slough, is now in poor health, having given so much to the sport over so many years.

Competition Statistics	GP	G	A	Pts	PIM
Wembley Canadians*	---	0	4	4	88
Wembley Monarchs	215	13	79	92	267
Wembley Lions	422	33	138	171	373**

* Excludes 1934/35
** Excludes 1938-40. GP 1935-40 excluded.

John 'Postie' ROST

Inducted 1991

The induction of John Rost provided the Hall's first father and son combination with John being the son of Sonny Rost.

John is there in his own right, not by filial connection. He has spent all his adult life immersed in hockey, first as a player, then coach, moving onto management then back to coaching.

He learnt to skate at the age of ten as well as the rudiments of hockey from his father, but there were no opportunities at Wembley. He took up hockey seriously five years later as a

John Rost holds a very special place in the British Ice Hockey Hall of Fame, being the first son of a Hall of Famer to be inducted alongside his father.

centre-ice with Streatham Maple Leafs. They played behind closed doors late at night, and he also practised with Richmond Ambassadors. With hockey ousted from both London rinks he joined the newly formed London Senators. In the club's opening match at Southampton on 8 December 1962 he scored, adding two goals the next evening at Brighton.

John was quickly signed on by Tigers, and again netted on his Brighton debut on 23 December in the 5-4 win over Southern All-Stars and joined Tigers for that winter's Continental tour. In the spring he was voted Most Promising Young Player by the All-Star selectors. He remained with the Sussex club until their rink closed in the summer of 1965. In three years he collected three Brighton, an Altrincham and a Southampton Tournament winners' medals, plus two from Cobley and Southern Cup triumphs. It was at Brighton that he got dubbed with his father's nickname of 'Postie' by the older players who knew Sonny had been the first to read the morning newspapers when at Wembley.

His first taste of coaching came when he formed his own team whilst at Brighton – Wembley Cougars – who played teams of a similar standard late on Sunday evenings following the Tigers match. Cougars soon became the Brighton Ambassadors.

He picked up games where and when he could, including a spell with Altrincham Aces during 1967/68. The following autumn he signed for his father's old club, the Lions, in their final season as amateurs. In his five challenge matches he scored two goals and served a minor penalty. John was a key component of the Wembley Vets, formed in 1970 as founder members of the Southern League. Three years later they merged with Sussex Senators, also homeless, as practice ice was at last secured at Streatham.

From 1972 until 1981 he gained ten All-Star ratings, eight for defence, including five 'A's and in 1972 and 1980 an additional 'B' and an 'A' as coach. These were spread across the years of the Southern League and, from 1979, the four years of the ICL senior league. From 1973 the Streatham club – he was chairman for fifteen years – took the lead and set the standard in developing regional hockey in England until the merger into an all-British set-up nine years later. He took over from Martin Harris in 1976 as the SL representative on the BIHA Council and was soon elected as a 'personal member'. Two years later he spent a couple of seasons as the first chairman of the seminal ICL. He served on the BIHA until summer 1995.

During this period, Streatham, with the added tag from 1976 of Redskins, collected league titles, cups and 'home' tournaments galore. Rost iced twice during 1982/83 before retiring.

The following season, which was the first of the HBL Premier Division, he coached Redskins to third place. Moving to youth development, he led Streatham Scorpions to the first British Under-16 championship at Wembley in April 1986.

Having played for England over five years of the 1970s annual clashes with Scotland, he went into team management with the British Under-19 team in 1979. After nine consecutive years at the European Championships the BIHA appointed him to manage the return of the Great Britain senior team to World competition at Pool 'D' in Belgium in 1989.

He made a brief return to coaching at senior level with Richmond Flyers of the EL during the club's last season of 1990/91, as their rink closed a few months later. With so many of his ex-teammates at Slough, from now on that's where John was to be found, coaching within the club's active youth development programme.

John Rost was born on 28 March 1944 at Islington, London. Away from hockey he worked in insurance, then for many years with the equipment suppliers W.H. Fagan & Son Ltd before following in his father's footsteps as a transport courier.

Although John retired from all hockey-related tasks at Slough in 2006, the tradition continues as his wife Pauline has been a hardworking and effective administrator in youth hockey at the Streatham and Slough clubs for many decades. Son Warren played in the British League and its successors and is now general manager to the EPL Jets.

But he will be hard put to equal his father's record of diversity and longevity in ice hockey, beloved of this sporting family.

Competition Statistics	GP	G	A	Pts	PIM
London Senators	3	2	0	2	0
Brighton Tigers	86	50	19	59	24
Wembley Vets	25	11	7	18	6
Streatham/Streatham Redskins	161	83	67	150	53

Blaine SEXTON

Inducted 1950

Blaine Sexton was instrumental in fostering awareness of ice hockey in both Britain and mainland Europe with his formation of London Lions.

Canadian by birth, but qualified by residence, he played on defence for Great Britain at the first Winter Olympics in 1924 at Chamonix, where they won a bronze medal. B.N. Sexton, as he was invariably referred to in the contemporary Press, scored three times in the 19-3 defeat of Belgium.

He contributed eight of Great Britain's 26 goals during January 1926 at the European Championships in Davos. France's *Le Mirror Des Sports* reported: 'Sexton is the star. Wearing a white sunshade he looks halfway between a jockey and a cinema director. His way of effortless gliding whilst rolling his shoulders, his rapid turns, his tricks... ensure his success.'

The following month in Paris he scored three of the six goals in Britain's win over Belgium. He was also in the British line-up at the first World Championships held in 1930. The last of his appearances for England came in February 1932 in the series with Boston All-Stars.

Blaine Sexton wearing 'D' or
automobile skates, *c.*1931.

In spite of an absence of ice rinks in southern Britain he founded the London Lions in
the autumn of 1924, taking them on many tours of the Continent during the next few years.
This team, of mainly expatriate fellow countrymen, contested the final of the 1924/25 Coupe
de Davos and made it to the quarter-finals of the prestigious Spengler Cup. They won the
first ever play-offs for the British League title in May 1930, with Sexton netting a singleton.
'Sexton at his very best as London Lions beat Glasgow 2-1 to win the Patton Cup,' reported

one newspaper. Lions, by reason of being undefeated, retained the club championship the following winter.

Equally at home on attack or defence, often playing the entire match, he captained Lions most years. By the late 1920s many of the outstanding players in England, if not Britain were members. These included club president William H. McKenzie, the first manager of the Harringay teams, and George Strubbe later with Queens and Earls Court. For some of the period James 'Robertson' Justice, a comic film star in the 1950s, was player-manager.

By the early 1930s, as more rinks opened, press coverage increased and Blaine was often named among the goalscorers. On 18 February 1933 he was one of just six players who made the journey to Manchester, where he netted in the 8-1 EL victory. With the demise of Lions in spring 1933 he signed for Queens. Next January he was with his new club in Switzerland. They won all six of their matches against top European sides for the St Moritz Trophy, with Sexton a rock on the blue line.

His last games, at the age of forty-three were with Queens in the southern section of the EL in the early part of the 1935/36 season. Probably the last player to still use the 'D' or automobile skates, an English magazine of the early 1930s called him: 'Perhaps the greatest showman ice hockey has ever seen.'

Blaine Nathaniel Sexton was born on 3 May 1892 and raised in Windsor, Nova Scotia. A prominent member of Windsor's Swastikas hockey team with his one-man rushes, he was also a noted footballer and horseman. Joining the Canadian Army he was posted to England in 1916 as an infantry officer. Twice wounded in action in France he transferred to the cavalry, to become the army's sabre champion.

After the war and two years back in Canada, where his English wife was not happy, they returned to England. Here he founded a canned food brokerage and developed a successful career in the food-importing business. His company was sold to the Guthrie Group in the early 1960s.

Blaine Sexton died at Folkestone, England, on 27 April 1966 aged seventy-three.

Roy SHEPHERD

Inducted 1999

Roy Shepherd is the only English-born-and-trained player to have been elected twice to the season ending All-Star teams of the pre-1960 semi-pro Canadian-dominated National Leagues.

His family moved to the Wembley area when he was three which led, just after the end of the Second World War, to him joining 300 boys for a try-out at the Empire Pool. He soon graduated to a regular place on the Wembley Terriers, partly interrupted by two years of National Service. In the team's six seasons in the Southern Intermediate League which commenced in 1949, he racked up 106 points from 57 matches in helping the team to four league titles. He set two individual scoring records for a defenceman.

As a burley rear guard he possessed a devastating open-ice body-check and a bullet-like low-level wrist shot from the point, which deceived many a netminder.

His first match for Wembley Lions came in the autumn of 1951 where he remained as a regular until the BNL folded nine years later. Roy was one of literally a handful of English lads to make the grade in pre-1960 pro hockey.

Probably his most impressive performance, and the one by which he is most remembered, occurred during the Soviet Union's first visit to Wembley on 1 December 1955. Roy nearly caused a diplomatic incident when two incoming forwards were laid out cold in the second period by crunching legal checks. After being removed from the ice by their comrades (they did not reappear that evening) the remainder of the Russians retired to their bench amid

Roy Shepherd of the Wembley Lions, 1951/52.

rumours of a strike. The Soviets came to Britain to learn the ways of the Canadian game and were taught to body-check by an Englishman.

A BNL winner's medal came in 1957 as he was voted onto the All-Star 'B' team for his contribution to the victory. Later that year he added an Autumn Cup medal to his collection. A second All-Star 'B' arrived in spring 1960.

With the collapse of that era's BNL he moved to Southampton Vikings – for two years of 'home' tournaments – to win the Southern Cup in his first season. The following winter he was appointed coach. He then moved east along the south coast to spend three years with Brighton. Tigers collected four trophies during 1962/63, and their own tournament and Cobley Cups from the next two campaigns. During three years at Brighton he was voted onto the All-Star 'A' sextet in 1963 and the 'B' team two years later.

With the closure of the Sports Stadium Tigers faded away. Roy signed for Wembley Lions in 1966 for their short seasons of challenge games until they too folded three years later.

His love of the sport continued into a fourth decade in the newly formed amateur Southern League, when he turned out with Sussex for two years from 1971. Despite having been off the ice for a while, his skills were recognised with an All-Star 'A'. He had one game with Streatham the next winter and spent 1974/75 with Bristol Redwings.

Hockey returned to Southampton in September 1976 as did Shepherd two months later, having been away from the rinks for a year. He stayed for two seasons, taking on the coaching role in the second, to contribute a total of 21 points over thirty-five games. Roy finally hung up the blades at the end of April 1978, at the age of forty-six.

His first international appearance was for England in November 1950 against Switzerland. The next week's *IHW* bore the headline: 'Shepherd shows promise.' His heavy body-checks proved too much for the Continentals as an all-native English squad won Pool 'B' of the World Championships at Liege in March 1952. The year before he competed in Group 'A' in Paris. Great Britain, with Shepherd, re-entered World play at Pool 'B' level in 1961. Twelve months later he flew with the team to the USA for seven games, one goal and two assists in the 'A' Pool.

Roy Shepherd was born on 4 August 1931 at Acton in west London. On leaving school he worked for a time in the family garage business as a motor mechanic and in the 1960s he set up his own garage in Brighton. In his younger days he was a keen golfer and a good hand at darts and table tennis.

Regrettably for such an active man, his health has deteriorated and he now resides in a care home.

Competition Statistics	GP	G	A	Pts	PIM
Wembley Terriers	57	48	58	106	78
Wembley Lions*	498	52	193	245	258
Southampton Vikings	81	37	58	95	51
Brighton Tigers	98	61	80	141	41
Sussex Senators/Tigers	17	15	18	33	8
Streatham	1	0	1	1	2
Bristol Redwings	5	2	2	4	2
Great Britain	23	4	2**	6	0

★ Excludes 1966-68 (challenge games),

★★ Excludes 1951, 1952 & 1961.

J.F.J. 'Icy' SMITH

Inducted 1988

John 'Icy' Smith is probably best known in sporting circles as the proprietor of Durham and Whitley Bay ice rinks and for his ownership of Durham Wasps with their Co. Durham only player policy.

At the age of twenty-three he decided to sell something that would not last – ice. He opened a second plant at Darlington where he entered public life and was soon mayor. He then moved to Durham to buy Bishop's Mill, installed a turbine powered by water from a diversion of the River Wear, to generate electricity. He turned that building into a factory producing ice.

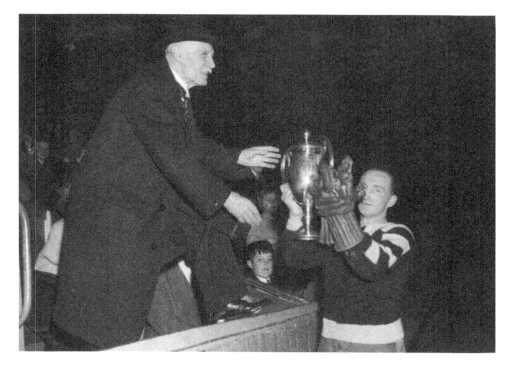

Icy Smith presenting the Northern Tournament Trophy in the early 1950s.

Towards the end of the 1930s improvements in fridges forecast the ending of commercial ice production, so with electricity freely available, Icy decided to build an ice rink. After earlier experiments with a mini rink, work commenced in June 1939. With the ice pad and freezing plant ready, the outbreak of war prevented erection of a permanent enclosure. Although opening in March 1940 for skating as an open-air rink, sun and rain frequently curtailed activities. Icy had seven posts driven through the ice, three down the middle and two at the ends, to support a 19,000 square feet tarpaulin roof. In November 1944 gales and later a fire destroyed the structure. Open-air skating resumed for a while, to cease in March 1946.

Early on, local lads with improvised sticks had played a form of ice hockey. With the advent of numerous RCAF airfields in the vicinity, a Canadian Services hockey league was soon established at Durham. The teams contained some high-quality players, some of whom married local girls to settle in the area.

In spite of post-war shortages, Icy managed to have a concrete and steel framed asbestos-cement-clad enclosed rink built in nine months. This facility, with tiered permanent benching, opened for business in December 1946.

Urged on by his son John, who had refereed many of the services games during the war, Icy gave his support to the development of a local ice hockey team. However, unlike other rinks, Icy insisted that his team should be based on players residing within Co. Durham. Equipment was improvised and twice-weekly training sessions were conducted by ex-RCAF man Mike Davey. Ten months after the roofed rink had opened 2,500 spectators turned up to watch Durham Wasps take on Kirkcaldy Flyers in the first of that winter's thirty-two challenge matches. By December attendances numbered 4,000 with hundreds more being turned away. Very soon the Hornets were formed for the less-experienced players.

The Northern 'Home' Tournament, a boon to senior amateur teams, was established in autumn 1948 and lasted until the early 1960s.

Icy founded a second rink at Whitley Bay in 1957 and as a beekeeper he duly named the new team Bees. The Northern Tournament now hosted games at both rinks – Whitley on Saturdays and at Durham the next evening.

He did not live to see his Wasps triumph in the 1980s and early 1990s during the era of the HBL but his dynasty lived on as the Durham and Whitley Bay rinks were run by his sons and later his grandsons.

John Francis James Smith, universally known in adult life as Icy was born in 1889 at Barnard Castle, Co. Durham, the thirteenth of fourteen children. From school he entered the family foundry business. Later in his life at Durham he served as a county councillor, Alderman and eventually Mayor of the City.

Icy died a tragic death, aged seventy-five, killed by a train at Jesmond, near Newcastle on 17 January 1964.

Floyd SNIDER

Inducted 1951

His original Hall of Fame citation stated: 'Floyd Snider is without doubt one of the greatest defencemen ever to play in Scottish hockey and if proof were needed, the fact that he has never once been overlooked for All-Star honours in five successive years should be sufficient.'

Snider, a Canadian, signed for Fife Flyers of the SNL, a virtually professional circuit, for the initial post-Second World War campaign of 1946/47. He stayed with the Kirkcaldy club, apart from one winter, through to spring 1954.

At 5ft 9in tall, and cool under pressure, he used brains rather than brawn and could often turn defence into attack. This is proven as his points totals never fell below 58 for his five All-Star seasons.

He was ninth in overall scoring in the 1948/49 Scottish Autumn Cup series, and third for his club with 20 goals, plus 47 assists as Flyers won both the Autumn Cup and SNL titles that season. The following year his total rose to 95 as Fife retained the league crown and added the Canada Cup to their silverware collection.

The year after his fifth consecutive All-Star selection (a 'B' in 1951, following two successive 'As'), his points production dropped off as Flyers failed to win any major trophies that winter or the next. Despite Fife's lack of success he piled up 71 points and was the team's fourth-best scorer the next season. Floyd then took a year out away from the Scottish rinks.

He was certainly missed as Flyers finished last in the Scottish Autumn and Canada Cups. He was recalled in time for the start of the SNL campaign but in spite of Snider's eight goals and 22 assist even he could not lift Flyers out of the cellar. According to Henry Hayes, coach for the following season – the club's first and last in the new BNL – Fife had had 'a team of mediocre quality.' Hopefully he excluded Snider from this undiplomatic comment to the 1954 *IHW Annual*.

A wily rushing defender with a skilful poke-check, like so many players, Floyd enjoyed golf off the ice. In Canada he was seen to be a smart at baseball. He was considered by his teammates at Kirkcaldy to be well mannered and a sharp dresser which stood him in good stead on the dance floor.

Floyd Snider resplendent as a Fife Flyer, 1948/49.

Floyd Snider was born in 1926 at Kingston, Ontario. He grew up on nearby Wolfe Island and from the age of seven or so was a 'rink rat'. Entering competitive hockey at twelve he moved up through the ranks to Kingston Vics before crossing the Atlantic Ocean as a twenty year old. He married Grace, a native of Kirkcaldy. who returned to the United Kingdom after Floyd died, aged fifty, from a brain anuerysm on 12 February 1976.

Competition Statistics	GP	G	A	Pts	PIM
Fife Flyers	334*	132	287	419	502

* Excludes 1946/47

Jimmy SPENCE
Inducted 2006

Jimmy Spence was one of ice hockey's finest Scottish-born-and-bred players during a twenty-three-year career.

His family moved to Perth when he was a year old as his father was appointed ice master at the newly opened rink. This gave the young Jimmy plenty of opportunity to hone his skating skills from the age of eight. Three years later he joined the pee-wee Panther Cubs before moving on to the intermediate Blackhawks.

As a centre-ice he proved naturally talented early on, scoring as a fifteen year old in his senior debut with the Canadian-dominated Perth Panthers. A year later he was offered a place with a junior team in Canada on the recommendation of his Glasgow-born coach Tommy Forgie but his parents considered him too young to make the trip.

With a regular place in Panthers' line-up from 1951 until the team pulled out of semi-pro hockey four years later, he accumulated a total of 310 points. In his first full year with the club he ended as their fourth-best scorer, moving up one place the next season and back to fourth in 1953/54. His 43 goals and 38 assists made him Perth's leading scorer and tenth overall in the league in the final campaign. This was a remarkable achievement for a forward who learnt his hockey entirely in Scotland. The lack of All-Star recognition seems less than natural justice.

With the demise of pro hockey at Perth he moved south to the English Panthers of Nottingham. His 71 points helped them win the double of Autumn Cup and BNL for 1955/56.

Her Majesty's armed forces grabbed Jimmy for two years of National Service with the Royal Signals, based near Paris. Apart from joining Edinburgh and Glasgow on their Continental tours he saw little ice time. Back on 'civvy street' he returned to Perth for the all-amateur Panthers and spells with Glasgow Flyers and Paisley Mohawks. In the winter of 1961/62 he came south again, signing for the newly formed Altrincham Aces where he spent two winters accumulating 108 points. During the first year Aces won their own 'home' tournament and the Southern Cup at Southampton. A handful of games followed for Fife Flyers between 1963 and 1966. During these years he received four All-Star ratings including two at 'A'.

Out of competitive hockey for some years he was persuaded out of retirement in autumn 1971 by Ian Forbes, coach of Dundee Rockets. On the Perth-based line with Sammy McDonald and Canadian Mike Mazur he was runner-up in Northern League scoring for consecutive winters. His total points from all competitions won him the Earl Carlson Trophy in spring 1973, when he retired at the age of thirty-eight. Astonishingly, in those two years back on the ice in fifty-two games of official NIHA competitions Spence scored 149 goals.

Twice selected for Scotland's Under-18 victories over England at Richmond, scoring three times in 1951, it would be ten years before he had that opportunity for Great Britain. He netted twice in Switzerland and his next chance came four years later in Finland, ending as Britain's top scorer with eight goals including three against Hungary in Great Britain's only victory. A further eight years passed before his final World Championship. This time it was

Jimmy Spence, a
naturally talented
centre-ice photographed
around 1964.

at Pool 'C' in Holland, his second marker coming in the 8–8 tie with Denmark for Britain's
only point.

But for the decline of the sport during the 1960s he would have achieved even greater
numbers and honours.

James Davis Spence was born on 21 March 1935 in Edinburgh. His other sports were
competitive swimming, football and cricket. He spent most of his working life as senior
electrician at Perth's Dewar's distillery.

He died suddenly at his home in Perth on 9 September 2004, aged sixty-nine.

Competition Statistics	GP	G	A	Pts	PIM
Perth Panthers	245	161	149	310	66
Nottingham Panthers	57	44	27	71	18
Altrincham Aces	38	68	50	108	8
Fife Flyers*	11	14	7	21	0
Dundee Rockets	52	149	93	242	28
Great Britain	18	12	3	15	4

* Excludes 1965/66.

Harvey 'Red' STAPLEFORD

Inducted 1986

Harvey 'Red' Stapleford first arrived in England in 1934, signing for Streatham to make major contributions to hockey both on and off the ice in his adopted country.

George Shaw, an established Streatham player persuaded Red, who had wanted to see the Continent, to come to England. One of the south London club's five class Canadians that season, they beat the two new Wembley teams to the EL title and the inaugural International Tournament. Here Red and his teammates overcame two French and two English teams plus Munich and Milan.

In a letter to a friend in Canada, written in the summer of 1935, Stapleford extolled the virtues of playing for Streatham:

> Last year we were all over the Continent. We flew to Berlin, and flew also several time [sic] from London to Paris. We also travelled for almost a month on the Continent in about six different countries. Simply marvellous trips… and all expenses paid while travelling. I would'nt [sic] have missed it for the world.

And, he adds, pay was £6 a week, over twice the then average wage.

The next winter the International Tournament was reduced to London-Paris with Streatham as finalists, losing out to Wembley Lions. Stapleford ended as third-highest scorer in the ENL and fifth in the London Cup, good enough to be named to the All-Star 'A' team. He took over from Carl Erhardt as team manager/coach early the next winter. He repeated his London Cup final points tally in 1937/38 although slipping to seventh in the league table.

For his final pre-war season he moved north-west across London to Wembley Lions. His new team pipped Harringay Greyhounds by one point to clinch the National Tournament. Stapleford contributed nine goals and two assists.

He spent the first two years of the war back in Canada in senior hockey with Stratford and London Streamliners. He joined the army and served in the infantry, rising to the rank of major. In August 1944 at the battle of the Falaise Gap in France he was wounded in the knee, thigh and shoulder. By early 1946 he was back on skates for the Canadian Reinforcement Unit in the Services League held at Wembley.

Returning to Streatham as player-coach for the first post-war league campaign he scored 13 goals and added 23 assists. The following winter he guided Streatham from the bench and in the next seven seasons his team won seven major trophies commencing with the National Tournament in 1947/48. Although not collecting any silverware, the next winter Red was named as coach to the All-Star 'A' squad. He also returned to the ice for the last time, to add 32 points to his career total for the club. The following winter Streatham became league champions and won the National Tournament with a 'B' rating for the coach. In 1951 the Autumn Cup was added to the collection with another ENL title in spring 1953 and a coaching 'A'. In his final year as coach Stapleford gained his third 'A' All-Star as Streatham again won the Autumn Cup and the revived London Cup.

The 5ft 9in, auburn-haired left-wing was a quick thinker, checking in both directions. A determined hard worker he hated to lose; off the ice he was quiet and humorous with a liking for the theatre.

As a coach he made Streatham the most consistently successful team in the immediate post-war era. He also helped British clubs by recruiting a stream of skilful Canadians of the quality the fans here appreciate.

When Streatham management decided not to enter the BNL in summer 1954 he coached on the Continent for a while, before returning to London as High Commissioner for the Government of Ontario.

Red Stapleford on the
Wembley ice during the
1938/39 season.

Harvey 'Red' Stapleford was born on 25 February 1912 at Windsor, Ontario, Canada. The family owned a wholesale provisions business producing poultry and early hockey for Red was with Stafford Midgets. In 1932/32 he contributed 28 points as a centre-ice for the home town Mic-Macs, moving during the next winter to the Grand Trunks, both in the Michigan-Ontario League. He impressed Detroit Red Wings who tried to sign him to a pro contract.

In England he married the daughter of Charlie Naughton – a member of the famous radio, stage and screen comedy act the 'Crazy Gang'. Their daughter Sally-Anne was five-times British figure-skating champion.

'Red' died in February 1993 in London.

Competition Statistics	GP	G	A	Pts	PIM
Streatham*	86**	112	88	200	162
Wembley Lions	---	23	13	36	---

★ Excludes 1934/35.
★★ Excludes 1935-38.

Coaching	GP	W	L	D	W%
Streatham	368	205	120	43	55.7

Gary STEFAN

Inducted 2000

Gary Stefan was a high-scoring centre-ice for twenty years, founder of Slough Jets, coach, rink manager, and a gold medal winner for Great Britain.

After playing junior hockey in Hamilton, Ontario, he was ignored by the professional draft. 'I was too small at seventeen, I shot up later,' he recalled. An aunt living in London persuaded him to come to England in the summer of 1980 and help out in her sports goods shop.

Before leaving Canada he had been contacted by the Richmond club in west London. His instant impact with Flyers earned him an 'A' team All-Star and the Wolf Elliot Trophy as top scorer with 70 goals in ICL competitions during 1980/81.

Fellow countryman Scott Bodger and the Goldstone family – both involved with the Streatham club – persuaded Gary to move south of the Thames to sign for Redskins. Five successful years gathered in a 670-points haul. A second successive Wolfe & Elliot, an All-Star 'A', and the Air Canada Trophy as 'Player of the Year' came at the end of the first winter. Redskins won the reinstated ENL, the Southern Cup and the ICL senior league. In the stormy play-off final Gary netted a trio in the 5-1 victory over Nottingham Panthers. A month earlier Streatham contested the first Heineken-sponsored British Championship play-off where he scored once in the 3-2 loss to Dundee.

In autumn 1982 Redskins joined Section B of the new British League with Stefan fourth in the nationwide scoring race and an All-Star 'B'. Six months later he topped the Autumn Cup points chart. Redskins lost out in the final on penalty shots to Dundee, after Stefan scored four of his team's six goals in regulation time. His one appearance at the Wembley finals weekend was in 1985. Here he collected an assist in Streatham's losing semi-final to eventual champions Fife Flyers.

Eighteen months on he accepted the salaried post of hockey co-ordinator and player for Slough Borough Council at their new facility in Berkshire, relocating to the nearby village of Burnham. Fittingly he scored Jets' first goals in both their opening away and home fixtures, on 28 September at Oxford, at 0.25 in the first period and on 4 October against his old club Richmond at 0.39, also in the opening frame.

'Reclassified' as a non-import the next season, he helped Jets head Division One for the first time before finishing as runners-up to Telford Tigers. Slough's first trophy came in 1988/89 with the revived London Cup, with Gary as top scorer on 59 points. A year later Jets won the Southern Cup and league title and two winters on tied with Fife for league honours.

Taking over as player-coach during 1992/93 was not an experience, he later admitted, that he wished to repeat. Returning the following winter to a purely playing role delivered a third Division One title. Play-off triumph meant he gained promotion to the HBL Premier Division. Stefan's final four years on the ice saw Jets win the Benson & Hedges Plate and the one-season Premier League, which became the BNL.

At Guildford on 31 January 1998 he scored at 9.04 to join Paul Adey (Nottingham) and Tony Hand (Murrayfield) in achieving 1,000 league points in the modern era of the sport whilst with the same club. At the age of almost forty this seemed a good time to retire. 'My body and my heart have been telling me it's time to quit,' was his honest comment to the *Ice Hockey Annual*. He had been a duty manager at the Slough rink for some time and was now the general manager.

The first of three successive trips to the World Championships came in 1990. Great Britain won Pool 'D' held in Cardiff where he contributed four goals and seven assists. Great Britain clinched the Pool 'C' gold medal two years later at Hull where he scored five times. In summing up those years he noted, 'I was proud to play for my adopted country.'

Gary Stefan was born on 23 June 1959 at Brantford, Ontario. Like most Canadian youngsters he first learnt to skate on double runners, aged four, assisted by his mother, on a

Gary Stefan of the Slough Jets in 1998, for whom he scored a combined 1,332 points (708+624).

farm pond. Two years later he had progressed to the family's 60 x 30ft-backyard rink where he was often joined on the ice by near neighbour Wayne Gretzky. In a team run by Wayne's father he guarded the nets for a season. He then exchanged places with his elder brother Greg who went on to a ten year career in the NHL with Detroit.

Retiring from rink management in 2000 he spent the next four years working for the now defunct BNL. In conjunction with Warren Rost, Gary set up Extra Time Sports Ltd. He can now be found at this sports equipment business located in Burnham High Street which opened in July 2005.

Competition Statistics	GP	G	A	Pts	PIM
Richmond Flyers	30	70	17	87	81
Streatham Redskins	197	436	234	760	644
Slough Jets	591	708	624	1,332	1,402
Great Britain	17	12	10	22	28

Sam STEVENSON

Inducted 1986

Sam Stevenson was one of the grand old men of Scottish ice hockey whose involvement with the sport spanned sixty years from player to youth coach.

His on-ice career commenced as a centre-ice at Glasgow's Mohawks in 1931, two years after the opening of the rebuilt Crossmyloof rink. The extensive ice surface in this building hosted all the Scottish League teams until the Perth rink provided a second venue from autumn 1936.

Mohawks won the league in his first season. He moved onto Dennistoun Eagles by autumn 1934, and two years later he was to be found in the colours of Kelvingrove. He completed his playing career with Glasgow Lions during 1937/38 who shutout Perth Blackhawks 3-0 in the March 15 final of the Mitchell Trophy.

After war service in the Lovatt Scouts Stevenson took over the management of the amateur Glasgow Mustangs in 1946. Two years later he moved into coaching with Mohawks. The team regularly competed in the Northern Tournament at Durham and were play-off semi-finalists in 1951 and finalists four years later. By the late 1950s his sons – Barrie and seven-year-old Robert – had also taken up the sport. The latter blossomed into one of Britain's finest centres prior to migrating to Australia.

Out of hockey for a brief period, Sam returned to Crossmyloof as team manager with the founding of Glasgow Dynamos in 1965. But he undertook any chore ranging from fund raising, club rep., to taping sticks and coaching the pee-wees. The most successful years were the late

Sam Stevenson spent sixty years of his life devoted to ice hockey – a career that began as a player and finished as a youth coach. Here he is in his mid-80s.

1960s and early 1970s, when they won the Icy Smith Cup in 1967, the Northern League play-offs for the Spring Cup in 1970 and were runners-up in the next campaign's Autumn Cup.

Although conditions at the aging rink were far from favourable, Sam remained fanatically loyal, resisting all efforts to move the club to nearby Paisley. Even after the formation of the British League his experience was required. At the age of eighty-three he again moved behind the bench for season 1984/85 as grandson Doug returned from Australia to sign for Dynamos.

The following year his beloved Crossmyloof closed, to be replaced by the Glasgow Summit Centre in Finneston. Here he continued to coach youngsters on Saturday mornings into the early 1990s.

In his playing days his frail physique led to him being dubbed 'Wee Sam', and the tag stayed with him through all the long years at Crossmyloof. His magnificent record of longevity and service to Scottish ice hockey is unlikely to be equalled for a very long time.

Samuel Barrie Stevenson was born in Glasgow on 20 July 1903. His early sporting successes were at diving and tennis. He lived about a mile from the rink that was his second home. His joinery shop business was also nearby.

He died aged ninety-two, on 4 August 1995.

Archie STINCHCOMBE

Inducted 1951

Archie Stinchcombe achieved almost every possible honour in British hockey. His greatest claim to fame was as a forward on Britain's 1936 gold medal winning Olympic team.

Encouraged by Red Stapleford of Streatham, who had been asked to track down English-born players in Canada, Stinchcombe signed for the south London club in autumn 1935. Within weeks of arriving he was recruited to the Great Britain team preparing for the following February's Olympics in Bavaria. Travelling on a Canadian-issued passport stamped 'British Subject by Birth' he played in six of the seven matches, sitting out the opening encounter with Sweden.

In his first winter in London his nine goals and six assist in the ENL – with a further 14 points in the London Cup – were sufficient to gain an All-Star 'B' selection. Twelve months on and the pace picked up with 35 league points. After three years at Streatham Archie moved to Wembley Lions to collect a National Tournament winners' medal. In the last campaign before war ended hockey for six years, he wore a Lions' sweater for the season-opening London Cup and National Tournament. In the ENL, where he scored 21 goals, his sweater bore the Monarchs' crest.

With hostilities at an end Archie shook the rust off his skates for Wembley Lions' challenge series during spring 1946. When competitive hockey resumed he signed for his first English club. He snapped in 34 goals for Streatham. The following winter, which was his last in London, his fifty-four matches yielded 17 goals and 29 assists.

In an article in an April 1947 edition of *IHW* by Bob Giddens, under the title: 'If We Had a Hall of Fame' he not only tipped Archie as an early nominee but also as a future coach. And that's just the role he took on when he moved to Nottingham in the autumn of 1948.

Icing for just seventeen games in his rookie player-coach campaign his efforts behind the bench were recognised with a season ending All-Star 'B'. A fallow winter followed, to be succeeded by Panthers' first league title, pipping Brighton by one point. Early in the season, with Panthers in the cellar of the Autumn Cup, Stinchcombe said: 'This is the best team I ever had' – from then on the laughs were all Archie's. He had remained behind the bench to collect a second 'B' rating from the experts. Donning the skates three times during 1951/52 he hung them up for good at season's end to concentrate on coaching.

Archie Stinchcombe on the
Wembley ice during the
1938/39 season.

With a bronze medal league finish the next spring he gained his third All Star 'B' as coach. Surprisingly, although he steered Panthers to their second ENL crown in four years in 1954, the experts failed to grant All-Star recognition. The following autumn the ENL and SNL combined to form the British League. Panthers were a creditable second behind run-away winners Harringay Racers. Four of Archie's boys made the All-Stars, Zamick and Strongman at 'A', both now fellow Hall of Famers.

After seven years on the ice and pacing the bench, Stinchcombe left the sport, although he still lived in Lace City.

The Olympic triumph of 1936 ensured Archie remained in Great Britain colours for the next two World Championships. His shot, considered the hardest in the ENL, provided five goals in London and again next year at Prague, for repeat European gold and world silver medals. Archie was recalled to the colours in 1948 in Switzerland. Britain never appeared likely to retain the Olympic crown and had to settle for sixth. Although not named as such, he was effectively the coach.

Stinchcombe skated with a galloping gait. He was a natural centre, although most coaches used him on the right-wing as he shot left, had a wicked snap of the wrists, and was a clean player with a high sense of sportsmanship. As a person he was blunt, forthright and hard working, as one would expect from his birthplace.

Archibald 'Archie' Stinchcombe was born on 17 November 1912 at Cudworth, South Yorkshire, England. Taken to Canada before the age of two his family settled in Windsor, Ontario.

First on skates in the backyard rink with his mother in goal, his hockey developed at high school. From the age of seventeen he spent three seasons with the local Walkerville Technical Juniors including a goal and an assist in 1932 for the Memorial Cup. The next couple of years were with Amherstburg Pioneers and Windsor Grand Trunks in the Michigan-Ontario League. He skated for Falconbridge Falcons of the Nickel Belt League during the winter before his Atlantic crossing.

Few people knew that Archie lost the sight in his left eye in a childhood accident. A mechanic by trade he worked with Sonny Rost in an aircraft factory during the Second World War. Following retirement from Nottingham he opened Mercury Sports on the Alfreton Road in conjunction with fellow Panther Les Strongman.

He died aged eighty-one, on 3 November 1994, at his Nottingham home in England. His son Martin is the proud possessor of his father's extensive Olympic memorabilia.

Competition Statistics	GP	G	A	Pts	PIM
Streatham	90*	92	114	206	24*
Wembley Lions	---	29	25	54	---
Wembley Monarchs	---	21	16	37	---
Nottingham Panthers	51	3	22	25	6
Great Britain	28	11	4**	15	---

★ Excludes 1935–38
★★ Excludes 1936 & 1948

Coaching	GP	W	L	D	W%
Nottingham Panthers	242	119	92	31	49.2

Les STRONGMAN

Inducted 1987

Les Strongman is synonymous with hockey in Nottingham. He joined Panthers for the beginning of their first post-Second World War season and when hockey returned after a twenty-year absence in 1980 he became the new Panthers' first coach.

With the revival of hockey after the war, Panthers' delayed ENL entry from 1940 saw coach 'Sandy' Archer gather together a team from around the Winnipeg area. From the opening fixture on 22 November 1946 – when the new team downed Wembley Monarchs 3-2 – Strongman became an established fans' favourite.

After two winters he was a little homesick for Canada. He played his final season there for Saskatoon Quakers, scoring 13 goals and contributing 17 assists in forty-six games. Returning to Nottingham in autumn 1949 he made a quick recovery from a skull fracture sustained mid-season. The following year Panthers, with Les as captain, won their first league title helped by Strongman's 61 goals and 41 assists. His first of three points centuries also gained him his first of seven All-Star accolades, this one at 'A'. The 'A' was repeated twelve months later.

In the final year of the ENL, Nottingham again lifted the league title, with Les notching 105 points to be elected to the All-Star 'B' team. He collected his 'A' twelve months later with Panthers runners-up in the rookie campaign of the BNL.

Increasing opportunities on the Continent lured Les to Zurich as player-coach for 1955/56. The following autumn he moved to London to win a BNL medal with Wembley Lions and a 'B' All-Star. As captain, he led Lions' Autumn Cup triumph for 1957/58 and gained his fourth 'A' in the end-of-season sextet. The following winter he was back at Lower Parliament Street for a third successive All-Star, another 'B' rating.

Les Strongman as captain
of Nottingham Panthers for
the 1951/52 season.

The Continent called again in 1959 as he commenced the first of six winters coaching Malmo FF in Sweden's Second Division. With the Scandinavian season finishing earlier than in Britain, he was able to spend the spring with Panthers, assisting the team to the experimental BNL play-off final.

From the autumn of 1965 Les was a regular weekend commuter to London as he donned a Wembley Lions jersey for their Saturday evening challenge games with Northern League teams. In the Southern Cup of 1966/67 and the one-off British Cup next winter he added 17 goals and 6 assists to his Wembley competitive-stats totals.

After Lions folded at the end of 1969 Les concentrated on his newsagents business situated almost opposite Nottingham's Ice Stadium. With the return of hockey to the Lace City eleven years later the new, initially amateur Panthers immediately sought his services to coach a new generation. Behind the bench he guided Nottingham to fourth in the Inter-City League and the Southern Cup. The following winter Panthers finished runners-up in a revived ENL and third in the Cup. From then on he coached the second-string Trojans and assisted the burgeoning youth-development programme. He served on the club management committee for many years and later as a director.

Leslie Strongman was born on 23 August 1924 in Winnipeg, Manitoba, of English parents from Market Harborough. At the age of eleven he was playing hockey with the local Lord Roberts and then White Seals, graduating to juvenile in 1941/42 with St James Canadians in the Manitoba Amateur League. Three and a half years in the RCAF followed as Warrant Officer Pilot in Coastal Command. Based mainly in Iceland he did spend four weeks in

England. He was a policeman in the Manitoba force before crossing the Atlantic in the *Aquitania* to join the newly formed Panthers.

Fifty-seven years later, in January 2003, he and his English wife Margaret sold their home by the River Trent and flew to Edmonton to live near their son and daughter who had already settled in Canada. Upon leaving he told Nottingham's *Evening Post*: 'My only regret is that Panthers stopped in 1960 and we had to wait twenty years for hockey to start again. I've had a great life in this country and I wouldn't change a thing.'

Competition Statistics	GP	G	A	Pts	PIM
Nottingham Panthers	507	401	329	730	330
Wembley Lions	125	118	59	177	42

Coaching	GP	W	L	D	W%
Nottingham Panthers	69	43	23	3	62.3

Ken SWINBURNE

Inducted 2006

To be inducted into the Hall of Fame one usually needs to be a player or a coach, or even a referee. Ken Swinburne was a trainer, assistant and then team manager, but his contribution to the sport in north-east England was considered to be worthy of special commendation.

One of hockey's unsung heroes, Ken never stepped onto the ice in skates, in fact he could not skate, but he still managed to collect an impressive tally of winners' medals as he worked behind the scenes with the all-conquering Durham Wasps of the late 1980s and early 1990s.

Initially a fan, he became a fixture on the Wasps' bench – and later with three Newcastle teams – where his reputation as a Mr Fix-it was legendary. Whether it was a piece of sticky tape, Elastoplast, a lace or a screwdriver, he would invariably have it to hand within seconds from the 'joiner's belt' around his waist. Former Durham player, coach and fellow Hall of Fame member Peter Johnson said he could never remember a time when Ken was unable to produce something for the required equipment repair.

Swinburne started watching Wasps with his dad as a seven year old and later travelled to the away games. The hockey habit became so deeply ingrained that in 1979 he began helping the team as a member of the bench staff carrying the sticks.

By 1984 he was assistant to team manager Brian Cooper – the father of Hall of Fame sons Ian and Stephen. Two years later he replaced Cooper senior, remaining in post, always as an unpaid volunteer, until 1996 when Wasps and the Durham rink were no more. During his time with Wasps they won the British League title in 1984-86, 1989 and 1990-92. They were play-off champions in 1986-88 and 1990-92, the Autumn Cup was also captured in 1984/85 and again during 1987-89. He estimated that he clocked up 300,000 miles of travel with Wasps including a European Cup match in Yugoslavia.

With the demise of Wasps he was not lost to hockey, moving a few miles north to the newly opened Newcastle Arena to serve as bench-manager with Cobras for two years from 1996. His title changed to 'player co-ordinator' with the advent of the Superleague-operated Riverkings in autumn 1998, they were play-off finalists in their second campaign. With the team's transition to Jesters in autumn 2000 Swinburne became team manager, although to his disappointment the owners ran out of money six months later.

For two decades his was a familiar face to almost everyone in British ice hockey, standing impassively on the bench chewing his wad of gum below his impressive moustache. Ken was

Ken Swinburne caught
on camera during
a Heineken League
play-offs weekend at
Wembley.

as popular at local rivals Whitley Bay as he was in Durham, and perhaps no greater tribute could be paid to him.

Kenneth Swinburne was born on 11 September 1941 at Inverness where his father was stationed with the British Army. A painter and decorator by trade he worked for Durham Council. His supportive wife Margaret, who washed the players' strips in the early years, said later: 'he didn't have time for hobbies outside of ice hockey.'

He died aged sixty-three on 6 May 2005 after a short illness.

James 'Tiny' SYME

Inducted 2006

James 'Tiny' Syme was an outstanding Scottish-born defenceman with Dunfermline and Paisley during the late 1940s and the 1950s. He was the only British-born-and-trained player to be selected to an All-Star 'A' team during the six years of the Canadian-dominated BNL of 1954-60.

'Tiny' came late to hockey, playing regularly from the age of nineteen with Dunfermline Royals in Scottish 'junior' hockey. Royals went undefeated in the inaugural 1945/46 Banner Trophy. Unlike today, 'junior' at that time was a label applied to the second tier of the sport in Scotland and was not related to a particular age group.

Tiny Syme in 1955 – the only British-born-and-trained player to break up the Canadian-dominated All-Star 'A' team during the BNL of 1954-1960.

His first outing with the 'senior' pro Vikings came on 26 January 1948 in a 3-3 tie with Falkirk. The local Press commented: 'Jim Syme tried hard, but he found himself a little out of his class.' From the following autumn he was a regular member of Vikings defensive quartet, averaging sixty matches a season. In 1949/50 and again four years later he helped Dunfermline win the Scottish Cup as well as the Canada Cup during 1950/51.

With Vikings taking a break from pro hockey, he and his brother, Tuck, also a defender, joined Paisley in September 1953. Previously very much underrated, here he blossomed under Canadian coach Keith Kewley to achieve an All-Star 'A' rating in his first winter at the East Lane rink. Pirates won the SNL title plus the Autumn and Canada Cups. The following winter Tuck left for Canada and Kewley made Tiny captain. Although Tiny's penalty minutes had initially risen above the 120 mark, as they had in his first three full campaigns at Dunfermline, they fell by half with the additional responsibility. His form increased and his spontaneous humour relaxed his teammates. It was in his final season in the All-British League that he gained the highest accolade by being named to the All-Star 'A' team, a unique distinction for a native British player. Fellow Pirate Bill Crawford recalled: 'Tiny was a helluva player, and a good captain. He imparted so much knowledge to young players…'

Selected for Scotland in the annual clashes with England in 1947 and again three years later when he gained a place, along with his brother, in Great Britain's roster for the 1950 World Championships held in London. With twenty-nine seconds remaining he netted Britain's second goal in their shut-out of Norway at Harringay. It was his only time with Great Britain.

The following winter Dunfermline would not release him and two years later IIHF rules considered him a professional and therefore ineligible.

A right-hand shot, his points tally was never high, but at 6ft 2in and weighing 195lbs the Tiny tag was a touch ironic. His no-nonsense rugged play made the opposition wary. Jimmy Thompson, a teammate from his Dunfermline days says of Syme, '… a really smart, intelligent bloke… Tiny was just a right happy-go-lucky fellow.'

James 'Tiny' Syme was born on 1 October 1926 in the coal-mining village of Blairhall, in west Fife. The family briefly moved to Canada when he was three but returned to Blairhall a year later due to the worsening depression.

He spent 1938 in Dundee where he attended Morgan Academy, then moved back to Blairhall where he won a bursary to Dunfermline High School. Although good at foreign languages and a fluent French speaker by the time he was twelve, he quit school as soon as he could help to deliver coal. Soon he followed his younger brother Tuck down the local coal mine to work on plant recovery.

He also followed his brother's example by emigrating with his wife and two children to Canada in the summer of 1957. Here he played senior 'A' hockey in Ontario with Strathroy Rockets. Employed as a manager at the Vick Chemical plant in St Thomas he moved with his job to Toronto in 1960. Nine years later the firm was taken over and he and his family relocated to London, Ontario, where he opened a bakery. Later Tiny worked as an insurance and car salesman.

He died at his home in London, Ontario, of an aneurysm on 22 August 1973, at the early age of forty-six.

Competition Statistics	GP	G	A	Pts	PIM
Dunfermline Royals	---	---	---	---	---
Dunfermline Vikings	324	21	63	84	580
Paisley Pirates	241	20	81	101	340
Great Britain	7	1	0	1	27

Tom 'Tuck' SYME

Inducted 2005

'Tuck' Syme was an outstanding Scottish-born-and-trained defenceman. In the eight seasons of 1946-1954 in the Canadian-dominated SNL he was the sole native player to be selected twice to the All-Star 'A' team.

He commenced skating at the nearby Dunfemline rink when he left school in 1942. Two years later he was approached at a public session by Johnny Rolland, son of a rink director, and asked if he would like to learn to play ice hockey. A strong skater as a sixteen year old he moved into Dunfermline Royals line up, helping the team to go undefeated in winning the inaugural Banner Trophy in spring 1946.

Tuck was promoted to the senior semi-pro Vikings in March 1947. Although ice time was limited he did notch two assists. For the next two winters he played in about half of Dunfermline's schedule, scoring a goal in each campaign. Season 1947/48 culminated, at the age of nineteen, in a trip with Great Britain to the Olympics in Switzerland.

He attributes his progress to his coach Keith Kewley, who was sufficiently impressed to recommend the young Scot to teams in Canada. In autumn 1948 Tuck gained a slot with Junior 'A' Guelph Biltimore, a farm team of the NHL New York Rangers. He retains fond memories of playing against Rangers at an exhibition game in Guelph.

Like fellow Scot Tony Hand nearly forty years later, a homesick Syme returned to Scotland to finish the season with Dunfermline, winners of the Simpson Trophy. From autumn 1949

Tuck Syme of Dumfermline
Vikings, *c.*1948.

he was a regular member of Vikings, partnering brother Tiny on the blue line. That winter
and the next, as the team won the Scottish and Canada Cups, Tuck notched up an identical
numbers of points at 23 and penalty minutes at 123. His first All-Star accolade, an 'A', came in
spring 1951. Two years on he gained a 'B' as Vikings captured the Scottish Cup.

With Dunfermline taking a year's break from senior hockey Tuck, along with his brother,
joined their previous coach Kewley at Paisley for the 1953/54 season. Named captain, he
played the best hockey of his career in his final season in Britain. Pirates won the Scottish
Autumn, Canada and Scottish Cups along with the SNL crown as Tuck gained his second
All-Star 'A' selection. In eight years of pro hockey his 13 goals were his highest number and
the 18 assists tied his previous best total.

Twice named to the British national team, he iced in all seven games at the St Moritz
Olympics in February 1948. The National Coal Board made a short film about him, which
was included in the weekly *Mining Review* newsreel. Two years later, he and his brother were a
formidable first line of defence as Britain achieved fourth place at the World Championships
held in London. An alternate captain he scored the second goal to bring the score back to 2-3
as Great Britain eventually defeated Sweden 5-4 at Earls Court.

Standing at 6ft 1in and weighing in at 190lbs with a left-hand shot, he was the highest-paid
professional sportsman in Scotland during his winter with Paisley. At £19 a week it was a lot
more than soccer players with Glasgow Rangers.

Thomas 'Tuck' Woods Syme was born on 15 May 1928 in the Fife coal-mining village of
Blairhall. When he was a baby his older brother could not pronounce Tom, it came out as
Tuck, and the nickname stuck. Leaving his Dunfermline school at fourteen he followed his
father into the local coal mine. Years later he said: 'I would have been in the mines all my life
it if hadn't been for hockey.'

In summer 1954 he tried Canada again, joining the Val d'Or Miners of the minor pro Quebec League. At $50 a week he had to combine hockey with working in the local gold mine. He recalls another exhibition game when the Miners were defeated 12-1 by Montreal Canadiens as he faced all-time greats 'Rocket' Richard and Jean Beliveau. Montreal management withdrew their invitation for Tuck to attend Canadiens training camp when they discovered he was twenty-seven. Soon afterwards he finished with hockey.

After serving in the CP railroad police he moved to California in 1960. For the next thirty years or so he worked as a troubleshooting linesman for a telephone company. Now retired, he and his wife live in Palmdale, just north of Los Angeles.

He told author David Gordon that induction into the Hall of Fame is: 'The greatest honour I've ever had.'

Competition Statistics	GP	G	A	Pts	PIM
Dunfermline Royals	---	---	---	---	---
Dunfermline Vikings	313*	33	67	100	450
Paisley Pirates	65	13	18	31	127
Great Britain	14	1	1	2	6

* Excludes 1946/47

Glynne THOMAS

Inducted 1991

Glynne Thomas came to prominence just after the semi-pro BNL folded in spring 1960, to gain numerous All-Star ratings. He was the first netminder in Britain to wear a protective moulded face mask.

Glynne learnt to skate at Richmond ice rink in west London in 1950 and took up ice hockey at the same time at the 'Young Britain' training sessions run by Canadian Greg Ward. He immediately moved into goal.

After a few games for Knights in the house league at the Thameside rink he graduated to Richmond Ambassadors in the Southern Intermediate League from season 1952/53. With limited ice time for practice, and games behind closed doors after public skating late on a Friday evening, Ambassadors struggled. From sixth in the rookie season Thomas's blocking helped lift Ambassadors three places for the next two campaigns. He guested for Liverpool Leopards on their 1954/55 Swiss tour and the next winter joined Oxford University for their annual trip to the Continent. The league limped on until spring 1959 reduced it to a handful of London teams, whilst Glynne spent two years National Service in the RAF.

Signing for Southampton Vikings in autumn 1961, who played most Saturday evenings, gave him the chance of regular competitive hockey. Glynne's first All-Star recognition came with a 'B' in 1961 and again next spring. With new owners Rank showing hockey the door Vikings transferred to Wembley to become the revived Lions. Successive 'A's followed although home games were mainly of the challenge variety after 1964. In the first year back at the Empire Pool Thomas back-stopped Wembley to victory in their London Tournament and Spring Cup 'home' tournaments. *The Hockey Fan* named him 'Player of the Year'. In early 1967 he appeared on television as Lions won the BBC *Grandstand* Trophy.

From spring 1964 he took to wearing a moulded-fibreglass protective face mask, similar to the one pioneered by Jacques Plante of Montreal Canadiens. Glynee's jaw had been broken in practice by a fierce shot from a teammate.

With Lions' demise at the end of 1968 a four-year lay-off followed before his comeback in autumn 1972 with the homeless Wembley Vets of the Southern League. The following winter the team merged with Sussex to form a new Streatham club.

Glynne Thomas as a Wembley Lion
during the 1963/64 season.

His averages were such that he was named to the Southern, then Inter-City All-Star team every spring, except his last season. Glynne collected Southern League winners' medals in 1973-77, in 1989 and in his final two years on the ice in the ICL. He back-stopped Redskins to four play-off championship triumphs and numerous 'home' tournament trophies. In his final season of 1981/82 he played around half the schedule. He retired, aged forty-six, on a high note with his seventh 'Netminder of the Year' trophy since returning to the ice ten years earlier.

International appearances came early. In March 1951 he shared the netminding in two England Under-18s encounters with the older Ambassadors at his home rink. Similar opportunities were limited or non-existent for many years. After selection for England 'B' at Brighton in November 1960 he gained a full England cap three months later. He had done enough in the 7-3 loss to Scotland to be appointed to Great Britain for their return to the World Championships after an eight-year absence. In his two outings he conceded four goals including holding group winners Norway 2-2 on the final day. The following winter he starred in two of England's victories over Scotland but declined Great Britain selection. He again played for England in 1969, 1974 and 1975.

Twelve years passed before he next donned a Great Britain shirt at the age of forty. His form at the Pondus Cup in Denmark in December 1975 secured his place with Britain at the Pool 'C' World Championships held in Poland three months later.

Keen eyes, sharp reflexes, agility, anticipation and a fine catching hand – plus a cool head – made Thomas one of the best, if not the best, goalie of his generation. Off the ice he is quietly spoken and friendly.

Glynne Thomas was born on 5 May 1935 at Acton, London. After secondary school he attended Willesden Technical College and served an apprenticeship as a woodcutting machinist. Now retired, he resides in north London.

Competition Statistics	GP	SoG	GA	GAA	SO
Richmond Ambassadors	---	---	---	---	---
Southampton Vikings	52	---	183	3.51	0
Wembley Lions*	41	---	216	5.26	0
Wembley Vets	7	173	15	2.14	3
Streatham/Redskins	111	2,476	182	1.63	23
Great Britain	6	156**	27	4.50	0

★ Excludes challenge games
★★ Excludes 1961

Nico TOEMEN

Inducted 1993

Nico Toemen came to live in Britain from his native Holland in August 1987 when he was recruited by BIHA President Fred Meredith to the salaried post of referee-in-chief.

The number and standard of match officers had fallen well behind the expansion of the sport. Toemen was tasked with setting an example on the ice and recruiting and training referees and linesmen to match the continuing growth of ice hockey at all levels. This he achieved, with the emphasis on youth and neutrality.

He first officiated in Britain at Wembley. In a two-man system Toemen took part in three games in November 1973 between the NHL Detroit backed London Lions and 'Dutch Internationals'. He returned twice more, in October 1983 at Dundee in a European Cup match and the next day as he handled his first BNL match at Murrayfield. Three years later he was back in another European encounter, this time at Durham.

Upon taking up his task, as he told the *IHN* in August 1998:

> I was scared [expletive deleted] when I saw the standard of refereeing then, the average age I think was about fifty years old. There was one good referee, Mickey Curry, and he was suspended… We had just fifty-seven officials, including linesmen and they did everything; they all refereed in the top and bottom leagues…

Toemen initially stayed at the London home of referee Alec Johnson before settling with his wife and two sons in Nottingham. From the beginning he attended BIHA Council meetings. Soon funded officiating seminars were regularly held around the country with pre-season long-weekend training camps. Emphasis was placed on physical fitness which included timed runs and skating exercises against the clock. Off-ice game supervisors and assessors (at one point there were as many as twenty-five) were appointed and supplied with report forms to complete and return to Toemen. He ensured that car mileage and game fees did not leave his volunteers out of pocket. Rinks were required to provide a dedicated secure room for the officiating crew. Six years later he had supervised the recruitment and training of over 230 on-ice officials at all levels. Sixteen were licensed by the IIHF to work international competitions.

Toemen continued to lead by example on the ice. By summer 1990 he had refereed fifty-nine BNL Premier Division matches plus three consecutive Wembley Championships.

Nico Toemen during his days as a referee. He was sometimes outspoken and controversial, but ultimately played a great role in improving the overall standard of match officials at all levels of the game in Britain.

Sometimes outspoken and controversial, he once had Durham's coach trying to kick down the door to the officials' room and clashed repeatedly with the Sheffield club.

Following a couple of mild heart attacks in the summer of 1992 he hung up his skates the next February to be appointed director of officiating. Simultaneously he was appointed by the IIHF as one of six supervisors of world officiating. During 1994 to 1996 he was the general manager of the Great Britain team in three World Championships and an Olympic qualifying tournament. From 1995 his domestic title changed to technical director, with additional responsibilities as the BIHA moved their head office to Holme Pierrepoint, near Nottingham. This operation incurred financial losses and he returned to Holland with his family in summer 1998.

Nico Toemen was born on 19 April 1958 at Tilburg in the Netherlands. His playing career began as a defenceman in his native town and progressed to the First Division. He started officiating whilst still a junior player, making his debut as a Premier Division linesman at the age of fifteen. Appointed to the international list at twenty-one he continued playing for another four years. In total he was assigned to twenty IIHF tournaments at all levels, including the senior World Championships as a linesman in 1977 and 1981. The highlight of his career must be the 1980 Olympics at Lake Placid. He lined the historic American upset over the USSR.

A bricklayer by trade, after leaving Britain he was employed for a while as a travelling salesman by a biscuit manufacturer. Toemen returned to ice hockey in 2004 as the Belgium IH Federation's referee-in-chief where he still oversees the sport.

Mike URQUHART

Inducted 2007

Canadian-born Mike Urquhart has been, and still is, a loyal servant to British ice hockey. For many years a useful utility player, he is now a successful youth coach at both domestic and international level.

At 5ft 11in tall, weighing 192lbs and with a left-hand shot he skated equally as well on defence or left-wing. Crossing the Atlantic in autumn 1982 to sign for Nottingham, he stayed for four years. His first season on the blue line ended with 44 points, fourth best for Panthers. Next year the points rose to 50. In his last season with Nottingham the club contested the English final of the Autumn Cup and the quarter-finals of the HBL play-offs for the first time. Mike contributed 58 assists.

The following autumn he moved to Oxford in HBL Division One, where he met his hockey-playing future wife Laura. Moving to Wales after four months he helped the rookie Devils into the Division Two promotion play-offs.

In the summer of 1987 he secured the post of assistant rink manager and player-coach at the newly opened rink in Chelmsford. He led Chieftains to runners-up in Division Two. Injuries kept him away from the ice for some time the following winter. The following season he stayed on the bench, guiding his team to an Autumn Trophy semi-final. Laura now ran the rink whilst Mike looked after the expanding youth development programme. Reclassified as a non-import, his return to the ice was a triumph as Chieftains won their first major silverware. Ten wins from eleven secured the Autumn Trophy in October. During his time in Essex he coached 164 games on and off the ice for a 55.4 win percentage. The Urquharts also staged Great Britain Women's European Championship qualifying games versus Holland in March 1989 in which Laura played.

After England and Wales, the winter of 1991/92 was spent in Scotland. The couple ran the Livingston rink and hockey, with Mike coaching the senior Kings to the Scottish League Division One title with sixteen wins from twenty matches. This took Kings through to the six-match HBL qualification play-offs, including a home-and-away clash with the rookie Sheffield Steelers.

In the summer Guildford club-owner American Barry Dow recruited Mike as player-coach. With the opening of the Spectrum complex delayed, sixteen home games were squeezed into eleven weeks. Mike returned to the ice with Flames for a total of 18 points, leading the team to the English League Conference B title. Crowds averaged over 2,000. Elevated to Division One South in the BIHA-inspired expansion and regionalisation of the British League, Mike's second season in Surrey proved traumatic. With three new imports Flames contested a quarter-final for the Autumn Trophy but by early 1993 financial problems surfaced, initially denied by Dow. Fans helped pay player's expenses as Flames finished fifth, three places above his old club at Chelmsford.

Mike Urquhart in his role as a Great Britain youth coach.

He next moved to nearby Bracknell as non-playing coach. Bees performed poorly to be relegated from the British League's Premier Division. His final season as a player was with Milton Keynes in the Premier Division during 1995/96.

His international coaching career commenced the next winter as assistant to the Great Britain Under-18s at the European Pool 'C' Championships in Romania. Great Britain gained promotion and the next winter Mike was head coach.

Five years later he returned as head coach as the young Brits won all five games in Lithuania to reach Division One. Although in April 2006 the opposition was just too strong for Mike's team, he was made assistant coach to the Under-20s for the following December. Winning all five games saw him as head coach for the Division One attempt in Italy in 2007. Victories over France, Kazakhstan and Norway kept his youngsters at the higher level.

Michael Urquhart was born on 9 April 1958 at Toronto, Canada. On skates by the age of six, one of his fondest memories is the winning of the international bantam tournament in Kamloops at thirteen. In his later teens he played ninety games in three stints with Kamloops Chiefs in the West Canada League. For Flin Flon Bombers in the same circuit he turned out thirty-four times during 1976/77, netting three goals and adding the same number of assists. College hockey followed for the Kamloops based Caribou Chiefs.

Now settled in Nottingham, Mike is employed as head coach of the award-winning youth-development programme at the National Ice Centre.

Competition Statistics	GP	G	A	Pts	PIM
Nottingham Panthers	148	92	176	268	321
Oxford City Stars	15	13	15	28	26
Cardiff Devils	9	22	36	58	12
Chelmsford Chieftains	79	102	126	228	132
Guildford Flames	66	17	26	43	77
Bracknell Bees	6	0	0	0	0
Milton Keynes Kings	43	1	3	4	6

Coaching	GP	W	L	D	W%
Chelmsford Chieftains	38	20	15	3	52.6
Livingston Kings	26	16	9	1	61.5
Bracknell Bees*	58	8	47	5	13.7
Great Britain under18	13	6	7	0	46.1
Great Britain Under-20	5	3	2	0	60.0

★ Includes six games as player-coach.

Alan WEEKS

Inducted 1988

Alan Weeks was ice hockey's highest-profile publicist for forty-five years as BBC Television's principal winter sports commentator. Whenever 'Auntie' screened ice hockey whether from the World Championships, Olympics, NHL or the domestic game it was invariably Alan's measured tones that accompanied the action.

His passion for ice hockey started as a schoolboy in Brighton. In the mid-1930s he watched Brighton Tigers at the local Sports Stadium. It was love at first sight and after war service he joined the staff of the Sports Stadium as assistant box office manager. A few months later he was appointed publicity manager and secretary to the Tigers, made their PA announcements and worked at the Sports Stadium until the building closed in 1965.

Alan Weeks, a broadcasting legend, signed this photograph for a fan in 1973/74 at a London Lions game.

It was BBC producer Peter Dimmock – who had played ice hockey pre-war for Wolves in Wembley's youth league – on hearing Alan over the mike at a Tigers match in 1951 who persuaded him to test for the BBC. He then went live during the third period to begin his long BBC career.

He wrote regular articles on the sport for the *Brighton and Hove Gazette* as well as other journals. As director he worked tirelessly to promote the 1973/74 NHL Detroit-backed Wembley Arena-based London Lions and was also president of the 1981/82 revived ENL, forerunner of the HBL. By 1985 he was a member of the BIHA Council, resigning briefly in 1988 due to ill health.

Rejoining as a 'consultant', he became a 'personal member' in 1992. In addition he fought long and hard for a replacement to his beloved Sports Stadium as an active member of the pressure group 'Brightice'.

In September 1959 Weeks joined the BBC *Sportsview* team, to cover thirty-five sports down the years. Among this total were football, gymnastics, snooker, swimming, and ice dancing – including Torvill and Dean's gold medal triumphs. He also attended five summer and seven winter Olympics. In April 1996 he received a lifetime achievement award from the Sportwriters Association of Great Britain, the first broadcaster to so honoured.

Alan Frederick Weeks was born on 8 September 1923 in Bristol, moving to Brighton when he was five. Educated at the local grammar school he joined the Merchant Navy as a sixteen-year-old cadet. Transferring to the Royal Navy two years later as a midshipman, it was his voice over the corvette's PA that informed the crew of imminent attack. He survived Arctic convoys to Russia in HMS *Renown* and two Malta runs, being demobilised in April 1946 as a Lieutenant RNR.

Away from the BBC and ice hockey he was a director of the Sports Aid Foundation from its inception in 1976, retiring as a governor in 1983. He was life president of Brighton and Hove Entertainment Managers; and a member of Lord's Taverners.

Alan was a modest man and one of life's true gentlemen. Fellow BBC commentator David Coleman paid this tribute to his colleague: '… to sit alongside him, especially at a high-speed Olympic ice hockey match was a humbling experience.'

A resident of Hove he retired from the BBC in March 1996 to die aged seventy-two from cancer after a short illness on 11 June the same year.

Jack WHARRY

Inducted 1994

Jack Wharry was for many years a stalwart of the Billingham club and a founder member of the English Ice Hockey Association. He was an efficient and effective administrator.

Like so many parents he first became involved with ice hockey through his two sons, Ian and Billy, soon after they joined their newly formed local club Billingham Bombers in 1974. His instant enthusiasm for this 'new' sport led him to become team manager and eventually club chairman. By 1988 he had stood down to become an honorary vice-president. These roles brought Wharry into close contact with those fulfilling similar functions and he found they had similar aims.

In 1982 representatives from the English regional associations then running the leagues followed the Scots' example and formed an English Association. Wharry was already a well-respected member of the hockey community in north-east England and a prime mover in uniting the expanding sport. He took on the thankless task of honorary treasurer. When he handed on the books in 1991 a grateful EIHA made him their president.

His calmly delivered hockey wisdom was now recognised nationwide. By 1987 he was a regular

Jack Wharry – 'ice hockey's favourite uncle'.

traveller to London to attend BIHA Council meetings as a 'Personal' member. The same year the EIHA appointed him as joint team manager of the England squad.

Following the inquest on the return of Great Britain in 1989 to the senior World Championships, changes were made for the next season. Alec Dampier was appointed head coach, with Wharry as assistant manager, for a second attempt to escape from Pool 'D', which was to be held in Cardiff.

With the job done he was promoted to general-manager for 1991 for the trip to Denmark in early April. A fifth-place finish provided the opportunity, twelve months later, for Jack and his boys to win promotion to the next level on home ice at Hull. In a slickly run tournament the Brits achieved a perfect five wins from five starts.

In his capacity as general manager, Wharry attended, on behalf of BIHA, the daily IIHF Directorate meetings for two consecutive World Championships. Regrettably fate intervened and he was not given the time to oversee the team in Pool 'B'.

Jack Wharry was born on 21 April 1926. For many years he was employed in the ammonia works section of the huge ICI chemical plant at Billingham.

His life was suddenly cut short by a heart attack at his home on 26 August 1992 at the age of sixty-six. BIHA Secretary David Pickles wrote, in a tribute in the following April's Wembley finals programme: '… many people in British ice hockey feel that they had lost their favourite uncle.'

In his honour for the seasons between 1992-94, the English Association renamed the Northern Section of their amateur English Conference the Wharry Division.

Ian WIGHT

Inducted 1993

Ian Wight, via his sponsorship agency – The Wight Company – was instrumental in securing ten years of lucrative Heineken sponsorship for British ice hockey.

He formed his company in 1979 and in the late 1980s it became Orbit International, based in Knightsbridge, London. Among his clients was Whitbread Plc, the well-established brewer,

Heineken lager being one of the brands they produced and distributed in the UK.

In the early 1980s Wight had received a presentation from the BIHA on ice hockey. This was around the same time as he had been commissioned by Whitbread's to find a sport which would be attractive to eighteen-to-twenty-four year olds. After being taken to Streatham to watch a game, he realised this was just the sport Heineken were seeking.

A spokesman for The Wight Company told *Marketing Week* in January 1988, 'When we were first looking for a sport to promote in 1983 we were looking for one with growth potential…'

Ian Wight, sponsorship agency founder, seen here in 1993.

Heineken sponsorship commenced with the second annual British Championships, held at Streatham in April 1983. This was a prelude to the prefixing of Heineken to a newly created Premier and Division One British League totalling twenty teams, facing off five months later. Thames TV covered the first Heineken finals but was soon superseded by the BBC with 'The Match of the Month' on Saturday afternoon *Grandstand*. During the next ten years Heineken invested nearly £2.5 million in the sport as a result of Wight's involvement.

Over the decade of the Heineken British League he put in an enormous amount of time at every level of the game to ensure its success. Former BIHA secretary Pat Marsh – who worked closely with him – said at the time of Ian's induction to the Hall: 'He was hooked on hockey from the start. What stands out in my mind is that he grasped the game so quickly. His enthusiasm, ideas and forthright personality sold the game totelevision, to Wembley and, of course, to Heineken.' He also organised for the BIHA the five-nation Olympic qualifying tournament held at Sheffield Arena in late August 1993.

Ian Wight was born in Belfast on 28 October 1941 and educated at the city's Campbell College, where he played football. He also gained a county cap at field hockey whilst still a schoolboy, and first watched ice hockey as an eight year old at Belfast's King's Hall. Although the puck flew off the ice hitting him on the head, it certainly did not put him off the sport.

Twenty-nine years ago he was one of the founders of the Stella Artois pre-Wimbledon tennis tournament at London's exclusive Queen's club. From executive director he took over, in 1995 as tournament director, retiring in June 2007. The previous December the Tennis Writers Association presented him with an award for his services to their sport.

He is an unassuming but quietly combative man when necessary, with a keen sense of humour. At sixty-six he is not in the best of health, but probably not quite ready for the fireside carpet slippers.

Bob WYMAN

Inducted in 1993 as a member of the Great Britain 1936 Olympic and World Champions

Bob Wyman was one of the two English-trained players in the 1936 Olympic gold medal winning team. He iced in the second match, a 3-0 defeat of Japan, held in the open air on the naturally frozen Riessersee Lake. He then joined Bob Bowman with the BBC radio commentary team.

Wyman learnt to skate and play ice hockey in the late 1920s and early 1930s at the six ice rinks then operating in London. He combined his first season in senior hockey with Grosvenor House Canadians during 1933/34 with success in speed skating.

He moved in October 1934 – with the majority of the Canadians – to the newly opened Empire Pool and Sports Arena at Wembley, staying two years then signing for Richmond Hawks of the ENL. Next season he is listed as an Earls Court Ranger. It's doubtful whether he enjoyed much ice time at any of the three clubs. A winter at Streatham with Princes in the lower standard London and Provincial League followed. The sport's only wartime season brought Wyman back to the ENL with Harringay Greyhounds.

As a defenceman weighing 148lbs, Hounds' coach Percy Nicklin said he had 'an accurate and formidable body-check as good as any Canadian.'

In the first season after hostilities ended, Bob dressed for a handful of Wembley Monarchs matches, finally finishing his hockey career three years later, aged forty, with Sussex in the inaugural Southern Intermediate League.

He represented Great Britain in the 1935 World Championships at Davos, scoring the only goal in the 1-0 win over France, helping to ensure the bronze medal. Recalled to the national side in 1938 at Prague and next year in Zurich, he kitted up for Great Britain twenty times at World events.

James Robert Wyman was born on 27 April 1909 at West Ham, London. Something of an athlete he became the English schoolboy long-jump champion at the age of fifteen. A holder of the British half-mile indoor speed-skating title, he won the national 440-yard outdoor crown at Rickmansworth Aquadrome during a cold spell in January 1934. This feat is depicted, in colour, on a Gallaher cigarette card. In the mid-1930s he resided in Ealing, west London, working in the motor car trade. During the Second World War he served in the Royal Navy as a lieutenant-commander.

Bob Wyman – one of just two English-trained players in the 1936
Olympic gold medal winning team – seen here in as a Wembley
Canadian during the 1934/35 season.

It's unfortunate for the Wyman story that the stats for his early days have vanished, a bit like
the man, whose trail goes cold after the late 1940s – though it is known he died in south-east
Surrey in the spring of 1978.

Competition Statistics	GP	G	A	Pts	PIM
Richmond Hawks	---	1	0	1	22
Princes	---	---	---	---	---
Harringay Greyhounds	---	2	3	5	---
Wembley Monarchs	9	0	0	0	0
Sussex	---	---	---	---	---
Great Britain	20	1	---	1	---

Victor 'Chick' ZAMICK

Inducted 1951

The greatest scorer, during the first post-war era of pro hockey in Britain, was without doubt 'Chick' Zamick of Nottingham Panthers.

In eleven years from 1947, Zamick, a 5ft 7in-tall, 140lb centre-ice accumulated 1,423 points in a period of generally low-scoring games. This feat was given recognition by the experts voting him onto nine consecutive end-of-season All-Star teams. Six were at category 'A', with a tenth, another 'A' in 1958.

In the summer of 1947, hearing that Sandy Archer, who grew up in Winnipeg, was in town recruiting, Zamick badgered the Nottingham coach for a chance to earn £15 a week playing in England. Two days prior to sailing Archer told him that, due to a late withdrawal, he was a Panther.

Chick proved an instant success on Lower Parliament Street, taking the scoring title in his first season with his deceptive body swerve and accurate left-hand shot. His hundredth goal entered the nets in December 1948 and his 600th just under six years later, with Panthers winning the ENL in 1951 and 1954.

He took the league points scoring crown six times, with highs of 112, and 169 for all competitions in 1954/55. Revered and respected by the Nottingham fans, some of whom wept openly when he took a tumble and broke an arm at the Ice Stadium in 1952. This was the only season when he totalled less than a hundred points, but only two less at 98! The Lace City voted him Nottingham's 'Sportsman of the Year' in 1949, beating international footballer Tommy Lawton and Test cricketer Joe Hardstaff. Two years later the Nottingham public again voted him their favourite sportsman.

Appointed player-coach in1955/56 he led Panthers to the Autumn Cup and league titles that winter. He continued in the same role for a further two seasons, then accepted a three-year contract to coach in Switzerland with Geneva–Servette.

Returning to settle in Nottingham in spring 1961 he kitted up later that year for the newly formed Altrincham Aces. Weekends in London two years on with Wembley Lions brought an illustrious career on British ice to an end, along with London Tournament and Spring Cup medals.

Wembley Lions defenceman Sonny Rost described Zamick to author Trevor Boyce '… as wide and stocky with plenty of muscle. His greatest asset was his marvellous shot which was always very low. The goalies had little chance as he could shoot on the move at high speed with a lightning quick release...' Often enduring rough treatment from opposing defenders he seldom retaliated, with less than two minutes in the penalty box every three games.

Victor 'Chick' Zamick was born in Winnipeg, Manitoba on 16 August 1926. His parents had emigrated from a small village in the Ukraine to produce twelve children in Canada. The 'Chick' nickname apparently derives from Chicklet chewing gum with twelve sticks in a packet.

He came late to hockey at twelve years old. From the local juvenile league he progressed three years later to the Sir John Franklin Midgets. In the Manitoba Junior League he spent fourteen games during 1943/44 with Winnipeg Air Cadets. The following winter with St Boniface Canadiens he scored 10 goals in 13 matches.

War service was cut short by injury and he was discharged, virtually dropping out of hockey for a while. He tried various jobs and earned a living as a flyweight boxer. Several of his brothers were also first-class fighters, both amateur and professional. Paul and Joe also played hockey briefly in Europe.

After a trial with Cleveland Barons of the AHL he joined St Catherines Falcons. Here his skills were honed by Rudy Pilous – a future coach in the NHL with Chicago, who had played in England with Richmond Hawks. In his thirty-two games for Falcons in 1945/46 'Chick' scored 19 goals and 23 assists.

Chick Zamick during the
1947/48 season spent with
Nottingham Panthers.

March 2000 saw a return to the Ice Stadium for Chick, this time without skates, as guest of
honour at Panthers last match in their original home before moving to the shiny new NIC.
He visited the NIC in November 2006 to help celebrate the Panthers' sixtieth anniversary
game.

Zamick, modest and serious, became a respected businessman in his adopted city with
business ventures ranging from dry cleaning to a sauna and the Plains Squash Club. Retiring
to Sevenoaks in Kent he later moved to north London to live with his daughter. He died on
9 October 2007 aged eighty-one after a long illness.

Competition Statistics	GP	G	A	Pts	PIM
Nottingham Panthers	624	778	645	1,423	192
Altrincham Aces	4	9	7	16	0
Wembley Lions	11	19	12	31	0

ICE HOCKEY HALLS OF FAME WORLDWIDE

Several nations, apart from Great Britain, have established an Ice Hockey Hall of Fame. Some are only in cyber-space, whilst others are physical entities where inductees are honoured, usually within an ice hockey museum displaying historic artefacts of the sport.

Not surprisingly, the one located at Toronto is the best known and largest. Listed below are those that the author is aware of; there may be others.

Most Canadian provinces also have a Sports Hall of Fame where hockey is naturally on prominent display.

Canada   Website: www.hhof.com/halloffame
Toronto: Established in 1945 there are currently 348 members. They are honoured within the Hockey Hall of Fame which is a superb tribute to hockey, both to the North American based National Hockey League and beyond. Major trophies and historic objects can be seen within this veritable homage to the heritage of hockey.

Bowmanville, Ontario   Website: www.total-hockey.ca
Total Hockey Museum – Brian McFarlane collection plus interactive exhibits.

Kingston, Ontario   Website: www.ihhof.com
International Hockey Hall of Fame. Opened in 1965. Historic artefacts, early sticks, etc.

Windsor, Nova Scotia   Website currently closed
Windsor Hockey Heritage Centre. opened in 1994 – Historic artefacts, equipment, shirts, skates, sticks, etc.

Finland   Website: www.jaakiekkemuseo/tampere.fi
Established in 1985 with 126 members at the last count. There is a physical presence within the Finnish ice hockey museum, which claims to be the largest in Europe. It can be found at the Vapriiki museum in the city of Tampere.

France   Website: www.azhockey.com
Established in 1961, cyber-space only.

Germany   Website: www.eishockeymuseum
There is a physical presence in the German ice hockey museum in the town of Ausburg.

International Ice Hockey Federation   Website: www.iihf.com
The IIHF Hall of Fame was created in 1997. Currently there are 157 inductees. They form a modest display within the Hockey Hall of Fame in Toronto.

<u>Russia</u>   website: none known

Founded in March 2004 with forty-four inductees. A physical presence is due to be formed within the new arena built in Moscow for the 2007 World Championships.

<u>Slovakia</u>   Website: www.hokejovasienslavy.sk

Founded in 2002. Currently there are twenty members who are honoured at a display within Bratislava Castle.

<u>United States of America</u>   Website: www.ushockeyhall.com

There is a physical Hall of Fame at Eveleth, Minnesota which opened in June 1973. Currently there are 123 members.

PRINCIPAL SOURCES

Books and Booklets

Beer, Anthony, *It's Funny When You Win Everything*, (Rover Publications, Abergavenny, 1994).
Bowman, Bob, *On the Ice*, (Arthur Baker Ltd, London, 1937)
Boyce, Trevor, *British Ice Hockey Players From The Golden Days*, (Yore Publications, Harefield, 1997)
Buchanan, Ian, *British Olympians*, (Guinness Publishing Ltd, Enfield, 1991)
Coleman, Jim, *Hockey Is Our Game*, (Key Porter Books Ltd. Toronto, 1987)
Drackett, Phil, *Ice Hockey World Annual 1953-54, 1954-55, 1955-56,* (Flick Publications Ltd; Ice Hockey World Ltd, London).
Drackett, Phil, *Flashing Blades*, (The Crowood Press, Marlborough, 1987)
Drackett, Phil, *Vendetta On Ice*, (Ice Hockey World, Norwich, 1992)
Drackett, Phil & Fill, Dennis, *Champions On Ice,* (Ice Hockey World, Norwich, 2000)
Erhardt, Carl, *Ice Hockey*, (W. Foulsham & Co. Ltd, London, 1937)
Giddens, Robert, *Ice Hockey World Annual 1948-49, 1950-51, 1951-52,* (London)
Giddens, Robert, *Ice Hockey The International Game*, (W&G Foyle Ltd, London, 1950)
Gordon, David, *Scotch On Ice,* (Tempus Publishing Ltd, Stroud, 2006)
Harris, Martin C., *Homes Of British Ice Hockey*, (Tempus Publishing, Stroud, 2005)
Hastings, Harold C., *Arthur Elvin: A Tribute*, (McCorquodale, London, 1958)
James C. Hendy, *The National Hockey Guide 1942,* (New York, USA)
Jonanovic, Rob, *The Official ISL Yearbook And Media Guide 2002-03*, (Pineapple Books Ltd, Nottingham, 2002)
Patton, B.M., *Ice Hockey*, (George Routledge & Sons Ltd, London, 1936)
Poplimont, Andre G., *LIHG Annuaire 1937*, (Anvers, 1937)
Roberts, Stewart, *The Ice Hockey Annual*, (Hove, 1976-2006)
Scherer, Karl, *1908-1979, 70 Years of LIHG/IIHF*, (Munich, 1978)
Stocks, Bernard, *The Herald Ice Hockey Annual,* (Glasgow, 1968-1972)
Wade, A.C.A., *The Skaters' Cavalcade,* (Olympic Publications Ltd, London, 1939)
Wade, Gordon, *Ice Hockey Yearbook Facts & Figures 1990/91*, (Southampton, 1990)

BIHA Record Book, hand-written ledger (now missing)
Ice Hockey Who's Who, author unknown, (Glasgow, 1946)
The Story Of Ice Hockey, author unknown, (Michael Mason, Westcliffe-on-Sea, 1948)

Journals

The Times
Ice Hockey World, 1935-40 & 1946-1958 & Feb./March 1985
Ice Skating, Oct. 1946

Speedway Gazette, 1948/49
The Hockey Fan, 1960-1965
The Ice Hockey Herald, June 1970 & 24 April 1971
Ice Hockey Newsletter, Jan. 1976
Ice Hockey News Review, 1981-2002
Ice Hockey Today, 1989

Match Day Programmes

Brighton Tigers, 1935-1939
Dundee, 16 April 1985
Earls Court, 1935-1939 & 1948-1953
Harringay, 1936-1958
Murrayfield Royals, 19 December 1957
Kingston (Ontario) Saints, 1946-47
Nottingham Panthers, 8 October 1948, 4 May 1952, 3 October 1952 & 5 November 1956
Richmond Hawks, 26 February 1935
Wembley, 1934-40 & 1946-1960
World Championships, 1990

Websites

Brighton Sports Stadium, www.mybrightonandhove.org.gov
Ice Hockey Journalists UK, www.ihjuk.co.uk
Nottingham Panthers History, http://homepage.ntlworld.com/peter.walch
Society of International Hockey Research (player database), www.sihrhockey.org

Other ice hockey titles published by Stadia

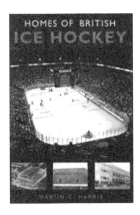

Homes of British Ice Hockey
MARTIN C. HARRIS

Ice hockey is currently one of the fastest growing sports in the world. Hectic, frantic and often quite violent, it naturally appeals to spectators and its popularity has taken off in the UK. This book looks at every venue ever to host the sport in England, Scotland, Wales and Northern Ireland. Containing a wealth of information on each building, including team histories, statistical information, architectural details and many illustrations, this is a fascinating book for anyone with an interest in the sport.

978 07524 2581 8

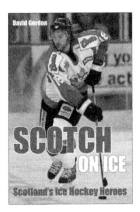

Scotch on Ice Scotland's Ice Hockey Heroes
DAVID GORDON

The players featured in this book are some of the finest ever seen on Scottish ice. Individuals like Billy Fullerton and 'Tuck' Syme were as outstanding in their chosen sport as any hero of football or rugby. This book tell genuinely significant stories such as Jimmy Foster's starring role in Great Britain's gold medal win at 'Hitler's Games' in 1936, or that of father and son duo Martin and Colin Shields, whose involvement in ice hockey has spanned five decades.

978 07524 3801 6

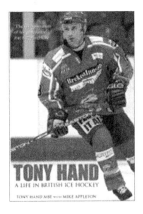

Tony Hand A Life in British Ice Hockey
TONY HAND WITH MIKE APPLETON

Tony Hand is the first British-born player to be drafted into the NHL and perhaps the finest ever to grace these shores. In his own words, Tony recounts his career; from winning and losing at Wembley to the highs and lows with the GB national team, his clubs and players. Find out why he didn't stick with Edmonton in the NHL, what really happens on a European tour and why he was banned for taking a cold remedy. An honest and revealing biography of a British sporting great.

978 07524 4478 9

If you are interested in purchasing other books published by Stadia or our other imprints, or in case you have difficulty finding any Stadia books in your local bookshop, you can also place orders directly through our website

www.tempus-publishing.com